Tell It Slant

CREATING, REFINING, AND PUBLISHING
CREATIVE NONFICTION

THIRD EDITION

Brenda Miller
and
Suzanne Paola

Mc
Graw
Hill

New York Chicago San Francisco Athens London Madrid
Mexico City Milan New Delhi Singapore Sydney Toronto

5 6 7 8 9   LCR   24 23 22

ISBN   978-1-260-45459-8
MHID   1-260-45459-2

e-ISBN   978-1-260-45460-4
e-MHID   1-260-45460-6

See the authors' *Tell It Slant* website at wp.wwu.edu/tellitslant/.

McGraw-Hill books are available at special quantity discounts to use as premiums and sales promotions or for use in academic programs. To contact a representative, please visit the Contact Us pages at www.mhprofessional.com.

Tell It Slant

Tell all the Truth but tell it Slant—
Success in Circuit lies
Too bright for our infirm Delight
The Truth's superb surprise
As Lightning to the Children eased
With explanation kind
The Truth must dazzle gradually
Or every man be blind—

—EMILY DICKINSON

Contents

Preface to the Third Edition of *Tell It Slant*   ix

PART I **Unearthing Your Material**

1 The Body of Memory   3

2 Writing the Family   23

3 "Taking Place": Writing the Physical World   33

4 Gathering the Threads of History   51

5 The Body of Identity   59

6 Writing the Arts   69

7 Glorious Facts: Research and the Research Essay   79

PART II **The Many Forms of Creative Nonfiction**

8 The Tradition of the Personal Essay   101

9 Innovative Forms: The Wide Variety of Creative Nonfiction   119

10 Mixed-Media, Cross-Genre, Hybrid, and Digital Works   137

PART III **Honing Your Craft**

11 The Particular Challenges of Creative Nonfiction   151

12 The Basics of Good Writing in Any Form   169

13 The Writing Process and Revision   193

14 The Power of Writing Communities   203

15 Publishing Your Creative Nonfiction   217

16 Putting on Our Editors' Hats   231

PART IV Anthology

Reading as a Writer   239

1 The Fine Art of Sighing   243
   Bernard Cooper

2 Leap   245
   Brian Doyle

3 Jumping the Fence   247
   Marjorie Rose Hakala

4 To Keep an Ear to the Ground   255
   Barbara Hurd

5 Of Smells   259
   Michel de Montaigne

6 On Touching Ground   262
   Jericho Parms

7 Perdition   269
   Kristen Radtke

8 The Night My Mother Met Bruce Lee   270
   Paisley Rekdal

9 The Coroner's Photographs   274
   Brent Staples

10 Because, the Ferguson Verdict   279
    Ira Sukrungruang

11 First   282
    Ryan Van Meter

12 Math 1619   286
    Gwendolyn Wallace

Appendix I: Good Habits for Healthy Writers   291

Appendix II: Resources for Writers   299

Credits   301

Index   303

Preface to the Third Edition of *Tell It Slant*

Feeling overwhelmed by data, random information, the flotsam and jetsam of mass culture, we relish the spectacle of a single consciousness making sense of a portion of the chaos. . . . The essay is a haven for the private, idiosyncratic voice in an era of anonymous babble.

—Scott Russell Sanders

Why *Tell It Slant*?

When Emily Dickinson wrote, "Tell all the Truth but tell it Slant/Success in Circuit lies," what did she mean? We think she meant that truth takes on many guises; the truth of art can be very different from the truth of day-to-day life. Her poems and letters, after all, reveal her deft observation of the outer world, but it is "slanted" through the poet's distinctive vision. We chose her poem as both title and epigraph for this book because it so aptly describes the task of the creative nonfiction writer: to tell the truth, yes, but to become more than a mere transcriber of life's factual experience.

The more you read and study, the more you will discover that creative nonfiction assumes a particular, creating *self* behind the nonfiction prose. When you set about to write creative nonfiction about any subject, you bring to this endeavor a strong voice and a singular vision. This voice must be loud and interesting enough to be heard among the noise coming at us in everyday life.

We see all the chapters in *Tell It Slant* as presenting a series of introductions, lessons, and sometimes provocations in the art of writing creative nonfiction. We aim to present the most comprehensive information about creative nonfiction possible, in an accessible form, with a sense of how these techniques have played out in the lives of working writers.

We also want all of the concepts we present to be translatable immediately into actual writing ideas, so each chapter begins with a short personal narrative to give you a sense of how we, the authors, have negotiated the territory. Because we recognize the limits of what we know, we have provided tips from many of the best nonfiction writers working today to expand our expertise in particular areas of creative nonfiction. At the end of each chapter, we provide a series of prompts to help you put into action the principles we've explained. Use them as starting points to "tell it slant" and create your own brand of creative nonfiction.

The Evolution of *Tell It Slant*

Since the first edition of *Tell It Slant* was published in 2003, creative nonfiction as a genre has been growing and shaping itself before our eyes. The term *creative nonfiction* was first used in English in the late 1960s, a fraction of a second in literary history. The term *lyric essay*, now so important in our genre, was introduced in 1997, by John D'Agata in the journal *Seneca Review.* All of us who are part of this living, growing genre still make our way through a young and exciting literary landscape.

In 2012, we produced an updated, second edition that responded to the exponential growth in the field, highlighting new forms and innovations while also looking in-depth at the tools you need to produce great writing.

Now, seven years later, we saw the need for a new, fully updated third edition that addresses how the field of creative nonfiction continues to evolve in a quickly changing world, even as we keep those basics of great writing, revising, and publishing in mind. Whenever it's time to update this book, we return to the job with renewed excitement. Part of that feeling is our love for this genre. Part of it, too, is how much, even in a few years, there is to talk about—how much has happened in creative nonfiction that's truly new. We continue to see great growth, formal experimentation, and much discussion about what this genre can and should do.

We would like to acknowledge here the essential input we received from Brenda's students in her Introduction to Creative Nonfiction course at

Western Washington University in winter 2019. They gamely read and field-tested many of the revisions and additions to this third edition, noting where we'd gotten it right and where we had some blind spots. Their detailed and insightful feedback put the finishing touches on this book, helping us make it even more relevant for today's readers.

Writing that falls under the rubric of creative nonfiction has always existed, of course, and we sprinkle historical readings throughout this book to remind our readers (and ourselves!) of this fact. But a great deal of very different literary work has historically been huddled under the umbrella of "the essay": meditation, memory, argument, opinion, vignette. Now we want to further explore this genre, theorize it, and play with it. What an exciting time to be here, in the world of creative nonfiction.

Highlights of the Fully Updated Third Edition

For this new edition, we have revised every chapter extensively, considering the relevance of each topic and example. We pulled some text, and added much more. Here are some of the highlights:

- Added a new chapter, "The Body of Identity," that more directly addresses such topics as race, sexual and gender identity, and disability.
- Expanded "The Body of Memory" to include issues of body image and illness.
- Expanded "The Five (or Six) Senses of Memory" section, with more discussion and examples on how to render memories in vivid, sensory detail, including the "sixth sense."
- Expanded "Writing the Family" to include more direct references to and examples of writing one's cultural identity.
- Revised and expanded our research chapter to include detailed discussion of techniques such as immersion, primary sources, research mapping, and more, making research both accessible and fun.
- Created a new anthology section at the end of the book, with a dozen powerful and formally diverse essays providing literary examples that range from the traditional essay to the graphic memoir.

- Added suggested reading lists at the end of each chapter to allow readers to easily put together their own creative writing course.
- Fully updated and expanded references to diverse creative nonfiction works and historical events throughout the book.
- Fully updated "Publishing Your Creative Nonfiction" to add more hands-on techniques, such as following the "breadcrumbs" left by other authors to find your dream editors and publications.
- Added a new chapter, "Putting on Our Editors' Hats," using our perspectives as editors to discuss what publishing looks like, and how submissions succeed, from the editor's point of view.
- Expanded our discussion of contemporary and emerging forms and strategies, including the "looping" essay, the video essay, flash nonfiction, the micro essay that can use platforms such as Twitter and Instagram, and the hybrid essay.
- Added an appendix, "Good Habits for Healthy Writers," that covers work–life balance, stress reduction, and practices that help you handle the difficulties of the writing life.

The Role of Our "Try Its"

For this new edition, we have also refreshed and revamped our writing prompts, called "Try Its." Our Try Its offer a way to begin new writing, a relief from blank computer screens, and a way of strengthening particular writing muscles. They'll engage you and move you beyond your literary comfort zones.

We carefully shape and field-test our Try Its. They are designed to help you move from taking in the concepts presented in each chapter to applying those concepts in your own work. These prompts, or writing challenges, are "exercises" in the sense that they may not always result in a finished essay; sometimes they're just practice. Unlike exercises on a piano or the like, though, our Try Its will often lead you to something new and complete. As writer Pamela Painter puts it, there is "nothing artificial about an exercise— except the origin of the prompt. What you write in response to that prompt becomes organically your own with the first words you write."

The *Tell It Slant* Website

We also offer with this edition a new book website, found at wp.wwu.edu /tellitslant/. For teachers—or for writers who would like to structure their own individual writing course—we have provided sample syllabi on the website, providing ways to use this book flexibly for different purposes in learning. We provide links to many excellent online readings and resources as well as blog posts aimed at the writing teacher and writing learner. We also offer classroom activities that can help instructors use specific chapters, readings, and Try Its to create a complete class.

You can contact Brenda and Suzanne through the book website or our Facebook page, with anything from questions about using the book to requests for classroom visits, in person or via videoconferencing programs. We want this book to work for you, whatever your slant may be, as a teacher, a learner, and a writer.

We believe that deep within you is a work of art only you can breathe into being. We can coach you and help you develop the muscles you need, but we trust that you will find, between the lines here, the prompts that spur only you, the book that begins where ours ends. Breathe deeply! Now let's begin.

TRY IT

What do you already know about creative nonfiction?

Have you read a particular book or short piece that, to you, embodies the genre of creative nonfiction? It may have been published in print or online. It may have been something you read on social media. It may have been something a family member or friend wrote in a letter or email. Write down your memories of this work or seek it out to read again. What makes this work memorable? What draws you to the writer's voice? What can you learn about the genre from this piece of writing?

FOR FURTHER READING

Throughout the book you will see suggested readings around particular topics. Here is a list of more general anthologies and resources that can also act as companions to *Tell It Slant*.

Resources Available Online

- *Assay: A Journal of Nonfiction Studies* (an online journal dedicated to a study of creative nonfiction)
- *Brevity: A Journal of Concise Literary Nonfiction* (an online journal that showcases a wide variety of contemporary flash nonfiction, along with craft essays and a blog)
- *Creative Nonfiction* (a print journal with extensive online content)
- *Hippocampus Magazine: Memorable Creative Nonfiction* (an online journal dedicated to creative nonfiction)
- *Quotidiana* (a website that houses classic essays in the public domain)
- *The Sun* (a print magazine that posts many of its creative nonfiction pieces online)

Print Resources

Anthologies of Creative Nonfiction

- *Waveform: Twenty-First-Century Essays by Women*, edited by Marcia Aldrich
- *The Next American Essay (A New History of the Essay)*, edited by John D'Agata
- *In Fact: The Best of Creative Nonfiction*, edited by Lee Gutkind
- *Short Takes: Brief Encounters with Creative Nonfiction*, edited by Judith Kitchen
- *Brief Encounters: A Collection of Contemporary Nonfiction*, edited by Judith Kitchen and Dinah Lenney
- *The Art of the Personal Essay: An Anthology from the Classical Era to the Present*, edited by Phillip Lopate
- *In Short: A Collection of Brief Creative Nonfiction*, edited by Mary Paumier Jones and Judith Kitchen
- *In Brief: Short Takes on the Personal*, edited by Mary Paumier Jones and Judith Kitchen
- *The Far Edges of the Fourth Genre: An Anthology of Explorations in Creative Nonfiction*, edited by Sean Prentiss and Joe Wilkins
- *The Fourth Genre: Contemporary Writers of/on Creative Nonfiction*, edited by Robert Root, Jr., and Michael Steinberg
- *Shapes of Native Nonfiction: Collected Essays by Contemporary Writers*, edited by Theresa Warburton and Elissa Washuta
- *The Touchstone Anthology of Contemporary Creative Nonfiction: Work from 1970 to the Present*, edited by Lex Williford and Michael Martone

- *The Best American Essays* series, published annually (each collection includes an Introduction by the guest editor that articulates key topics in creative nonfiction)

Print Journals Specializing in Creative Nonfiction
- *Creative Nonfiction: True Stories, Well Told*
- *Fourth Genre: Explorations in Nonfiction*
- *River Teeth: A Journal of Nonfiction Narrative*

PART I

Unearthing Your Material

If there's a book you really want to read, but it hasn't been written yet,
then you must write it.

—Toni Morrison

1

The Body of Memory

Memory begins to qualify the imagination, to give it another forma-
tion, one that is peculiar to the self. . . . If I were to remember other
things, I should be someone else.

—N. Scott Momaday

In my earliest memory, I'm a four-year-old girl waking slowly from anesthe-
sia. I lift my head off the pillow and gaze blearily out the bars of my hospital
crib. I can see a dim hallway with a golden light burning; somehow I know in
that hallway my mother will appear any minute now, bearing ice cream and
7-Up. She told me as much before the operation: "All good girls get ice cream
and 7-Up when their tonsils come out," she said, stroking my hair. "It's your
reward for being brave." I'm vaguely aware of another little girl screaming for
her mother in the crib next to mine, but otherwise the room remains dark
and hushed, buffered by the footfalls of nurses who stop a moment at the
doorway and move on.

I do not turn to face my neighbor, afraid her terror will infect me; I can
feel the tickling urge to cry burbling up in my wounded throat, and that
might be the end of me, of all my purported bravery and the promised ice
cream. I keep my gaze fixed on that hallway, but something glints in my
peripheral vision, and I turn to face the bedside table. There, in a mason jar,
my tonsils float. They rotate in the liquid: misshapen ovals, pink and nubbly,
grotesque.

And now my mother has simply appeared, with no warning or announce-
ment. Her head leans close to the crib, and she gently plies the spoon between
the bars, places it between my lips, and holds it there while I swallow. I keep

my gaze fixed on her face, and she keeps her gaze on mine, though I know we're both aware of those tonsils floating out of reach. The nurses pad about, and one of them enters the room bearing my "Badge of Courage." It's a certificate with a lion in the middle surrounded by laurels, my name scripted in black ink below. My mother holds it out to me, through the bars, and I run a finger across my name, across the lion's mane, across the dry yellowed parchment.

—Brenda

The Earliest Memory

What is your earliest memory? What is the memory that always emerges from the dim reaches of your consciousness as the *first one*, the beginning to this life you call your own? Some of these early memories have the vague aspect of a dream, some the vivid clarity of a photograph. In whatever form they take, they tend to fascinate us.

Memory has been called the ultimate "mythmaker," continually seeking meaning in the random and often unfathomable events in our lives. "A myth," writes John Kotre, author of *White Gloves: How We Create Ourselves Through Memory*, "is not a falsehood but a comprehensive view of reality. It's a story that speaks to the heart as well as the mind, seeking to generate conviction about what it thinks is true."

The first memory then becomes the starting point in our own narratives of the self. "Our first memories are like the creation stories that humans have always told about the origins of the earth," Kotre writes. "In a similar way, the individual self—knowing how the story is coming out—selects its earliest memories to say, 'This is who I am because this is how I began.'" As writers, we naturally return again and again to these beginnings and scrutinize them. By paying attention to illogical, unexpected details, we just may light upon the odd yet precise images that help our lives make sense, at least long enough for our purposes as writers.

The prominent fiction writer and essayist David James Duncan calls such autobiographical images "river teeth." Based on his knowledge that knots of dense wood remain in a river years after a fallen tree disintegrates, Duncan creates a metaphor of how memory, too, retains vivid moments that stay in mind long after the events that spurred them have been forgotten. He writes:

> There are hard, cross-grained whorls of memory that remain inexplicably lodged in us long after the straight-grained narrative material that housed them has washed away. Most of these whorls are not stories, exactly: more often they're self-contained moments of shock or of inordinate empathy. . . . These are our "river teeth"—the time-defying knots of experience that remain in us after most of our autobiographies are gone.

Virginia Woolf had her own term for such "shocks" of memory. She calls them "moments of being," and they become essential to our very sense of self. "I hazard the explanation," she writes, "that a shock is at once in my case followed by the desire to explain it. . . . I make it real by putting it into words." Woolf's early moments of being, the vivid first memories from childhood, are of the smallest, most ordinary things: the pattern of her mother's dress, for example, or the pull cord of the window blind skittering across the floor of their beach house. The memories that can have the most emotional impact for the writer are those we don't really understand, the images that rise intuitively in our minds.

"Imagistic Endurance"

In order to flesh out those "shocks of memory" or "river teeth," you must develop the ability—and the patience—to stay with the memory as long as you can, filling in the details using your imagination (see Chapter 11, "The Particular Challenges of Creative Nonfiction," for a discussion of the relationship between memory and imagination). The poet Jenny Johnson has called this skill "imagistic endurance," likening the act of sustaining our attention on images to the stamina an athlete must cultivate. Of course, it's possible to go overboard in this direction, but in the drafting process it's useful to keep training your writing muscles to *keep going*. You never know what might turn out to be important.

Many writers will use present tense to suspend a moment in time, allowing space for this sustained attention. (For an example of this technique, see "First" by Ryan Van Meter in our anthology.) For one thing, it's more difficult to summarize in the present tense; by virtually "re-inhabiting" a memory, both writer and reader can allow the scene to unfold more deeply, and unexpected details might arise that could lead to new discoveries. (You don't necessarily need to *keep* the material in present tense, if this tone doesn't work for your piece, but by drafting in the present tense, you may be able to slow down enough to unearth new material.) Often these scenes are left to speak for themselves; the writer refrains from *telling* us how to interpret the scene, instead providing images as clues that allow the reader to make connections.

For example, in her short personal essay "Behind the Screen," Jo Ann Beard sustains her attention on a small passage of time in her childhood: a Fourth of July evening when she is banished to the screened-in porch because she's having an allergy attack. She needs to watch the activities from afar, separate from her family. From this observation post, she reports every movement her family makes, first looking closely at her older sister, who wears:

> a pop-bead necklace, a Timex wristwatch, a mood ring, and a charm bracelet that makes a busy metallic rustle every time she moves her arm, which she does frequently. On the charm bracelet, between a high-stepping majorette and a sewing machine with movable parts, is a little silver book that opens like a locket to display the Teen Commandments. . . . Every few minutes she raises and lowers her right arm so the charm bracelet, which I covet, clanks up to her elbow and then slides slowly and sensuously back down to her wrist. She doesn't bother turning around to see how I take this. She knows it's killing me.

Beard zooms in on the smallest details (down to the specific charms on the bracelet!), and she allows these details to build a picture of the era (mood rings) and family culture (Teen Commandments), without the author needing to state this information directly. She then turns this laser gaze on her younger brother, her mother, and her father, and all the while we can feel her isolation behind that screen, as well as the buildup to the fireworks that, when they arrive, lead to a charged, suspended moment:

> The sky is full of missiles. All different colors come out this time, falling in slow motion, red and blue turning to orange and green. It's so beautiful, I have to close my eyes. My family joins the neighbors in oohing. Suddenly, as the delayed booms are heard, I have to lean forward and put my head on my knees, inhaling the scent of Bactine and dirt. Everything is falling away from me. I open my eyes.

As you can see in this excerpt, a sustained exploration—set in the present tense with attention to small sensory details such as the smells of Bactine and dirt—can create a vivid child's perspective and voice.

In his memoir, *House Built on Ashes,* José Antonio Rodríguez builds his story bit by bit, creating small, self-contained scenes of key memories from his childhood, and the reader experiences it all from inside the child's point of view. For example, in an early chapter titled "milk," Rodríguez remembers a flash encounter with his mother that has stayed with him all these years. He had been running through the house chasing a lizard and didn't hear his mother tell him to stop. Notice how he gives the background to the scene in past tense, but the essential moment slows down to present tense:

> I don't know why I didn't hear her, but I didn't. Then I got tired. I came in for a flour tortilla. I grabbed one from the stack, felt it warm in my hand. . . . And that's when she said it, turning a tortilla on the griddle, like she's always doing, her arm over the stove and her head over her shoulder, her chin up, like picking a fight: I don't love you anymore.
>
> I walk back, away from her. She looks at me that way, like to look at me hurts her eyes.
>
> I sit on the ground on the other side of the table, stare at the dirt, hard brown. This morning I was spooning milk from a cup so it would last longer than gulping it like water. That was happening, that was here. Amá loving me was always happening, like milk that never runs out, that was here too. But now it is not happening. It has stopped. . . .
>
> The piece of tortilla in my mouth tastes like raw dough and it sticks in my throat. I want to spit it out, but I'm not supposed to waste food. Little ants with their little stings walk trails on the ground, move around my bare feet splotchy with sweat and dirt and backsplash from peeing.

Again, the small details—tortillas on the griddle, the dirt floor, the mother at her station—all provide information about the child's family and environment. The shock of separation from the mother, though it takes just a moment in real time, is so impactful it needs to have room on the page to expand. We stay with the narrator in that suspension of time when he feels he has lost his mother's love forever. Thankfully, in this memory, the mother relents almost right away, pats his head and says, "C'mon, I do love you." The child is relieved, but also transformed a bit by this rift, and he ends the short chapter by returning to the image of "a tortilla puffy and light like a cloud. She taps it and it deflates slowly, steam escaping through a little tear."

Note how in all these examples, the authors rely on strong sensory details to build these scenes, creating images using smell, sound, touch, and taste, in addition to sight. (See later in this chapter, "The Five (or Six) Senses of Memory," for more details on this essential writing skill.) You can practice building your imagistic endurance by trusting your memory, and your intuition, to give you the material you need to start building your own story, one "river tooth" at a time.

Metaphorical Memory

A metaphor is a way of getting at a truth that exists beyond the literal. By pinpointing certain images as symbolic, writers can go deeper than surface truths and create essays that work on many levels at once. This is what writers are up to all the time, not only with memory but with the material of experience and the world. We resurrect the details to describe not only the surface appearance, but also to make intuitive, metaphorical connections. For example, the tortilla deflating in Rodríguez's memory reflects the deflation the child feels in that moment.

As we saw in the last section, many writers allow early memories to "impress themselves" on the mind. They do not dismiss them as passing details but rather probe them for any insights they may contain. They ask not only "what?" but "why?" Why does Beard remember that moment of isolation from her family, and why was her child self so affected by the fireworks on that particular evening? Why does Rodríguez remember that quick moment of estrangement from his mother? The memories are insistent enough that these writers spend the time necessary to embody these bits of their childhood on the page and, through the writing, perhaps discover some themes that will permeate their work, such as finding one's place in the family, or understanding the rickety nature of love.

Muscle Memory

There is a phrase used in dancing, athletics, parachuting, and other fields that require sharp training of the body: *muscle memory*. Once the body learns the repetitive gestures of a certain movement or skill, the memory of how to execute these movements will be encoded in the muscles. That is why, for instance, we never forget how to ride a bike.

One cannot speak of memory—and of bodily memory in particular—without trotting out Marcel Proust and his famous madeleine. Proust dips his cookie in lime-blossom tea, and *Remembrance of Things Past* springs forth, all six volumes of it.

The body can offer an inexhaustible store of memories to begin any number of essays, each of which will have greater significance than what appears on the surface. Sometimes, what matters to us most is what has mattered to the body. Memory may pretend to live in the cerebral cortex, but it requires muscle—real muscle—to animate it again for the page.

The Five (or Six) Senses of Memory

By paying attention to the sensory gateways of the body, you also begin to write in a way that naturally *embodies* experience, making it tactile for the reader. Readers tend to care deeply only about those things they *feel* in the body at a visceral level. We experience the world through our senses. We must translate that experience into the language of the senses as well.

Smell

"Smell is a potent wizard that transports us across thousands of miles and all the years we have lived," wrote Helen Keller in her autobiography. "The odors of fruits waft me to my southern home, to my childhood frolics in the peach orchard. Other odors, instantaneous and fleeting, cause my heart to dilate joyously or contract with remembered grief."

We all have this innate connection to smell. Physiologically, we *do* apprehend smells more quickly than the other sensations, and the images aroused by smell can act as beacons leading to our richest memories, our most private selves. Smell is so intimately tied up with breath, after all, a function of our bodies that works continually, day and night.

Smells can also evoke a place in your memory quite effectively. For example, in Joan Didion's essay "Goodbye to All That," she recreates her experience of moving to New York as a young woman. Her senses take in everything, and smells are especially potent. She remembers "the warm air smelled of mildew" and "I could smell lilac and garbage and expensive perfume." Or in the Michel de Montaigne essay, "Of Smells" (see Anthology), smells become the animating force behind some of his strongest (and characteristically quirky) opinions.

Taste

Food is one of the most social gifts we have. For example, in "A Thing Shared," food aficionado M. F. K. Fisher uses something as simple and commonplace as the taste of a peach pie—"the warm round peach pie and cool yellow cream"—to describe a memory of her father and sister the first time they found themselves alone without the mediating influence of the mother. The food acts as more than mere sustenance; it becomes a moment of communion:

> That night I not only saw my father for the first time as a person. I saw the golden hills and the live oaks as clearly as I have ever seen them since; and I saw the dimples in my little sister's fat hands in a way that still moves me because of that first time; and I saw food as something beautiful to be shared with people instead of as a thrice-daily necessity.

This scene becomes an illustration of how we awaken to one another. It's less about her own family than about the fleeting moments of connection that can transpire in all families, in one way or another. (See Chapter 2, "Writing the Family," for more examples of how memories of food can be an effective way into writing about family.)

Sometimes taste can be evoked not only through the act of eating, but also by noticing a taste on the tongue. The taste of fear, for example, is often metallic, and strong emotion or illness can lead to a sensation of sourness. Or you can have a taste linger long after a meal is finished. For example, in his essay "Afternoon of an American Boy," E. B. White remembers his first date—an awkward, tense, and hilarious occasion—this way: "In my dream, I am again seated with Eileen at the edge of the dance floor, frightened, stunned, and happy—in my ears the intoxicating drumbeat of the dance, in my throat the dry, bittersweet taste of cinnamon." He ends the paragraph on that image, emphasizing the flavor of cinnamon, but also emphasizing how such memories are often "bittersweet."

Hearing

Sounds often go unnoticed. Because we cannot consciously cut off our hearing unless we plug our ears, we've learned to filter sounds, picking and choosing the ones that are important, becoming inured to the rest. But these sounds often make up a subliminal backdrop to our lives, and even the faintest echo can tug back moments from the past in their entirety.

For example, in his short essay, "The Fine Art of Sighing" (see Anthology), memoirist Bernard Cooper uses a sound as subtle as a sigh to elucidate his relationship to his family, himself, and the world. He describes how his father sighs, how his mother sighs, and how he, himself, sighs. And, paradoxically, by focusing in on this small, simple act, Cooper reveals much larger things: his mother's dissatisfaction with domestic life, his father's gruff sensual nature, and Cooper's ambivalence about his own body and sexuality. He writes:

A friend of mine once mentioned that I was given to long and ponderous sighs. Once I became aware of this habit, I heard my father's sighs in my own and knew for a moment his small satisfactions. At other times, I felt my mother's restlessness and wished I could leave my body with my breath, or be happy in the body my breath left behind.

Music is not so subtle but rather can act as a blaring soundtrack to our emotional lives. Think about the bonds you formed with friends over common musical passions, the days spent listening to the same song over and over. Sometimes you turned up that song as loud as you could so that it might communicate to the world—and to your deepest, deafest self—*exactly* the measure of your emotion. We often orchestrate our memories around the music that accompanied those pivotal eras of our lives. When you have the soundtrack down, the rest of life seems to fall into place. (See also Chapter 6, "Writing the Arts," for further discussion on the role music can play in our writing.)

Touch

Hospitals rely on volunteers to hold babies on the infant wards. Their only job is to hold and rock any baby that is crying or in distress. The nurses, of course, do not have time for such constant care, but they know this type of touch is essential as medicine for their patients' healing. As we grow, we are constantly aware of our bodies, of how they feel as they move through the world. Without this sense we become lost, disoriented in space and time.

Remember Rodríguez's childhood memory from earlier in this chapter? He often uses the sense of touch as a way to evoke the atmosphere in which he grew up. For example, in his chapter titled "dark loud," he describes a typically hot night in his home, where he sleeps in a bedroom with eight brothers and sisters. His mother lies next to him, fanning him with a shirt:

> Oh, the fanning is like a big bowl of beans just for me. She runs her hand through my hair that feels wet and slithery like earthworms matted against my forehead. She raises it and blows softly and this feels good, like it is the first time. I try to turn my body because it gets hot lying on one side. I want to cool my back but there's no room, shoulders and elbows and backs press against me like angry, pin me down.

Sometimes an essayist can also focus on the tactile feel of objects as a way to explore deeper emotions or memories. For instance, in his short essay "Buckeye," Scott Russell Sanders focuses on the feel of the buckeye seeds that his father carried with him to ward off arthritis. They are "hollow," he says, "hard as pebbles, yet they still gleam from the polish of his hands." (See also Chapter 8, "The Tradition of the Personal Essay," for more about "The Object Essay.")

Sanders then allows the sensation of touch to be the way we get to know his father:

> My father never paid much heed to pain. Near the end, when his worn knee often slipped out of joint, he would pound it back in place with a rubber mallet. If a splinter worked into his flesh beyond the reach of tweezers, he would heat the blade of his knife over a cigarette lighter and slice through the skin.

Such sensory details bring the reader into the father's body, feeling the pound of that mallet, the slice of the skin. He never needs to tell us his father was a tough man; the images do all the work for him. These details also allow us to see the narrator, Sanders, watching his father closely, and so this scene also conveys at least a part of their relationship and its emotional tenor.

Sight

How do you see the world? How do you see yourself? Even linguistically, our sense of sight seems so tied up in our perceptions, stance, opinions, personalities, and knowledge of the world. To see something often means to finally understand, to be enlightened, to have our vision cleared. What we choose to see—and *not* to see—often says more about us than anything else.

Visual scenes can be rendered from various distances. We can have an extended view, taking in the scenery, the environment, the exterior details; and we can have a more focused view, zeroing in on particular details of people and places. You might think about it in cinematic terms, the way a camera will often give an "establishing shot" of the scene, then gradually move in to show the viewer the important details in a close-up.

Sometimes, when we are in unfamiliar territory or intuit that we may be in danger, our senses heighten, and this awareness can be translated into a highly visual scene on the page. For example, in her memoir *I Am, I Am, I Am: Seventeen Brushes with Death,* Maggie O'Farrell articulates several key moments in time when she felt her mortality, and she renders these moments in minute detail. For example, in the first chapter, titled "Neck" (all the chapters are labeled after body parts that were involved in the incidents), she remembers a time she met a man alone on a hiking trail. She drops us right into the scene, with no introduction or buildup:

> On the path ahead, stepping out from behind a boulder, a man appears.
>
> We are, he and I, on the far side of a dark tarn that lies hidden in the bowl-curved summit of this mountain. The sky is a milky blue above us; no vegetation grows this far up so it is just me and him, the stones and the still black water. He straddles the narrow track with both booted feet and he smiles.

I realize several things. That I passed him earlier, farther down the glen. We greeted each other, in the amiable yet brief manner of those on a country walk. That, on this remote stretch of path, there is no one near enough to hear me call. That he has been waiting for me: he has planned this whole thing, carefully, meticulously, and I have walked into his trap.

I see all this, in an instant.

This scene is cinematic in its rendering: we can see every detail clearly, from the man's booted feet (up close) to the "stones and the still black water" (extended view). She gives us a brief flashback to establish context, then returns to the charged moment at hand. The scene *feels* dangerous, but she never mentions the word "danger." She, thankfully, avoids being harmed by this man (who does, indeed, turn out to be quite dangerous), but she allows the reader inside this moment where we don't yet know the outcome.

Of course, this is an extreme example, but we all have moments that have "struck" us in some way. We have visual details engraved in our memories, and we can render those details in visual terms on the page.

"Sixth" Sense

When we say we have a "sixth sense" about something, we usually mean that we are gaining information that isn't obvious to our five physical senses. We're intuiting an emotion, an intention, or an outcome; or we are feeling the presence of forces beyond our everyday control. For example, take a look at the short graphic memoir "Perdition" by Kristen Radtke (see Anthology). The scene—a moment that shows the undercurrents of a relationship between mother and daughter—is built almost entirely on the "sixth sense."

When you practice rendering your memories in highly physical details, often these details will give rise to an intuitive sense as well. And as the older narrator looking back on a scene, this present knowledge may also color your perception of the memory and allow for a subtle prediction of what will happen in the future. You might even be able to use *future tense* to show this mature awareness, with phrases such as "I don't yet know" or "I didn't know then" inserted into the memory. (For an example of this technique, see "First" by Ryan Van Meter in our Anthology.)

Look back at the examples given throughout this chapter and see if you can find the "sixth sense" functioning in the scenes. What are the narrators' intuiting? What kind of knowledge arises in their bodies?

Body Image

As you practice calling up and articulating memories using the body as a vehicle, you may find yourself grappling with issues of body image. Many people have struggled with perceptions of their bodies throughout their lives, and thinking about their bodies may also evoke memories of deep trauma.

For example, to open her memoir *Hunger: A Memoir of (My) Body,* Roxane Gay writes: "I wish I could write a book about being at peace and loving myself wholly, at any size. . . . But I soon realized I was not only writing a memoir of my body; I was forcing myself to look at what my body has endured, the weight I gained, and how hard it has been to both live with and lose that weight. I've been forced to look at my guiltiest secrets." Such an exploration goes beyond the personal narrative; it reaches out to connect with others. Gay goes on to say: "This is a memoir of (my) body because, more often than not, stories of bodies like mine are ignored or dismissed or derided."

In her innovative essay "People Are Starving," Suzanne Rivecca manages to transform the issue of body image from a personal narrative to a communal story. She shows how her experience of an eating disorder is enacted in various ways among so many others through strategic use of the first-person plural ("we") point of view. As the essay progresses, each paragraph shows both how food and eating function so differently in each person's life, but how united the "we" becomes through this focus on body image:

> Before there was pretty or ugly, before there was virginal or slutty, there was fat or skinny. We saw what happened to the girls who were fat, even if they were barely fat at all. Everything they did and said was discredited and illegitimate by default. If they were sad, they got laughed at. If they were happy, they got laughed at. Nothing they had could be pure. There was no margin for error.

Body image is so complex; it encompasses body size, clothing, skin, hair, and a multitude of other aspects that affect the way we move through the world. It can be challenging to delve deeply into this material, but such an exploration can yield great rewards—for yourself and others.

Illness Memoir

As we write about our bodies, illness—both physical and mental—can naturally emerge as an important subject for autobiographical writing. Experiences of illness often lend themselves to memoir because they are such decisive turning points and have so much impact on our lives.

In writing an illness memoir, it can be tempting to overwhelm the reader with step-by-step medical information, because *all* this information was relevant to you. Readers will be more likely to connect to the story if you can prune that information down and find the key moments or concrete objects that allow us deeply into your experience. For example, when Brenda was writing about a miscarriage, she found herself writing, instead, about a needlepoint kit her mother had given her. These words came out: "As I recovered from surgery, I thought only of that needlepoint, each stitch, one after the other, and mounds of color gradually developed under my hands . . . [My mother] knew that sometimes only the simplest actions are feasible, and those are the ones that lead us out of illness and back into the world."

As with other autobiographical topics, illness can often lead to an examination of issues that go beyond the personal. You may be breaking silences, or helping remove the isolation and stigma someone with a similar illness may experience. In *Pain Woman Takes Your Keys, and Other Essays from a Nervous System,* Sonya Huber writes:

> This is a collection of unconventional essays on chronic pain; my goal with these essays was not to fix or provide advice (most of us have had too much of that) but to explore the landscape. Pain is a territory known by those who are in that land. I am in a small corner of it, and the more I see of its vastness, the more I realize how little I know. . . . I hope with these essays to add to the growing literature about what pain is and how it is experienced, imagined, and expressed so that its universal burden can be shared.

These last words speak to why we write and read any type of memoir. Yes, we care, to a certain extent, about the details of an individual life, but to hold our interest and have an impact, a personal narrative must be written in such a way that the author reaches beyond the self and connects to more communal concerns.

Try It

1. First Memories

Write a scene of an early memory, perhaps your first memory. What calls out for further examination? What in this scene seems to matter to you? What are you leaving out? If you get stuck, keep repeating the phrase "I remember" to start off your sentences; allow this rhythm to take you further than you thought you could go.

2. "Imagistic Endurance"

Once you have written down your memory, go back with this checklist in hand, and see how many more sensory details you can include. Don't worry about going overboard or about "making things up." Your memory holds more than you thought possible!

- What did this memory *look* like? (details of colors, clothing, objects, people, etc.)
- What did this memory *sound* like? (What might you have heard in the background? Music, nature sounds, city sounds, conversations, sounds of the household, etc.)
- What did this memory *smell* like? (smells that might have been present, such as odors of cooking, nature, city, perfume, laundry, etc.)
- What did this memory *taste* like? (taste in your mouth from food or emotion, eating food, taste of the air, etc.)
- What did this memory *feel* like? (tactile sensations on the skin, textures of objects or nature or people, etc.)
- What kind of *intuition* does the character experience? (a new understanding, a sense of what is really going on with the people around her, a prediction of what will happen in the future, etc.)

3. **Metaphorical Memory**

    Go back and look at your early memory writing. Ask yourself "Why?" Why did you remember what you remembered? Why did that moment arise? What kind of theme or idea is suggested by the details in this memory?

    Once you have a theme or idea or emotion in mind, what other memories and/or scenes might also relate to this theme? Brainstorm a list. This list can provide you with lots of good material for further writing.

4. In the preface to his anthology *The Business of Memory*, Charles Baxter writes, "What we talk about when we talk about memory is—often—what we have forgotten and what has been lost. The passion and torment and significance seem to lie in that direction." What have you forgotten in your life? What are the moments that keep sliding out of reach? Write for twenty minutes, using the phrase "I can't remember" to start off each sentence. Where does such an examination lead you?

    You may find that by using this exercise you can back into the scenes and images you *do* remember but never knew how to approach. You can write some very powerful essays based on this prompt, exploring material that seemed too dangerous to examine head-on.

    > **VARIATION:** After you've lighted on some events or times you can't fully articulate, do a little research. Ask others about their memories of that time. Find documents or photographs that may shed some light on the issue. After you've gathered enough evidence, write an essay that focuses on the way your memory and the "reality" either differ or coincide. Why have you forgotten the things you did?

5. How many different "firsts" can you remember in your life? The first meal you remember enjoying, the first smell you remember wanting to smell again, the first day of school, the first book you remember reading by yourself, the first album you ever bought, the first time you drove a car, the first kiss? How does your memory of these "first" events color your perception of yourself? What kinds of metaphors do they generate for your life story?

THE SIX SENSES OF MEMORY

Smell

1. Gather articles that you know carry some smell that is evocative for you. One by one, smell them deeply, and then write the images that arise in your mind. Write quickly, allowing the smell to trigger other sensory associations.

2. Which smells in your life are gone for you now? Which ones would you give anything to smell again?

> **VARIATION FOR A GROUP:** Each person brings in an object that carries some kind of strong smell and takes a turn being the leader. Keep the object hidden until it is your turn. The rest of the group members close their eyes while the leader brings this object to everyone and asks them to smell deeply. Each person immediately writes the images and associations that smell evoked. Share these writings with each other and see how similarly or differently you reacted to the same odor.

Taste

1. Try to remember the first meal you consciously tasted and enjoyed. Describe this meal in detail; make yourself hungry with these details. Who ate this meal with you? If you can't remember any such meal, imagine one.

2. If you were to write a life history through food, what would be the "touchstone" moments, the meals that represented turning points for you? Which meals have you loved? Which meals have you hated? Which meals marked important transitions in your life?

> **VARIATION FOR A GROUP:** Have "food exploration" days set aside for your group meetings. On these days, one person is responsible for bringing in an item of food for everyone to taste. After exploring the sight, textures, and smells, taste it. Describe this food in detail, then go on to whichever images and metaphorical associations arise.

Touch

1. Take an inventory of the scars or marks on your body. How were they received? How do these external scars relate to any internal "markings" as well?

2. Find an object that you consider a talisman, something you either carry with you or keep in a special place in your home. Hold it in your hand, and with your eyes closed, feel all its textures. Begin to write, using this tactile description to trigger memories, scenes, and metaphors.

> **VARIATION FOR A GROUP:** Each person brings in such an object for a "show-and-tell," explaining the story behind the item. Pass these things around the room for everyone to examine, and then write based on *someone else's* talisman. What did it feel like in your hand? How does it trigger memories of your own?

Hearing

1. Try creating a scene from your childhood using *only* the sense of hearing. What music is playing in the background? Whose voice is on the radio? How loud is the sound of traffic? Try to pick out as many ambient sounds as you can, then begin to amplify the ones you think have the most metaphorical significance. What kind of emotional tone do these sounds give to the piece?

2. Put on a piece of music that you strongly associate with a certain era of your life. Using this music as a soundtrack, zero in on a particular scene that arises in your mind. Try writing the scene *without mentioning the music at all*, but through your word choices and imagery and sentence structure convey the essence of this music's rhythm and beat.

> **VARIATION:** Do the same thing, but this time use fragments of the lyrics as "scaffolding" for the essay. Give us a few lines, then write part of the memory those lines evoke in you. Give us a few more and continue with the memory, so that the song plays throughout the entire piece.

Sight

1. Using a photograph of yourself, a relative, or a friend, describe every detail of the scene. Then focus on one object or detail that seems unexpected to you in some way. How does this detail trigger specific memories? Also, imagine what occurred just before and just after this photograph was taken; what is left outside the frame? For instance, write an essay with a title such as "After [Before] My Father Is Photographed on the *U.S.S. Constitution*." (Insert whichever subject is appropriate for the photographs you've chosen.)

> **VARIATION FOR A GROUP:** Repeat the preceding exercise, but then trade photographs with your neighbor. Which details strike you? How does any part of the scene remind you of scenes from your own life? Perform a number of these trades around the room to see which details leap up from other people's photographs.

2. Look at a memory piece you've already written. What kind of sight distances do you use? Extended view? Close up? Try revising this scene (or create a new one) using various sight distances.

Sixth Sense

1. Go back to a scene you've already written and see if you can use language that heightens the sixth sense. Words such as "I don't yet know . . . ," or "perhaps . . . ," or "I don't know why . . . ," can signal that you are entering territory beyond the physical facts of the moment.

BODY IMAGE

1. Has body image been an issue in your life? Try to pinpoint early memories that speak to a "before and after" with this topic. When did you feel at ease with your body? When did that change? As with any early memory writing, use both fact and imagination to populate these scenes with concrete, sensory detail.

2. Using the example from Suzanne Rivecca's essay "People Are Starving" as a model, write your experience of body image in the first-person plural ("we") point of view.

3. Take a concept from Roxane Gay, and write a memoir piece from the point of view of your body.

ILLNESS MEMOIR

1. Call up a memory of a time when you were ill: either an ongoing chronic illness or a momentary one. Focus your attention on the objects that surrounded you during that time. Give your reader a full picture of your environment, and allow the concrete things of this environment to lead you to new memories, new ideas, new understanding.

    For example, in *The Sound of a Wild Snail Eating,* Elisabeth Tova Bailey turns her attention on a tiny snail she finds in a pot of wild violets a friend brings her as she recuperates from a serious illness. We never find out much about the illness itself; rather, that time in bed, with only a wild snail for company, provides the author with a space to examine how one's world shrinks in times of vulnerability and isolation.

FOR FURTHER READING

In Our Anthology
- "The Fine Art of Sighing" by Bernard Cooper
- "Of Smells" by Michel de Montaigne
- "Perdition" by Kristen Radtke
- "First" by Ryan Van Meter

Resources Available Online
- "Goodbye to All That" by Joan Didion
- "People Are Starving" by Suzanne Rivecca
- "Buckeye" by Scott Russell Sanders

Print Resources
- *The Sound of a Wild Snail Eating* by Elisabeth Tova Bailey
- *The Business of Memory,* edited by Charles Baxter
- *The Boys of My Youth* by Jo Ann Beard
- *Truth Serum: Memoirs* by Bernard Cooper
- *Slouching Towards Bethlehem* by Joan Didion
- *River Teeth* by David James Duncan
- *The Art of Eating* by M. F. K. Fisher
- *Hunger: A Memoir of (My) Body* by Roxane Gay
- *Pain Woman Takes Your Keys, and Other Essays from a Nervous System* by Sonya Huber
- *The Story of My Life* by Helen Keller
- "Needlepoint" by Brenda Miller in *Season of the Body*
- *The Names* by N. Scott Momaday
- *I Am, I Am, I Am: Seventeen Brushes with Death* by Maggie O'Farrell
- *Remembrance of Things Past* by Marcel Proust
- *House Built on Ashes* by José Antonio Rodríguez
- *Essays of E. B. White* by E. B. White
- *Moments of Being* by Virginia Woolf

2

Writing the Family

One thing that we always assume, wrongly, is that if we write about people honestly they will resent it and become angry. If you come at it for the right reasons . . . if you treat them with complexity and compassion, sometimes they will feel as though they've been honored, not because they're presented in some ideal way but because they're presented with understanding.

—Kim Barnes

My brother is swinging the bat and I'm bored in the stands, seven years old. My mother has given me a piece of paper and a pen that doesn't have much ink in it. I've written, "I have two brothers. One is a little one. One is a big one. There are only two girls in our family. One is me. One is my mother." The mothers sit all around me, their straight skirts pulled tight across their knees. My brother is swinging the bat and wiggling his hips on the other side of the mesh. Where is my father? I squint to see him near the dugout, his hands cupped around his mouth. My brother swings the bat, and the ball sails, sails, sails out of sight. Everyone stands up, cheering, but I stay seated long enough to write: "The big brother just made a home run and I think that's all I'll write. Goodbye." My brother prances around the bases, casually slapping the hands held out in high fives as he trots past third. The catcher already sulks unmasked against the backstop. My brother casually taps his foot against home.

On that scrap of paper, I naturally turn toward the people in my life as a way to begin a description of that life. As a child, it's nearly impossible to think of myself as an individual separate from my family.

—Brenda

23

Situating Yourself in Relation to Family

From the minute we arrive in the world, we're put at the mercy of the people who care for us. And we might find the rest of our lives taken up with dual, contradictory impulses: to be an integral part of this clan and to be a separate individual, set apart. Our families, however they're configured, provide our first mirrors, our first definitions of who we are. And they become our first objects of love, anger, and loyalty.

When we say the word "family," we often mean our biological families—our families of origin. But we can also think of other families we create throughout our lives—our families of choice. We also often have friends that feel and act more like family. For the purposes of writing about this topic, you can define "family" as it best fits for you.

In writing about family, it's often tempting, especially when you're dealing with emotionally charged material, to try and encompass *everything* in one essay. Such a strategy will leave you, and your readers, numb and exhausted. Ask the small questions. Focus on small details that show a bigger picture. For example, in "Reading History to My Mother," Robin Hemley spurs a complex essay about his mother by focusing first on her eyeglasses:

> My mother owns at least half a dozen glasses, and I know I should have sorted through them all by now (we tried once). . . . On her dresser there are parts of various eyeglasses: maimed glasses, the corpses of eyeglasses, a dark orphaned lens here, a frame there, an empty case, and one case with a pair that's whole. This is the one I grab and take out to my mother who is waiting patiently, always patient these days, or perhaps so unnerved and exhausted that it passes for patience.

In this memoir, Hemley will detail the decline of his mother's physical and mental health as she advances in age, and he chronicles his own ambivalent responses to caring for her. This subject will lead into even bigger ideas about how we recreate our histories as part of our love for one another. Rather than approach such things head-on, Hemley wisely turns to the small, physical things first—those eyeglasses—as a way to not only create a convincing scene, but also to plant the seeds for the emotional material to come. Those mangled, mixed-up eyeglasses signal the state of mind we'll be invited to enter.

The Biographer

When we're writing about family, sometimes it's helpful to think of ourselves as biographers, rather than autobiographers. This slight shift in perspective just might be enough to create the emotional distance necessary to begin shaping experience into literature on the page. It will also allow you to take a broader view of your subject that encompasses community, culture, and history.

As Tarn Wilson articulates in her essay "Go Ahead: Write About Your Parents, Again," we write about more than just our own families when we do so with curiosity and a desire to understand our families in new ways. We can also see our family members shaped by the historical context in which they lived. She writes:

> If I step back from my fears, I know that when we write honestly and richly about our families, we also write cultural history. While wrestling with my memoir about my hippie parents' attempt to live off the land in the Canadian wilderness in the early 70s, I discovered that to truly understand my mother and father, I had to know the forces that shaped them: the assassinations of John F. Kennedy and Martin Luther King, Jr.; the divisions and disillusionments of the Vietnam War; the rise of modern feminism; the movement toward an eco-spirituality. I began to see my parents not merely as individuals making choices, but as players in a larger cultural movement.

Sometimes it helps to take this biographer's stance as a necessary distancing device. For example, in Brent Staples's essay "The Coroner's Photographs" (see Anthology), Staples assumes a reporter's role, using the coroner's statistics and graphic photos as a way to begin dealing with his brother's violent death. Because the subject holds so many emotional land mines, Staples uses this structure to step back from the scene, but at the same time he's able to give us intimate physical details of his brother, such as the way his second toe "curls softly in an extended arc and rises above the others in a way that is unique to us." Not until the very end of the essay do we hear a direct emotional reaction from the narrator; rather, he allows the facts to speak for themselves.

Sometimes it's helpful to imagine our relatives as they might have been before we knew them as mother, father, grandmother, and so on. In Paisley

Rekdal's essay "The Night My Mother Met Bruce Lee" (see Anthology), she allows herself to imagine in vivid detail her mother as a sixteen-year-old girl:

> Age sixteen, my mother loads up red tubs of noodles, teacups chipped and white-gray as teeth, rice clumps that glue themselves to the plastic tubs' sides or dissolve and turn papery in the weak tea sloshing around the bottom. She's at Diamond Chan's restaurant, where most of her cousins work after school and during summer vacations, some of her friends, too. . . . My mother's nails are cracked, kept short by clipping or gnawing, glisten only when varnished with the grease of someone else's leftovers.

We then move from this imaginative scene into a real one closer to the present day. The contrast between the two scenes allows for a level of character development that might otherwise be impossible.

Family and Cultural Identity Through Food

As we saw in Chapter 1, "The Body of Memory," sensory details are key to developing our memories on the page. And look back to the Paisley Rekdal quote in the preceding section; note how she turns to the sensory details of food to immediately evoke a picture of her mother's situation as a young woman. Whether you're writing about family relationships for the first time or for the hundredth time, food can often serve as an especially effective portal to describe and articulate both your familial and cultural identity.

For example, in her essay "There's No Recipe for Growing Up," Scaachi Koul describes her upbringing through a focus on specific foods she had throughout her childhood and into the present day. After describing the foods her mother prepared for the Hindu holiday of Diwali, Koul goes on to describe the everyday foods of her childhood:

> Food is a big part of any Indian holiday, but in my parents' home, hearty homemade Indian food was a fixture every day. Nightly, we had mounds of basmati rice, baby eggplants stewed in spices that I'd hold up to my face like bejeweled earrings, collard greens and turnips (gross, until I grew up). Best of all were the nights where she made Kashmiri rogan josh, a lamb dish she'd

whip together in a pressure cooker that was perennially broken, the whistle propped up with a wooden spoon and screaming every five minutes on a Saturday afternoon.

Notice how specific Koul is in her detailed descriptions of the food in her home (and of that "perennially broken" pressure cooker!), and how that food defined the culture of her growing up. She immerses us in these details, without extraneous explanations, so that we experience her household from the inside out.

As the author digs deeper into her memories, we are led, inevitably, to an imagining of what will happen when her mother is no longer with her. The essay then transcends a personal story into a universal concept: "When you emigrate, you end up the last person to touch a lot of your family history."

This longing to connect to one's cultural identity through food—especially in the light of a family member's imminent or recent death—is quite common and creates a bond with the reader. Through an author's attention to sensory detail—and a strong individual voice—these moments can stand above the rest. For example, in Ruby Tandoh's essay "From Soup to Nuts," she describes the transformation she experiences after her grandfather's death:

> I had been happy enough at school to let people twist my Ghanaian surname into knots—Ruby Tandoori, Ruby Tango—and make jokes about the ashy colour I went in the sun, or the woolly tangles of my hair. I hadn't really known what Ghana meant to my family or who my extended family even was. . . . But when Ransford died I found that I never wanted to be that rudderless or that acquiescent to people's everyday bigotries ever again. I wanted a taste of my heritage; I wanted to know who I was.

There are, of course, an infinite number of ways to handle family material in creative nonfiction, but many writers turn to memories of eating because food—whether it be abundant or scarce—is so elemental to family and cultural life. Food can become, on the page, not only sustenance for the body, but also fortification for some of the deepest (and most complex) memories of family we hold.

The Obstacle Course

When we write about family, we set ourselves up for a plethora of ethical, emotional, and technical issues that may hinder us from writing altogether. It's one thing to write about your sister in your diary; it's quite another to write about her in an essay published in a national magazine. And when we set out to write about family, we are naturally going to feel compelled to break long silences that may have kept the family together in the first place. Many creative nonfiction works take on issues of child abuse, incest, alcoholic parents, and other emotional issues. When you sit down to write, you might also feel obligated to write about traumas of your family history. You might feel these are the only issues worth tackling in literature.

Family is always an enormous subject, and as writers, we must find a way to handle this topic with both aplomb and discretion. If your family history is particularly charged, it will be even more essential for you to find the smaller details that will lead the way into a successful essay. For example, as noted in Chapter 1, Bernard Cooper focuses on the sound of his family's sighs to describe crucial differences between his father, his mother, and himself in his essay "The Fine Art of Sighing." Paisley Rekdal focuses on her mother's fingernails "varnished with the grease of someone else's leftovers." You might find yourself drawn to take on big issues with your family. But they must arrive on the page less as issues and more as scenes, images, and metaphors that will evoke a strong response from the reader.

Permission to Speak

While drafting your essay, you must instinctively drown out the voices that tell you *not* to write. Your mother, father, sisters, and brothers must all be banished from the room where you sit at your desk and call up potentially painful or embarrassing memories. But once you know you have an essay that is more for public consumption than private venting, you have some difficult decisions to make. How much of this is really your own story to tell?

Writers deal with this dilemma in a variety of ways. Some merely remain in denial, convincing themselves that no one—least of all their families—will ever read their work. Some go to the opposite extreme, confessing to their families about their writing projects and asking permission to divulge certain stories and details, giving them complete veto power. Some, such as Frank McCourt with *Angela's Ashes*, wait until the major players have died so that they can no longer be hurt by the exposure or pass judgment on the writer. Some decide that writing about this material in a nonfiction form is just too risky and decide to present their work as fiction instead. Some writers change the names of their characters—some even write under a pseudonym—to protect both themselves and their families.

However you choose to negotiate these tricky issues, remember that your story *is* your story to tell. Yours is not the *only* story or perspective on family or on your community, but it is a perfectly valid voice among the chorus. In her essay "Writing About Family: Is It Worth It?" Mimi Schwartz reminds us that "a memoirist, in particular, must think of truth as having a small 't,' not a big one—as in *my* truth rather than *the* truth." And if you examine this truth with a healthy sense of perspective and with literary skill, you may be surprised at the reactions you evoke among your subjects. They may feel honored to see themselves couched in a work of literature. (See also Chapter 11, "The Particular Challenges of Creative Nonfiction.")

Here is how Robin Hemley dealt with these issues when he wrote and published "Reading History to My Mother."

> I think this is one of the few essays I haven't shown my mother. . . . I don't think that one needs to show everything one writes to those involved—sometimes one can actually do more harm than good with the full-disclosure impulse. Sometimes, one acts more out of one's own need for absolution rather than actually considering the feelings of the person to whom the disclosure is made. . . . We write for many different reasons, and often our best work is dangerous, edgy, and guilt-inducing. Sometimes we feel it's worth sharing with others, whether the reasons are literary or therapeutic, and I don't think we should necessarily engage in self-censorship simply because we might be unwilling to share our work with the person(s) the work deals with. . . . I'd say that my decision was made of equal measures of love and cowardice.

Love and cowardice might aptly describe all of us when we find ourselves writing about family or about those close to us in our communities. Complex emotions beset us in this endeavor, and we must remain aware of them before they ambush us altogether.

Our Motives

If we are going to write successfully about family, our motives must be more than simple exposure of family history and secrets. We must have some perspective on our experience that spurs the essay beyond our own personal "dirty laundry" and into the realm of literature.

Our role as writers can be that of the witness. We continually bear witness to those around us, and sometimes our job is to speak for those who have never spoken for themselves. When we write about our families or take on the mantle of the biographer, we are really writing (and forging) community. As Terry Tempest Williams writes, in her essay "A 'Downwinder' in Hiroshima": "I think about . . . how much we need to hear the truth of one another's lives. . . . The Japanese have a word, *aware*, which speaks to both the beauty and pain of our lives, that sorrow is not a grief one forgets or recovers from but is a burning, searing illumination of love for the delicacy and strength of our relations."

TRY IT

1. Try to reconstruct the names of your matriarchal or patriarchal lineage. For instance, what is the name of your mother, your mother's mother, your mother's mother's mother, and so forth? How far back can you go? Naming them brings them to life and enables you to begin writing about them. Where do the names come from? Does your own name have any "inheritance" attached to it? What are the stories behind the names? Are you adopted? How does this affect how you construct your sense of lineage?

   VARIATION: Circle one of the names that intrigues you for whatever reason, then do some research on this person. Find photographs, letters, or birth certificates—whatever might be stored in a family archive. Begin an essay that builds a portrait of this person from the name outward.

2. Describe every member of your family in terms of a part of the body. For instance, describe the hands of your mother, father, siblings, grandparents, and yourself. How are they alike? How are they different? If necessary, imagine the details. For instance, imagine your grandmother's hands as they were before she was a grandmother. Which traits emerge in your own physical makeup? Which ones do you hate? Which ones do you love?

3. As Paisley Rekdal did, begin an essay by imagining the life of someone close to you—a family member, friend, mentor—before you knew them. Use your imagination coupled with your experience of this person. Use any clues that may exist: objects from the past, documents, photographs, and so forth to form a portrait of this person before you were in the picture. Then complete the essay by contrasting this portrait with the person you know today. How are they different or similar?

4. Write a list of the foods you remember most from your childhood. Use as many sensory details as you can to evoke how this food was a backdrop to your growing up.

5. Write a paragraph or two starting with the line: "I would love to taste again. . . ." Use this phrase to evoke what you miss the most from family meals or other food experiences. See if this opening might lead you to other details or people you miss (or don't miss) in your family history.

6. Gather with some friends to create a potluck based on key foods from your cultural and/or familial histories. Encourage storytelling at the table. Perhaps write an essay based on this present-day experience as a platform for evoking memories of the past.

7. Create a picture of your family based on some simple gesture: the way they sigh, laugh, cry, and so on. Begin with a vivid description of this gesture, then describe your father, your mother, yourself, or any other family members. Try to see how examining these small gestures reveals larger details about the family.

8. Try writing a family story you think you know well in a voice other than your own. Use the point of view of another family member and see how the story changes or which details now become important.

9. The writer and philosopher John Berger has said: "I have always thought that household gods were animals. Sometimes visible and sometimes invisible, but always present." Begin an essay by writing about the animals in the life of your family. What role did a particular animal play in the family dynamics? You can begin by describing the way this animal arrived in your life, using the types of sensory details and scenes you've been practicing in other work.

FOR FURTHER READING

In Our Anthology
- "The Fine Art of Sighing" by Bernard Cooper
- "The Night My Mother Met Bruce Lee" by Paisley Rekdal
- "The Coroner's Photographs" by Brent Staples
- "First" by Ryan Van Meter

Resources Available Online
- "There's No Recipe for Growing Up" by Scaachi Koul
- "From Soup to Nuts" by Ruby Tandoh
- "Go Ahead: Write About Your Parents, Again" by Tarn Wilson

Print Resources
- *Open House: Writers Redefine Home,* edited by Mark Doty
- "Reading History to My Mother" by Robin Hemley in *Fourth Genre: Explorations in Nonfiction,* Spring 1999
- *This Is the Place: Women Writing About Home,* edited by Margot Kahn and Kelly McMasters
- "Writing About Family: Is It Worth It?" by Mimi Schwartz in *The Writer's Chronicle,* Oct./Nov. 2001

3

"Taking Place": Writing the Physical World

> If you live in a place—any place, city or country—long enough and deeply enough you can learn anything, the dynamics and inter-connections that exist in every community, be it plant, human, or animal—you can learn what a writer needs to know.
>
> —GRETEL EHRLICH

I am writing about the first place I remember living, casting around for a way to write about it that fits in with what I've learned is acceptable in the literature of place. Elizabeth, New Jersey: people who know the city shudder and mention the rows of smokestacks craning along the side of the New Jersey Turnpike. I spent my early years there, and along with a rickety shore bungalow, it's the place I have the most visceral childhood attachment to. But when I think of the writing of childhood place, I think of Vladimir Nabokov's *Speak, Memory*, with the majestic beauty of pre-Revolutionary St. Petersburg; of Annie Dillard's wooded rambles in *An American Childhood*. How do you write about a vacant lot glinting with glass, where I spent many ecstatic hours as a child, a cemetery where my brother and I played? It was as scary and luminous a childhood as any other. Does place matter only when it carries its own transcendent beauty? How do you memorialize the seemingly unbeautiful?

After many false starts, I begin writing about my early home by reflecting on the city's name. "Elizabeth," I write, "had a Queen's name. Every land's an extension of the monarch's body, a great green *I Am* of the royal person, and Elizabeth's city showed she'd been gone a long time. It was gassy and bad-smelling as any dead woman."

The Elizabeth of the city, I learned much later, was not Queen Elizabeth, as I'd thought, but some other woman. No matter. It was what I believed at the time of writing, and what I believed, for some reason, as a child. The interest of the place was not in its beauty, its own transcendent qualities, but the way it bounced off my life and the lives of those around me: the character it became.

—SUZANNE

Start Looking

Where are you reading this book? Put it down for a second and look around you; take into account what is both inside and outside the space you're in. In your mind, run over the significance of this place. Are you somewhere that has meaning for you because it is the place you grew up or because it is not? Does this place represent freedom or responsibility? Is it someplace temporary for you or permanent? When you force yourself to look around carefully and openly, do you thrill to the natural beauty or respond to its urban excitement? Or are you somewhere now you feel you could never call home?

Our responses to place are some of the most complex we'll ever experience. Our sense of visual beauty, our psychological drive for comfort and familiarity in our environment, and our complex responses to loaded concepts such as "nature" and "home" embed place with layers of significance. Although fiction writers typically have the importance of location and setting driven into them, it is easy for nonfiction writers to forget that they, too, must be situated physically. We find that an essayist with a wonderful story to tell—a story, say, of a magician father, or a troubled sibling—will typically leave out the vital backdrop of the story: a small town, a gritty city, or a town in which the family's story unfolds against a background of open-mindedness, or misunderstanding.

Where We're Writing From

We, Brenda and Suzanne, landed—through various tracks—in the smallish city of Bellingham, Washington, under a volcano called Mount Baker that is presently giving off steam from under-earth vents called *fumaroles*. On the one hand, our lives are peaceful. We teach classes, write, attend a film or concert now and then, and work on this book. On the other hand, every few years the mountain issues this fleecy reminder that it has more control than we ever give it credit for. Under its crust is enough molten rock to turn our lives into something else entirely.

Environments tend to function as informing elements that we take for granted and edit out of our stories until they act up. We who live here may notice that people become quieter and more lethargic during our gray, rainy winter months, bursting back into exuberant life when the sun returns. Nevertheless, it takes a certain amount of awareness to relate the way our lives unfold to the fact that we live here, in the maritime Northwest, rather than somewhere else. Locating your nonfiction is essential—in the words of writer Sarah Van Arsdale, setting is "the very particular time and place that acts as a kind of beaker in which the story can heat, bubble, and blend."

Setting Scenes: Place as Character

Would *Jane Eyre* have been the same book without her tale unfolding against the backdrop of Thornfield, that gabled mansion with its nests of crows? Would Huckleberry Finn's adventures have had the same resonance without the silvery roil of the Mississippi River? Your own story needs the same depth of field. One useful way to judge your own scene-setting is to think of place as a character unto itself. In the excerpt from the essay "Elizabeth" at the start of this chapter, the city takes on the character of a woman: an aging, decayed figure against which the children's exploits take on an incongruous irony.

In E. B. White's essay "Good-Bye to Forty-Eighth Street," the author is attempting to move out of a New York City apartment that becomes its own mulish and willful character. He describes the place as "mournful" and in need of coaxing to allow him to move out, as in this passage:

> For some weeks now I have been engaged in dispersing the contents of this apartment, trying to persuade hundreds of inanimate objects to scatter and leave me alone. It is not a simple matter. . . . During September I kept hoping that some morning, as by magic, all books, pictures, records, chairs,

beds, curtains, lamps, china, glass, utensils, keepsakes would drain away from around my feet, like the outgoing tide, leaving me standing silent on a bare beach.

In spite of White's claim that his New York possessions are inanimate, they become characterized as animate and moving—mournful, restless as a tide, yet refusing to leave. His careful itemization of the types of material things he owns only makes their resistance feel more overwhelming.

Writing About Home

For nonfiction writers, particularly memoirists, the place of childhood has a critical importance. It is the primal map on which we plot life's movements. It is the setting of the rich mythology that is earliest memory, the enchanted forest in which our benighted characters wander, looking for breadcrumbs and clues and facing down their demons. If you draw your earliest place of memory—a bedroom, say, or a favorite hiding place in an apartment or a yard—you will, by the highly selective and emotional process of memory, be drawing an emotional landscape of your childhood.

Maybe you remember the deep, sagging chair that attracted and frightened you because it was sacred to your father and he sank into it in the evening, angry from the day's work. Or perhaps you remember the table where your family sat around and ate kimchi, which none of your friends ate and of which you learned to be vaguely ashamed. Maybe you recall the soft woolly smell of your covers at night or the dim blue glow of a nightlight. This is home, the place where the complex person you are came into being. And understanding the concept of home and its physical character is key to understanding the many different individuals you'll write about in your nonfiction.

When Home Is Away

Bharati Mukherjee, an Indian-American writer, says home to her is a place she has never been and that no longer exists in a national sense. At the time of her father's birth, his village was in India. Now it is part of Bangladesh. As do some women of Indian descent, she defines her home patrilineally, making her a citizen of an unknown place, bearing ethnic claims that no longer make any sense. In her essay "A Four-Hundred-Year-Old Woman," she writes:

> I was born into a class that did not live in its native language. I was born into a city that feared its future, and trained me for emigration. I attended a school run by Irish nuns, who regarded our walled-off school compound in Calcutta as a corner (forever green and tropical) of England. My "country"—called in Bengali *desh*, and suggesting more a homeland than a nation of which one is a citizen—I have never seen. It is the ancestral home of my father and is now in Bangladesh. Nevertheless, I speak his dialect of Bengali, and think of myself as "belonging" to Faridpur.

Later, Mukherjee writes that for her, "the all too real Manhattan [her present home] and Faridpur have merged as 'desh.'"

For most Americans, the terms *home* and *native* are probably loaded with connotations we rarely pause to tease out. We—Brenda and Suzanne—for example, celebrate different holidays. We bake our traditional breads—challah and panettone—and mark rites of passage with chopped liver or the dried fish called *baccala* without much awareness of how those foods reflect what was available and affordable in our families' countries of origin, or the poverty and threat reflected in the fact that our not-too-distant forebears came to be here. There are stories in these deeply personal, everyday connections and disconnections in American lives. (See also Chapter 2, "Writing the Family," and Chapter 5, "The Body of Identity," for further discussion on approaches to writing your cultural identity.)

Writing About Nature

If we think of place as character, we should add that no "character" comes with as many preconceptions as nature. Drawing energy from early writers like Thoreau, American essayists have always had a particular affinity with nature writing. This country in its present incarnation is relatively new, and created on land belonging to indigenous peoples who have been pushed to the margins and driven from their lands. The waves of immigration to these shores mean that, for many people, their country of origin—the so-called "old country"—and languages of origin are still part of daily experience. For much of its life, this country has defined itself by its wilderness, by the sense of frontier to be explored and frequently controlled.

American nature essayists such as Emerson and Thoreau were called *transcendentalists* because of their belief that nature would allow humans to rise above, or transcend, the limits of civilization. And even as the American wilderness vanishes, literature faces the question of what we have lost with it, along with the buffalo, sequoia, and deep old-growth forests breathing so recently out of our past.

In his classic memoir *Walden; or, Life in the Woods*, Henry David Thoreau's declarations become a charge to nature writers and nature seekers for generations to come: "I went to the woods because I wished to live deliberately, to front only the essential facts of life, and see if I could not learn what it had to teach, and not, when I came to die, discover that I had not lived." American literature's historic distrust of civilization (think of *Huckleberry Finn*) has created a particular reverence for nature writing in our country. Writers like Thoreau teach us that recording the experiences of the individual removed from society—one-on-one with the physical world that created him or her— provides an avenue to "live deep and suck out all the marrow of life."

Thoreau's approach to nature—as a way of paring life down to its essentials, finding oneself—continues in the work of writers such as Wendell Berry. Berry describes how on a hiking trip, "Today, as always when I am afoot in the woods, I feel the possibility, the reasonableness, the practicability of living in the world in a way that would enlarge rather than diminish the hope of life."

To Berry and Thoreau, nature represents life at its most basic—life at the bone. But in the literary world, few subjects are as complex in their symbolic structure as nature. To Wordsworth, it was the ultimate muse, the "anchor of his purest thoughts." To others, it's simply the ultimate power.

What does nature mean to you? For those with a nature-writing bent, it's deceptively simple to wax rhapsodic about the cathedral beauty of old-growth forests or the piercing melodies of the thrush. In other words, we tend to approach nature writing first and foremost as description. While fine description is dandy, it tends to wear thin after a while. Even if your prose about the soft rosy beauty of the alpenglow is first rate, if you don't move beyond that, readers are likely to want to put your writing down and go see for themselves.

What holds readers in the works of writers like Berry and Thoreau is the sense of a *human consciousness* moving through nature, observing it, reacting to it, and ultimately being transformed by it. Thoreau's description of his cottage at Walden Pond is instructive:

> I was seated by the shore of a small pond. . . . I was so low in the woods that the opposite shore, half a mile off, like the rest, covered with wood, was my most distant horizon. For the first week, whenever I looked out on the pond it impressed me like a tarn high up on the side of a mountain, its bottom far above the surface of other lakes, and, as the sun arose, I saw it throwing off its nightly clothing of mist, and here and there, by degrees, its soft ripples or its smooth reflecting surface was revealed, while the mists, like ghosts, were stealthily withdrawing in every direction into the woods.

Notice how Thoreau embeds his basic concept of living in nature as stripping human life bare in this very description. Not only is it beautifully poetic, but we see Walden Pond looming huge in front of him, throwing off its obscuring mists, as a kind of mirror for Thoreau's consciousness, coming clear in nature and throwing off the layer of fog of human convention.

Robin Wall Kimmerer is a botanist, a writer, and a member of the Citizen Potawatomi Nation. In her book *Braiding Sweetgrass: Indigenous Wisdom, Scientific Knowledge, and the Teachings of Plants*, Kimmerer tells the stories of various plants and other natural phenomena using both her traditional teachings and current scientific ones, privileging neither.

> Our stories say that of all the plants, *wiingaashk*, or sweetgrass, was the very first to grow on the earth, its fragrance a sweet memory of Skywoman's hand. Accordingly, it is honored as one of the four sacred plants of my people. Breathe in its scent and you start to remember things you didn't know you'd forgotten.

A little later in the book, Kimmerer lets us see how this ancestral knowing interweaves with her teaching:

> On Mondays, Wednesdays, and Fridays at 9:35 a.m., I am usually in a lecture hall at the university, expounding about botany and ecology—trying, in

short, to explain to my students how Skywoman's gardens, known by some as "global ecosystems," function.

Kimmerer argues in the book that different wisdom traditions, including science, often tell similar narratives in different ways. She calls for reciprocity and regeneration between plants and humans, and openness to learning from every source that seeks to understand ecological balance. Thoreau and Berry see nature as something to travel to, something to be attained—Kimmerer's approach is to pay homage to all of the ways in which she and the natural world are already connected. (See also Barbara Hurd's essay "To Keep an Ear to the Ground" in our Anthology for another example of effective nature writing.)

Writing About Animals

Of course, nature consists of more than landscape. It is also the creatures that inhabit that landscape. Diane Ackerman, a naturalist who writes nonfiction, described writing about animals this way: "Each of the animals I write about I find beguiling in and of itself, but in all honesty, there is no animal that isn't fascinating if viewed up close and in detail." And we humans, too, are animals, ones who find in their fellow creatures everything from a glimpse of a very different way of being in the world to a surprise kinship.

Strong writers can mine that fascination, even with animals that may not seem like what environmentalists call "charisma species," as Jill Christman does in her essay "The Sloth." Standing in an outdoor shower after the tragic death of her fiancé, Christman sees a three-toed sloth, "mottled and filthy . . . hung by his meat-hook claws not five feet above my head in the cecropia tree." The sloth in all of its earthy glory is tangibly present, both deeply other from and deeply connected to the author, its presence "as slow as grief."

Annie Dillard often notices, with deep curiosity, the animals in her environment. For example, in her essay "Living Like Weasels," she describes a surprise encounter with this creature: the weasel she comes upon has "two black eyes I didn't see, any more than you see a window." Experiencing a sudden glimpse into the weasel's mind, Dillard experiences it as "blank" and foreign. If she could be more like the weasel, she imagines, "I might learn something of mindlessness, something of the purity of living in the physical sense and the dignity of living without bias or motive." The encounter leads her to examine the notion of wildness, and to yearn for that kind of primal energy in her own life. The weasel draws her in through its deep difference.

Marjorie Rose Hakala, in "Jumping the Fence" (see Anthology), writes about the behavior of animals in zoos. She begins the essay with the concepts of confinement and escape, and details a story of her mother who, by making eye contact with a musk oxen, caused the animal to charge her and damage its fencing. But further in, Hakala switches tone: she presents a scene of peaceful integration between a group of penguins and the woman who feeds them.

> One of the birds got harried away by its fellows, and the keeper went after it, crouched down, and fed it some pieces of fish while keeping the others away. Some of the penguins made a little noise, honking like geese or braying like donkeys, but the keeper ignored them and went about her work, peaceful and long-legged like a heron among the squat penguins. She ignored the people watching her, and we were quiet in return. . . . The zookeeper looked like she belonged in there, like she had crossed a barrier that none of us could cross.

Note in this essay how carefully the imagery unites all of the beings in this scene. These are not isolated creatures with clear borders—the penguins sound like geese and donkeys, and the zookeeper stands among them "like a heron." Without making a heavy-handed move away from her tales of restriction and escape, one in which "a zoo animal you can't look at is failing the most basic element of its job," Hakala offers the possibility of human-animal connection. It is an approach that contrasts with Dillard's celebration of the weasel's radical difference.

Writing About the Environment

In an issue of the literary journal *Granta* devoted to the "new nature writing," editors explained their subject this way: "For as long as people have been writing, they have been writing about nature. But economic migration, overpopulation, and climate change are transforming the natural world into something unfamiliar. As our conception and experience of nature changes, so too does the way we write about it." For instance, critics have coined terms like "Superfund Gothic" to describe a natural world in which industrial chemicals interfere with the characteristics of fish and wildlife.

In "An Entrance to the Woods," Wendell Berry goes beyond merely describing the woods or the way in which his hiking and camping experience lends perspective to his own human existence. As a nonfiction writer who is constantly pushing himself to examine with the broadest possible lens what exists at the tips of his fingers (which all good nonfiction writers do), he asks himself how he as a human being embodies the larger interaction of human and nature. It's an interrelationship that's become problematic in the twenty-first century, as we face global warming and the last century's outpouring of industrial pollution.

While in the woods, Berry hears the roar of a car in the distance and writes, "That roar of the highway is the voice of the American economy; it is sounding also wherever strip mines are being cut in the steep slopes of Appalachia, and wherever cropland is being destroyed to make roads and suburbs." It is a wonderful moment in the essay, of opening out and refocusing from a simple, enlightening natural experience to a critique of human intervention in the natural order of the ecosystem. Kimmerer also notes the environmental damage done to her people's homeland, writing, "Today, the land where the Peacemaker walked and the Tree of Peace stood isn't land at all, but beds of industrial waste sixty feet deep."

Typically, a writer sitting down to compose a nature essay such as Berry's would erase that car motor from his or her record of this occasion, simply leave it out; it is tempting in nonfiction to pare down our experiences to those sights and sounds that make a unified whole. A passing mention of the noise as an anomaly—out of tone with the peaceful surroundings—would also be a natural move to make. It would be a far less important and less honest tack, though, than Berry's turn, which was to discuss how these woods in the essay exist in uneasy, threatened relationship to the human-dominated world around them.

Travel Writing

Often, a sense of place comes into sharp focus when we travel off our own turf and into lands foreign to us. In the context of travel, "place" begins to seem not so much the land itself, but everything and anything associated with the land: its people, animals, food, music, religion—all the things that make up life itself.

Pico Iyer, a well-known travel writer, sums it up this way: "We travel, initially, to lose ourselves; and we travel, next, to find ourselves. We travel to open our hearts and eyes and learn more about the world than our newspapers will accommodate." Your task, as a good travel writer, is to both pay attention to the details of place and to render these details in a voice that is wholly your own. You must situate yourself as both participant and observer, ready to learn and move beyond your own preconceptions.

This mandate requires you to find a purpose for your writing *above and beyond* the travel experience itself. If you expect the travels themselves to carry the weight of narrative interest, you will end up with an essay that looks disconcertingly like: "First I went here, then I went here, and look what an amazing/horrible/fascinating/soul-searing time I had!" Eventually, no one will care. The places themselves may be intrinsically fascinating, but if you render them into flat landscapes, you'll be left with the lame protest, "Well, you just had to have been there."

In a way, the demands of travel writing can epitomize the challenges of any kind of creative nonfiction writing. How do you shape or draft the work so that the experience becomes *more* than itself? Critic Paul Fussell answers that question this way: "Successful travel writing mediates between two poles: the individual physical things it describes, on the one hand, and the larger theme that it is 'about' on the other. That is, the particular and the universal."

For example, to come back to Pico Iyer, his books not only describe his travels into places as diverse as the L.A. airport, Burmese temples, and suburban Japan, but they also often become inquiries into the effects of globalization on the world's cultures. Born to Indian parents in England, then living for a long time in California, Iyer brings with him his innate awareness of how modern cultural boundaries have begun to blur. He begins his book *Video Night in Kathmandu* with a description of how Sylvester Stallone's movie character Rambo had infiltrated every cinema in Asia during his visit there. By using this one specific example as a focus, he sets the tone and purpose for the book. "I went to Asia," he writes a few pages into the first chapter, "not only to see Asia, but also to see America, from a different vantage point and with new eyes. I left one kind of home to find another: to discover what resided in me and where I resided most fully, and so to better appreciate—in both senses of the word—the home I had left."

You will find that good travel writers avoid the pitfalls that lead to self-serving or clichéd writing. They also show awareness of themselves as outsiders who may very well carry with them an ingrained colonial or privileged perspective. In much of the beginning writing we see about travel, writers fall into clichés about the people of the lands they visit, or see them as stereotypes. They also complain about other travelers, with little awareness of their own culpability in tourist culture. Their attention to place becomes myopic and misses the point.

The other pitfall in travel writing is for the voice to become too much like a guidebook, commenting on mundane details that are not very interesting. As Fussell puts it: "Guidebooks are not autobiographical but travel books are, and if the personality they reveal is too commonplace and un-eccentric, they will not be very readable." As with any good creative nonfiction, the *self* must be wholly present in the work, a voice that engages us to take this trip along with you, to stand at the windows and gaze out at what you, *and only you*, choose to show us.

Witnesses to Our World

In Chapter 2, "Writing the Family," we discuss nonfiction as a literature of *witness*—the sense that, in a world flooded with activity and change and information sources the public growingly distrusts (rightly or wrongly), the individual voice may provide the ultimate record. In the last decades nothing has changed faster than the environment. The world's population has burgeoned, and technology has developed the ability to clear lands, pollute the air, and drive species to extinction in record time. Your life has witnessed the eclipse of hundreds of thousands of species, even if they passed out of this world without your awareness. (The current rate of species extinction is matched only by that of the age of the dinosaurs' demise, sixty-five million years ago.) Your life has also seen the destruction of much natural land and its replacement with human-made habitat, even if this fact, too, only barely crossed your consciousness.

For example, if you can remember a time when Rhode Island spent winters buried under several feet of snow—now replaced by light snows and rains—you may be a witness to the phenomenon of global warming. Or, if you remember rivers thick with migrating salmon, or chasing frogs as a child—creatures that have seen drastic species declines—you have witnessed the current loss of species diversity. Perhaps you have simply noticed that where you live, the last decade has contained most of the area's historic high temperatures. There is a reason nature writing has become so urgent in our era—both the need to record what is left and the need to chronicle what we are losing. Take your role as a witness seriously; think of your writing as a way to capture the changes you've lived in the natural world.

TRY IT

1. For ten minutes, write down every detail of the surroundings you can remember from your morning "commute." Whether this be a walk to school, a bus ride, a drive to your office, or simply moving from one room to another—what are the details, images, snippets that come to mind?

   Now, write a new paragraph that begins with the line: "I've done this _____ (walk, bus ride, drive, etc.) a thousand times, and every time I notice _____." Write down what seems to stay the same, and what changes with the seasons.

   Now write a new paragraph that begins with this line: "Years from now, when I no longer have to do this _____ (walk, drive, bus ride, etc.), I'll miss _____." Write down what you think you'll remember most vividly and why.

2. Since many of us are focused on our phones as we move through the day, think about the digital world as part of your environment. Can we consider the life on our screens as a "place" that is parallel to our physical surroundings? Can you capture the sense of living in these twin places at once?

3. Isolate a single room or outdoor place that to you forms the most essential place of childhood. Quickly write down every element of the place you can remember with as much detail as possible. What were the patterns of the things you see? Are they old or new? Which odd details do you remember (e.g., a gargoyle-shaped knot in the wood, a gray rug with a dark stain the shape of Brazil, and so forth)? Now fill in an emotional tone for each detail. Did the wallpaper make you feel safe

or frightened? What were your favorite things in this place to look at? Your least favorite? Why? What felt "yours" and what felt other? Assemble these specifics into an essay about the emotional landscape of your childhood, moving about the room, letting your essay function as an emotional "camera."

4. Many of us, like Mukherjee, find our sense of "desh" blends real and distant—maybe unseen—places. Is your family one of the many in this country that embodies a divided sense of home? What does "home" mean to you, your siblings, your parents? Many contemporary American families are very transient now. As one of our students, whose father had been transferred multiple times as she grew up, put it, "home is where there's a room for me to unpack my things." Think about whether there's a single place—a physical location—your family defines as "home," or what you do as you move around to bring the sense of home with you. If you're adopted, your birth family, whether you know them or not, may represent another concept of home. Consider writing an essay in which you unpack the complex layers of meaning in the word *home*, with specific references to all the possibilities.

5. Is there an "old country" in your family profile? How does it affect your family culture, traditions, or modes of interacting? Write about the ways your family's country or countries of origin cause you to see yourself as different from others in your area, perhaps straddling several very different cultures.

6. Examine a piece of your writing and scrutinize place as character. Is your setting a developed character? What kind of character is it: positive, nurturing, menacing, indifferent? Imagine the setting of a scene as a silent character, shaping and adding nuance to the action surrounding it.

7. Using the passage we quote in this chapter from E. B. White's "Good-bye to Forty-Eighth Street" as a model, describe a home environment, past or present, by the objects that inhabit it. You can use the same plot—packing up to move—as a way into the essay. How can you fully get across the character of this place through your descriptions?

8. Write a biography of a place. Choose a street, a forest, an airport (possibly look at Pico Iyer's essay on the Los Angeles airport, "Where Worlds Collide," for guidance), a shopping center, any place that has character to you, whether positive or negative. Write a profile, a "character study," of that environment.

9. Can you articulate what your own vision of nature is? If the outdoors draws you and brings you a special kind of knowledge or contentment, can you put into words what that connection consists of? What would your metaphor be of the human-nature interaction that is, in many ways, the ground of our lives here on Earth? Can you think of a time when you went into a natural setting to make a difficult decision, work something out in your mind, or somehow come to feel more "yourself"? What led you to that place? Did it help you in the way you wanted?

10. In this era of accelerating change, we ask you to think of your life as a piece of living history. Looking at your life as an intersection of personal history and the environment that surrounds you, to what can you bear witness? Write for about ten minutes, associating freely and spontaneously, about a place of your childhood, a place that for you defines your childhood—the porch of your house, a creek, the fire escape of an apartment, a special place in the woods. What did the place smell, taste, feel like? Include, but don't limit yourself to, the natural elements: air quality and odor, trees, wildlife (including insects).

    Now write for ten minutes on what this place is like now, whether from your own current experiences of it or from what you've been told. How has it changed? What is gone now that was there before? What is there now that wasn't there before? Think of yourself as a living history of this place—what changes did you find between the place of your childhood and the place of your adulthood? Do these changes reflect any changes in your own life?

    As you compare these two writings, see what larger elements emerge. Have you and the place of your childhood changed in tandem or gone in different directions? Are you a witness to changes that reflect larger—perhaps dangerous—currents of change in our contemporary world? Think about it: even seemingly small things, like the loss of much of our amphibian life, such as frogs, will alter over time the nature of the planet we live on. Think about your writings in the largest possible sense: often this short exercise unlocks a valuable essay.

11. If you have a travel diary or blog, go back to it now and pull out sections that give highly sensory descriptions of place: the feel of the air, the taste of the food, the sounds, the smells. Type these out in separate sections, then arrange them on a table, seeing if you can find a common theme that may bind an essay together. What can you construe as the greater purpose for your travels? How can you incorporate that purpose into your travel writing? What is the one image that will emerge for metaphorical significance?

12. Take a day to travel your hometown as a tourist. Pretend you've never seen this place before and wander with all your senses heightened. Take a notebook with you and write down your impressions. How can you make the familiar new again?

> **Variation for a group:** As a group, take this trip together. Then compare notes and see how different eyes perceive different things. Take some time at the end of the day, or a few days later, to write together and see where these sensory impressions might lead.

13. Read Marjorie Rose Hakala's "Jumping the Fence," Annie Dillard's essay "Living Like Weasels" or Jill Christman's essay "The Sloth." Then think of an encounter you have had with a wild animal that you found personally meaningful. As with Hakala, the creature can be seen in a zoo, or other confined place; add the creature's situation to your meditation. Freewrite on this moment, considering the following questions: How can this creature work as a metaphor for you? How has your encounter with this animal marked you, changed you, or caused you to see yourself differently? How do this creature's actions mirror yours? How are you fundamentally different? What finally haunts you about this moment?

14. Think of animals we see often, perhaps, with an eye toward reinvigorating our view of them: deer, squirrels, opossums, crows. Use research, if you need more concrete information. Even the creatures we see every day have fascinating aspects to them: opossums are the only North American marsupials. Crows have documented tool use and a sophisticated language.

15. Pull out an essay you've already written and check to see if locations and physical settings are established. Can we hear how a key conversation was heightened by the silence of a forest clearing? Do we see and smell the banyan trees of South Florida rather than the cedars of the Northwest? If you write of a town or a city, is its physical location and socioeconomic character clear?

For Further Reading

In Our Anthology
- "Jumping the Fence" by Marjorie Rose Hakala
- "To Keep an Ear to the Ground" by Barbara Hurd

Resources Available Online
- "The Sloth" by Jill Christman
- "Living Like Weasels" by Annie Dillard

Print Resources
- "Elizabeth" by S. (Paola) Antonetta in *Body Toxic*
- *An Entrance to the Woods* by Wendell Berry
- *An American Childhood* by Annie Dillard
- *Video Night in Kathmandu* by Pico Iyer
- *This Is the Place: Women Writing About Home,* edited by Margot Kahn and Kelly McMasters
- *Braiding Sweetgrass: Indigenous Wisdom, Scientific Knowledge, and the Teachings of Plants* by Robin Wall Kimmerer
- "A Four-Hundred-Year-Old Woman" by Bharati Mukherjee in *The Writer on Her Work*
- *Speak, Memory: An Autobiography Revisited* by Vladimir Nabokov
- *Istanbul: Memories and the City* by Orhan Pamuk
- *Walden; or, Life in the Woods* by Henry David Thoreau
- "Good-bye to Forty-Eighth Street" by E. B. White in *Essays of E. B. White*
- *The Best American Travel Writing,* published annually, various editors
- *The Best American Science and Nature Writing,* published annually, various editors

4

Gathering the Threads of History

History is nothing more than a thin thread of what is remembered stretched out over an ocean of what has been forgotten.

—Milan Kundera

I am working on a short essay about a strange summer I had when my brother worked for the New Jersey Department of Environmental Protection, running tests on water samples that had been held up for years. He drove a tiny, two-seater Fiat Spider, the car of choice that year. My start: "It's my brother's Spider summer. Not dog days but spider days. My brother has a blue Fiat Spider. It has no backseat but I ride in the back anyway, rolled up in the ten inches or so under the rear window. Spiders aren't much more than human-sized tins so this is risky but it doesn't matter. Let me be a bottle rocket."

What follows is the revised beginning, after a quick search on major events of the year (1974) and surrounding years. I did this search primarily on the internet, on History Central's "this year in history" service, bringing up forgotten memories: "It's my brother's Spider summer. Not dog days but spider days. It's 1974 and things have been crashing. Nixon's resigned or is going to and a few years ago Apollo 13 crash-landed when an oxygen tank blew. (Astronauts in there like Spam in a can, Chuck Yeager said.) Karen Silkwood's about to crash. My brother has a blue Fiat Spider. It has no backseat but I ride in the back anyway, rolled up in the ten inches or so under the rear window. Spiders aren't much more than human-sized tins so this is risky but it doesn't matter. I am a lost person. Let me be a bottle rocket."

When I add these historical details—the space program, the death of Karen Silkwood—my story becomes enriched and begins to expand outward: connections move back and forth, between the closeness of the car and of space capsules, the sense of questing and uncovering and yet danger that marked that time. The reference to Karen Silkwood adds a reference to those who ask difficult questions, particularly environmental ones, as this book goes on to do. The imminent resignation of President Nixon captures the sense of chaos and rebellion, embodied in these teenagers, so prevalent in our country at that time.

—SUZANNE

Our Historical, Universal Selves

As the preceding experience shows, each of us exists in both a private and a public way. We're all at once son or daughter, lover, sister, brother, neighbor—the person who must have chocolate cereal in the morning and who absently puts the milky bowl down for the cat to lick. We're also pieces of history. We have created digital culture, with all the implications of lives lived in virtual games, social network postings, and tweets. We are also the people who have lived through economic downturns and Mideast wars.

To look at what it means to exist and be human, and who we are as a species, we must look at history. That historical frame is one that may simply enrich your story. Or—as the Kundera quote shows—writing creative nonfiction focused on history might have a deep ethical implication. Sometimes using our own experience of history is a way of preventing that destructive forgetfulness that Kundera describes.

For example, in "Because, the Ferguson Verdict" by Ira Sukrungruang (see Anthology), the author uses a repetitive, chant-like structure to connect racial violence he experienced as a child with the shooting of black teenager Michael Brown by a white police officer in Ferguson, Missouri. "Because someone scrawled on our driveway, *Chinks Go Home*, in shaving cream," Sukrungruang writes, and he winds up to, "Because we share this body of history, which joins—never separates—us." Sukrungruang embodies the act of remembrance, as well as acknowledging that what happens to us reflects in some sense the history in which we're embedded. Consider your life. What indelible larger moments have affected you?

What Will Be Your Stories?

Consider yourself as you exist in this historical moment. Doing so will involve acknowledging what historical and social changes—as well as intractable problems—you have witnessed.

We all have moments when we think, "These are the stories I will tell my grandchildren." Sometimes what we've experienced is tragic. Brian Doyle wrote "Leap" (see Anthology) after the terrorist attacks of September 11, 2001. Doyle said in interviews about "Leap" that he hesitated about writing the essay, feeling it was not his story to tell—he had neither witnessed the event nor personally lost anyone. Ultimately, Doyle focused on victims at the World Trade Center who jumped from upper stories of the burning building hand-in-hand:

> But a man reached for a woman's hand and she reached for his hand and they leaped out the window holding hands.
>
> Jennifer Brickhouse of New Jersey and Stuart DeHann of New York City saw this from far below.
>
> I try to whisper prayers for the sudden dead, and the harrowed families of the dead, and the screaming souls of the murderers, but I keep coming back to his hand and her hand nestled in each other with such extraordinary ordinary succinct ancient naked stunning perfect simple ferocious love.

Over and over again in "Leap," Doyle cites those, like Brickhouse and DeHann, who saw the leaping victims—he becomes in effect a witness's witness. Doyle cannot speak to the attack as a whole; nothing can encompass such loss. He tells us how the poignant detail of strangers jumping while holding hands becomes a small act of redemption, of love, in the tragedy.

History has occasions that are joyful as well as somber. Such an occasion can be as simple as a groundbreaking election or a medical breakthrough. Your historical moments don't have to carry weight beyond what they reflect about society at this time and even what they say about our popular culture. Suzanne once turned a corner in New York City and saw the Rolling Stones filming a music video in front of a crowd of gaping fans (with whom they did not interact!). While this event is hardly newsworthy in the sense a presidential election is, it speaks volumes about contemporary celebrity culture.

First Actors

As creative nonfiction writers, we occupy the ticklish position of being both the authors and, much of the time, the subjects of our own work. We are shaper and protagonist—from the Greek *protos* (first) and *agonistes* (actor), that is, the person who generates the action of a drama—and we must learn to assess ourselves as protagonists with all the objectivity we can muster. Everyone who sits down to write is, in some sense, a *privileged observer*—a writer who has had experiences and witnessed events any reader would be fascinated by, if the writer can learn to uncover and record them.

The French memoirist and novelist George Sand wrote, "Everyone has his own story, and everyone could arouse interest in the romance of his life if he but comprehended it." Any of you could write a book that would be treasured in two hundred years, as we treasure the best pioneer diaries, if we could all learn, as those authors did, really to *see*.

We take many things about ourselves for granted—and take for granted, too, their societal implications. Gender, race, religion, class, ethnicity, sexual orientation—these aspects of ourselves govern our social interactions in ways that are unique to our moment in history (see Chapter 5, "The Body of Identity"). Part of your social self is always historically determined. Race, religion, sexual orientation, and so on, along with all the other small—or not so small—pieces of your history and identity make you you. Did you go to religious school? Have you lived in a commune? Do you have children? Are you from a marginalized group? What assumptions about you do others arrive at based on these simple facts of your life? The aspects of yourself that have led to the greatest challenges, even discrimination, can be among the most rewarding to put under the lens of your nonfiction writer's scrutiny.

In Sui Sin Far's 1909 essay "Leaves from the Mental Portfolio of a Eurasian," Sin Far describes becoming aware of her status as a biracial child in the early twentieth century United States. In one scene, a man examines her at a party:

> [A] white-haired old man has his attention called to me by the hostess. He adjusts his eyeglasses and surveys me critically. "Ah, indeed!" he exclaims. "Who would have thought it at first glance? Yet now I see the difference between her and other children. What a peculiar coloring! Her mother's eyes and hair and her father's features, I presume. Very interesting little creature!"

I had been called from play for the purpose of inspection. I do not return to it.

The power of Sin Far's description lies in how skillfully she lets the story tell itself: the man who examines her, adjusting his glasses as if looking at a laboratory specimen. He discusses her as she stands there, as if Sin Far's race renders her beneath comprehension. Sin Far's dry comment that she does "not return" to her play makes it clear how devastating her awareness of herself as racially different becomes.

A contemporary essay, Jenny Boully's "A Short Essay on Being," describes a similar encounter:

Two older, white women are sitting on chairs in front of us and ask where we are from. We say we're from Valley-Hi, because that's the section of San Antonio where we live. No, they say, what's your nationality? We had never heard that word before, and although we had never heard that word before, we answered that we were Thai, although our nationality was American.

Again, through a simple but meticulous description of the encounter, Boully gives her readers a vivid sense of the dislocation it created in her as a child. The fact that the questioning women used "where are you from?" as a veiled way of asking the author her race—and that they could not accept her answer—shows how deeply race mattered to these women.

Unless you exist alone on an uncharted island—and are never discovered!—the elements of your life are reverberant with historical significance because you live in a communal group whose attitudes and choices are historically shaped. We've all experienced meeting someone who claimed to be ordinary while finally slipping into the conversation that he or she had sung opera as a child or—like one person we remember—come of age living inside the Statue of Liberty with his Park Service father. The world he grew into, literally seen through the eyes of the Statue of Liberty, is not the same world the rest of us know.

It's important for you as a writer, particularly a nonfiction writer, to think through what is different and important in your world, and what historical events formed the canvas for the fine brushstrokes of your own life. You can easily check the highlights of particular dates and years using historical online and print resources.

The "When" in Addition to the "What"

Here is the opening of James Baldwin's famous essay about racism and family, "Notes of a Native Son":

> On the twenty-ninth of July, in 1943, my father died. On the same day, a few hours later, his last child was born. Over a month before this, while all our energies were concentrated in waiting for these events, there had been, in Detroit, one of the bloodiest race riots of the century. . . . On the morning of the third of August, we drove my father to the graveyard through a wilderness of smashed plate glass.

Notice that the author's attention operates like a moving camera, panning between familial and national tragedy. Family events come first; then, as if his gaze is forced away, Baldwin takes in the larger chaos of the country's rioting. Right at the start of the essay Baldwin carefully states the season and the year; it's a hot summer month during World War II. Part of the race frustration building up to the riots described here arose from black GIs risking their lives overseas and coming home to face the same old racism, a fact that would have been clear to Baldwin's contemporary audience. By the end of the paragraph, the rioters' smashed glass has become a "wilderness," as if that landscape equals the natural landscape about to close over Baldwin's father's body. The essay accomplishes an unforgettable weaving of personal tragedy with the period that spawned it.

Always keep in mind the extent to which history is the individual writ large, and the individual life is history writ small. Understanding what shapes how you perceive the world—and how you are perceived—is critical to using your own experiences to create strong nonfiction.

Try It

1. You will likely be the last person to recognize what's fascinating—and deeply significant—about you. Your friends will see it, and if you're lucky your family will too. If you're normal, you will brush off their interest, tell them it really wasn't so different—you just don't see what all the fuss is about that last night on board the *Titanic*.

Here's a tool to help you along: a checklist to start yourself off with, whether you choose to answer on paper, in a journal, or in the privacy of your own head. This checklist is designed to elicit a greater awareness of the historical events that have shaped your life, and also a greater awareness of your *social self*—you as conservative or liberal, member of a disadvantaged group, Buddhist, activist, Rosicrucian. While considering these questions, it's important to remember that this social self *always* functions in a cultural and historical context.

a.   Which event of national or world importance do you remember most clearly? How did you hear of it, and what did you hear? What were other people around you doing? What was going on in your own life that this event bounced off of, resonated with, or formed a strange contrast to? Use all of your senses to recreate this memory.

b.   Which aspects of your life do people around you consistently find most interesting? What questions do they ask you? What can you tell them that satisfies, or dissatisfies, them?

c.   Try to imagine your own life as someone five hundred years from now might view it. What about your life—the place you live in and the historical unfoldings you've witnessed—do you believe that person would find most interesting? (Hint: What do you find most interesting about life in the past?) How are you a privileged observer?

d.   Get in the habit of thinking of yourself in the third person—seeing yourself move through the world as a protagonist—at least once a day. Narrate your daily story to yourself in the third person. As an objective listener (and, to some extent, you can be one), what interests you?

Dating a Significant Event

This is the exercise that helped Suzanne expand her description of the summer of 1974.

1.   For the first part, write a description of several paragraphs about a scene or event you consider critical in your life. It should date from at least a few years in your past and can be from childhood. As in most writing exercises, write quickly and do not censor yourself. Be as specific and detailed as possible, using all your senses.

2.   Now use a list of chronologies to date your experience with a corresponding national or world event. Don't worry if you feel you weren't thinking about the event at the time; your obliviousness to it may be part of what makes the essay fascinating.

3. Once you find a historical corollary, write as many connections, real or metaphoric, as you can. (Suzanne might have written "secrets, cover-ups, crashing, underground corruption, apathy.") In an essay, draw together the two links to show how a critical moment in your life unfolded against a corresponding moment in history. Don't feel the need to justify to yourself immediately why something feels important. If your gut tells you it's important, then surely it is.

4. Using Ira Sukrungruang's essay "Because, the Ferguson Verdict" (see Anthology) as a model, draft an essay triggered by a recent news headline that has some relevance for your own life. Use the word "Because" (or another word) as a refrain, and list all the ways your life has specifically been affected by similar issues.

FOR FURTHER READING

In Our Anthology
- "Leap" by Brian Doyle
- "Because, the Ferguson Verdict" by Ira Sukrungruang

Resources Available Online
- "Notes of a Native Son" by James Baldwin
- "A Short Essay on Being" by Jenny Boully
- "Leaves from the Mental Portfolio of a Eurasian" by Sui Sin Far

Print Resources
- *The Fire Next Time* by James Baldwin
- *A Small Place* by Jamaica Kincaid
- *Istanbul: Memories and the City* by Orhan Pamuk
- "Late Victorians" by Richard Rodriguez in *Days of Obligation*
- *Assassination Vacation* by Sarah Vowell

5

The Body of Identity

The body offers deep truths all its own. Different truths, truths of difference.

—Stephen Kuusisto and Ralph James Savarese

I have a disability, one that others aren't always able to see. Recently I mentioned this disability to a new friend. She leaned toward me and said, in a half-whisper, "Well, don't worry, I would never have been able to tell."

I realized this person felt she was being kind. But there are painful assumptions loaded into this comment, one that I've heard versions of many times before: my diagnosis is one that I should want to keep hidden. I should feel reassured and flattered that it doesn't "show." What about those times when I cannot hide? How should I feel about myself had she noticed?

I began, in response, to explain to this person why she may not have found my disability obvious in that context. Then I stopped and changed the subject. More dialogue would have made her uncomfortable and probably elicited more comments on how well I "manage." Like so many disabled people, I made the choice to drop sharing a fact of my identity and divorce myself from a key part of who I am. The choice to stay quiet is a choice I've made before, and not one I'm especially proud of. But like so many people who exist outside the mainstream in their bodies, their minds, their loves, their identities, I need to ration my emotional energy. This won't be the last such conversation.

As much as writing may put us deep within our own psyches, we are still embodied beings in the world. For some of us, our experience within the world can put us in the "different" category—it can be fraught. This happens

59

though differences are socially constructed, may be based on biased standards of normalcy, and related to negotiating a social sphere that may care little for accessibility and inclusion. I can't speak for anyone else, but writing my disability—taking readers to a place that may be new to them, yet loaded with assumptions—can feel overwhelming. As writer Nancy Mairs puts it, "Some realities do not obey the dictates of language."

As writers, perhaps at least partly memoirists, if we deal with biased social assumptions about our identities, we deal with them in our work as in life. What do we tell? When is telling painful? How much empathy and understanding can we expect from our audience?

—SUZANNE

As we saw in Chapter 1, "The Body of Memory," we can often locate our personal, autobiographical material in our experiences of the body. As you continue to practice how to focus on sensory images as a way to remember and translate experiences to the page, you may also find yourself drawn to write about bigger issues of identity that bodily memories can evoke. When you're exploring such territory—one that can have implications far beyond the personal—you might experience a sense of vulnerability as you grapple with finding the right voice, form, and structure for conveying your authentic experience.

Racial Identity

Race is an area of writing that may be especially difficult to approach, but it's also a subject that is more necessary than ever. We need to try to understand one another's lived experiences as fully as we can. One way some writers have approached exploring racial identity is through the body, which creates a visceral experience for both writer and reader.

For example, in his memoir *Between the World and Me,* Ta-Nehisi Coates begins by bringing his black body front and center into the narrative. Written as a letter to his son, Coates opens the memoir with this line: "Last Sunday the host of a popular news show asked me what it meant to lose my body." He goes on to describe the cultural, political, and social context in which he is writing this letter to his son, who is fifteen:

I am writing you because this was the year you saw Eric Garner choked to death for selling cigarettes; because you know now that Renisha McBride was shot for seeking help, that John Crawford was shot down for browsing in a department store. And you have seen men in uniform drive by and murder Tamir Rice, a twelve-year-old child whom they were oath-bound to protect. . . . And you know now, if you did not before, that the police departments of your country have been endowed with the authority to destroy your body.

By containing this work as a letter to his son, Coates's voice can be, by turns, intimate, adamant, and sorrowful. He uses specific examples from his own life and the life of black people at large to get across what it means to live in a black body during his family's lifetime.

In a special issue devoted to race, the online journal *Brevity* sought work that could describe—in brief, vivid essays—the authors' lived experiences in racially diverse bodies. The guest editors, Joy Castro and Ira Sukrungruang, interviewed each other to create a craft essay that described their own interest and experience with how racial identity plays out in literature, and in creative nonfiction in particular. Sukrungruang writes:

> In literature, race wasn't about color alone. It wasn't about difference. In literature, race is made complicated. Race is seen through a myriad of views. Played out not only through violence and hate and injustice, but love and understanding and empathy.

One of the writers featured in this issue, Danielle Geller, writes about her Navajo identity, and the complications that arise by being both seen and unseen as a Native American. In her essay "Blood; Quantum," Geller details all the various ways she has been identified by both strangers and family alike. She writes:

> But once, as I sat in the empty hallway of my middle school, an older man stopped in front of me and said: Are you Native American? I'd bet anything you are. When I said yes, he just smiled and moved on. . . . And once, when I told the Mexican man on the bus that I was not Latina but Native American, he asked me to what degree, and when I said half, he said: Good. That means the blood isn't too thick. But once, when I came home with a barbell

through my tongue and a ring through my nose, my white grandmother said, in disgust, "It must be the *Indian* in you," which was always cheerlessly funny to me because I never felt Indian at all.

How might you focus on and articulate your own experience of race? In our Anthology, you will find several examples of how writers employ various formal techniques to contain stories of racial identity. In "Math 1619," for example, Gwendolyn Wallace couches her experience in the form of a math test to get across how it feels to be a marginalized black student. (This technique is called a "hermit crab" essay: borrowing another form to tell your story. See Chapter 9, "Innovative Forms: The Wide Variety of Creative Nonfiction," for a discussion of hermit crab essays.)

Also in our Anthology: Ira Sukrungruang's "Because, the Ferguson Verdict" uses the trigger of recent news headlines to create a collage that lists his own experiences of racial injustice and discrimination. In "The Night My Mother Met Bruce Lee," Paisley Rekdal imagines herself into the experience of her mother as a young woman who experienced societal constraints because of her race. Look to these essays—and others from our suggested reading list at the end of this chapter—to glean ideas about how to find a way into this subject for yourself.

(See also Chapter 2, "Writing the Family," for ideas on how to explore cultural identity, which can be closely linked to racial identity.)

Gender and Sexual Identity

For many writers, the subject of gender and/or sexual identity has become central to much of their autobiographical writing. Our collective knowledge and terminology around gender identity keeps deepening, expanding, and becoming more complex the more such diverse personal stories gain attention. And no one approach is deemed "correct." Some writers will start in childhood, seeking insight. In Ryan Van Meter's essay "First" (see Anthology), an early childhood recollection shows a crucial turning point in his awareness of his sexuality. In his memoir *Firebird*, poet and nonfiction writer Mark Doty also remembers a childhood marked by family tension and a growing awareness of his sexual orientation.

Some writers will begin closer to their adult experiences of gender and sexuality. For example, in Barrie Jean Borich's memoir *My Lesbian Husband: Landscapes of a Marriage,* she explores how language cannot fully express the nuances of her spousal relationship. First published in 1999, before gay marriage was made legal in the United States, Borich's book examines the lexicon and rituals of marriage as they might apply to her and her partner of many years, Linnea. "Are we married?" she asks throughout the chapter titled "When I Call Her My Husband," and the two women cannot come up with a satisfactory response. In an intimately rendered scene, we are allowed to witness their interchange, and also the larger societal issues that press into their intimacy:

> Linnea rolls over, shooing away the cat, resting her belly alongside my hip as her chin nuzzles my shoulder. "I think you're my wife," she says.
>
> I laugh and squeeze in closer, turn so I can kiss the soft exposed flesh below her ear. She is completely serious and not serious at all, in that queer way we learn to roll with a language we are at once completely a part of and completely excluded from.

This interchange leads to the heart of this chapter and of the book as a whole. The word "wife" does not fit Linnea the way it does Barrie, and so she ventures to call Linnea "husband," appropriating this term for their own use:

> When I call Linnea my husband I mean that she's a woman who has to lead when we slow dance, who is compelled to try to dip and twirl me, no matter that I have rarely been able to relax on a dance floor since I stopped drinking. She leads me between the black walls of a gay bar, our faces streaked with neon and silver disco light, to air so dark Linnea's black leather belt and both pairs of our black boots seem to vanish, leaving parts of us afloat in the heavy smell of booze and cigarettes.

As we've seen with memoirs centered on any kind of topic, the best writing will use scene and sensory details to fully engage readers and let us into their singular experience. Notice how Borich allows us into this representative moment in time, using intricate details to get across the depth of their intimacy.

Kate Carroll de Gutes also provides this vivid glimpse into her identity in the essay "Sir, Ma'am, Sir: Gender Fragments." In a series of vignettes put together as a collage, de Gutes shows us how she has often been defined by gender nonconformity. It begins:

> I was 9 the first time I was mistaken for a boy. I stood in the candy aisle of Long's Drugs store, trying to decide between a Big Hunk, a Charleston Chew, or Milk Duds. It was winter, I know that much, and I wore a blue quilted coat with a white faux fur-trimmed hood. I hated that hood, but my mother was adamant about girly clothes. She didn't want me mistaken for a boy.

After several of these examples that move through time up to the present day, de Gutes steps back for a longer view: "We see gender because it's what we are conditioned to see."

Think about how your own identity has been marked by gender or sexual orientation. How have you named yourself or chosen the pronouns you use? What are the key memories or turning points that show your own evolution or understanding of this aspect of your identity?

Our Bodies of Difference

In the introduction to his anthology *Staring Back: The Disability Experience from the Inside Out*, Kenny Fries notes that "throughout history, people with disabilities have been stared at. Now, here in these pages . . . writers with disabilities affirm our lives by putting the world on notice that we are staring back." Being heard as whole persons, for any group existing on the margins of our culture, is an act of courage and of resistance. The disabled are often objects of the stare not just in public spaces, but in the pages of literature, frequently depicted as objects of pity, cheap inspiration, and literary gawking.

People who are disabled write from a position of having bodies, or minds, of difference. There is, of course, no one disability, and no one aesthetics of disabled authors. Nor is there one correct way of designating disability. Self-naming may be an act of claiming and of recovery. Nancy Mairs, an author who wrote extensively of her experiences with multiple sclerosis, gives us this passage from the essay "On Being a Cripple":

> First, the matter of semantics. I am a cripple. I choose this word to name me. I choose from among several possibilities, the most common of which are "handicapped" and "disabled." I made the choice a number of years ago, without thinking, unaware of my motives for doing so. Even now, I'm not sure what those motives are. . . . People—crippled or not—wince at the word "cripple," as they do not at "handicapped" or "disabled." Perhaps I want them to wince.

While we cannot, and should not, ascribe any one quality to authors because they are disabled, it's hard to escape the way that those with minds and/or bodies of difference will mostly be defined, as author Kenny Fries puts it, by the "nondisabled gaze." Nancy Mairs describes how disabled characters are nearly always defined by their disability, rather than appearing as complete persons. The act of "staring back," or recognizing and reversing that gaze, may be part of these writers' strategies. Disability as a culture of its own, and disability as a social construct often created by lack of accessibility, may also be part of the projects of disabled authors.

TRY IT

1. What assumptions do others make about you? Write a list of qualities—good, bad, or neutral—people think they see when they see you. How might these qualities be related to race, ethnicity, religion, appearance, who you do or don't love? Consider, as Suzanne does in the opening of this chapter, times when you might want to correct assumptions, and times when you don't.

2. Related to the preceding activity, freewrite using the title "Self-Portrait Through the Eyes of _____." Choose different people in your life, including strangers, to fit into this title. You can continue with the most promising of these freewrites or write an essay sequence.

3. Using the example given from "Between the World and Me" as a model, try writing your experience of identity in the form of a letter to someone you love.

4. Using Ryan Van Meter's "First" (see Anthology) as a model, can you remember a turning point in your life when you became aware of your sexual orientation or gender identity? Call up a specific memory and recreate it using concrete detail. What themes arise? How could you use this theme for further writing?

5. Think of a personal "territory" you inhabit. Where are you positioned within this territory? What do you see?

   (See also the Try Its in Chapter 2, "Writing the Family," for ways to approach writing your cultural identity. See Chapter 9, "Innovative Forms," for ideas on ways to use nontraditional forms to contain your story, as Wallace does in "Math 1619.")

FOR FURTHER READING

In Our Anthology
- "The Night My Mother Met Bruce Lee" by Paisley Rekdal
- "The Coroner's Photographs" by Brent Staples
- "Because, the Ferguson Verdict" by Ira Sukrungruang
- "First" by Ryan Van Meter
- "Math 1619" by Gwendolyn Wallace

Resources Available Online
- "How We See One Another: Our Guest Editors Castro and Sukrungruang in Conversation" at *Brevity*
- "Blood; Quantum" by Danielle Geller
- "On Being a Cripple" by Nancy Mairs

Print Resources
- *My Lesbian Husband: Landscapes of a Marriage* by Barrie Jean Borich
- *Gender Outlaw: On Men, Women, and the Rest of Us* by Kate Bornstein
- *Truth Serum: A Memoir* by Bernard Cooper
- *Firebird: A Memoir* by Mark Doty
- "Sir, Ma'am, Sir: Gender Fragments" from *Objects in Mirror Are Closer Than They Appear* by Kate Carroll de Gutes
- *Between the World and Me* by Ta-Nehisi Coates
- *Staring Back: The Disability Experience from the Inside Out,* edited by Kenny Fries
- *Bad Indians: A Tribal Memoir* by Deborah A. Miranda

- *A Mind Apart: Travels in a Neurodiverse World* by S. (Paola) Antonetta
- *If You Knew Then What I Know Now* by Ryan Van Meter
- *Shapes of Native Nonfiction: Collected Essays by Contemporary Writers*, edited by Theresa Warburton and Elissa Washuta

6

Writing the Arts

Culture is like a magnetic field, a patterned energy shaping history. It is invisible, even unsuspected, until a receiver sensitive enough to pick up its messages can give it a voice.

—GUY DAVENPORT

I've put up a new picture, a photograph bought for me at an Edward Weston exhibit last April. The composition shows a young woman, all in black, posed against a high, white fence. She half turns toward the camera; her right hand lies tentatively across her heart. The shadow of a leafless tree (I imagine it to be a young oak) curves up and over this slight figure. Actually, it does more than curve; the shadow arches behind her in a gesture of protection. Almost a bow of respect.

Why do I like this picture so much? I glance at it every day, and every day it puzzles me. What draws me to those dark, shaded eyes? What holds me transfixed by the movement of gray shadows over the straight white planks, the drape of the black coat, the white hand raised to the breast in a stunned gesture of surprise?

These questions led me to write the first essay I ever published, titled "Prologue to a Sad Spring," after Weston's own title of the photograph I describe. In this essay, the photograph's mysterious title becomes a meditation on what it means to have a "sad spring," on how our lives are full of losses never memorialized in photographs. It's a short essay, with a circular design that leads the reader back to the appeal of black-and-white photography and to this particular photograph that started the rumination in the first place. Though it's a simple piece, with simple ambitions, it remains a favorite essay in my repertoire. It feels almost like a gift, an ephemeral connection between myself and the woman in this photograph, a distant communiqué between a writer and a photographer who would never meet.

—Brenda

The Visual Arts

With old glass-plate daguerreotypes—the earliest form of photography—if you tilt the plate just slightly, the image disappears and the photograph becomes a mirror, an apt metaphor for how the creative nonfiction writer can approach art. Through a close observation of particular paintings, sculptures, or photographs, you can reveal your own take on the world or find metaphors in line with your obsessions. At the same time, you will elucidate that artwork in such a way that the piece will forever after have a greater significance for your reader.

For example, in the essay "Inventing Peace," art historian and journalist Lawrence Weschler closely analyzes a Vermeer painting to understand what is happening during the Bosnian war crimes tribunal in The Hague. He compares the serene, almost dreamlike settings of Vermeer with the atrocities the judges in The Hague, just minutes from the Vermeer exhibit, hear about every day. One particular painting, *The Head of a Young Girl* (popularly known as *Girl with a Pearl Earring*), intrigues him. He explicates this painting for us:

> Has the girl just turned toward us or is she just about to turn away? . . . The answer is that she's actually doing both. This is a woman who has just turned toward us and is already about to look away: and the melancholy of the moment, with its impending sense of loss, is transferred from her eyes to the tearlike pearl dangling from her ear. . . . The girl's lips are parted in a sudden intake of breath—much, we suddenly notice, as are our own as we gaze back upon her.

Weschler closely studies this painting, interpreting the details as he unfolds them for us one by one. He creates a speculative narrative that brings this painting to life. In a speculative narrative, the writer infuses a painting or any situation with a story that arises from both fact and imagination. For instance, it is clear in Weschler's description that the *facts* of the painting exist as he relates them—the parted lips, the pearl earring—but he allows himself to speculate on the *meaning* of those details. He brings his own frame of mind to bear on the portrait; this interpretation sets up the themes for his piece.

In Jericho Parms's essay "On Touching Ground" (see Anthology), she begins by describing an Edgar Degas bronze sculpture housed in the Metropolitan Museum of Art: "Horse Trotting, Feet Not Touching Ground":

> Deep within the galleries of the Metropolitan, a glass wall case barely contains the wild form of a racehorse. Veiny grooves mark the horse's flank and haunches, its powerful shoulders, crest, the forelock of its mane. The tail extends like a petticoat train in its cantering wake. Head high, the horse is poised, proud.

The specific, vivid, and active details in this description bring the artwork to life on the page, and they also provide the writer a foundation for several associative leaps. The essay will travel beyond the gallery to memories of working with her grandfather on the family ranch, to researched material about wild mustangs, to other artwork about horses, and other bronzes by Degas. It becomes a richly textured braided essay that relies on visual art as the grounding thread. Parms said in an interview with the magazine *The Normal School*: "For me, viewing art is an exercise of attention, a process of giving myself over to observation and allowing new ideas and meditations to surface as a result of the simple act of looking."

Another way of working with art is to allow the viewer to gaze on the images with you. In *A Postcard Memoir,* Lawrence Sutin pairs his personal writing with images from old postcards. He looks for small, unexpected details that give rise to his own memories and meditations. (See Chapter 10, "Mixed Media, Cross-Genre, Hybrid, and Digital Works," for further discussion on using other media in your creative nonfiction.)

The Moving Image Arts

The moving image arts—such as film, television, YouTube videos, music videos, even video games—create a vital and visible part of our cultural expression.

Remember Paisley Rekdal's "The Night My Mother Met Bruce Lee" (see Anthology) from Chapter 2, "Writing the Family"? The essay invokes pop culture images of the Chinese and the Chinese-American, particularly the narrator's mother, whose school guidance counselor advises her not to go to Smith, "hinting at some limitation my mother would prefer to ignore." At the same time, a cook in the restaurant where the mother works tells her he comes from Hong Kong and hence is "*real* Chinese." Rekdal embeds that sense of cultural limbo—appearing Chinese to a white guidance counselor but an assimilated American to a recent immigrant—in the artifice of kung fu movies.

In the essay, mother and daughter bond watching the martial arts film *Enter the Dragon*:

> Bruce Lee narrows his eyes, ripples his chest muscles under his white turtleneck.
>
> "I knew him," my mother tells me. "I worked with him in a restaurant when I was in high school."
>
> "Really?" This is now officially the only cool thing about her. "What was he like?"
>
> "I don't remember. No one liked him, though. All that kung fu stuff; it looked ridiculous. Like a parody."

Rekdal pays close attention to the film itself in this piece; her prose follows the film's use of lighting—the way Lee's chest "seemed outlined in silver," mirroring the way Rekdal's mother's face "twists into something I do not recognize in the television light." It's as if the cultural distortion created by the movie and movies like it distorts the mother even in the eyes of her daughter. Note that Rekdal has been careful to look at the techniques of the films in question and use them throughout her essay—not just the kung fu itself, which becomes picked up by the restaurant chef, but kung fu films' visual style of bright color and exaggerated gesture.

You can also take a more analytical approach to television and film, exploring what they mean in terms of culture and society. For example, Bill McKibben, in his book *The Age of Missing Information*, performs an experiment in which he has friends record every channel on a Virginia cable network for twenty-four hours, then he goes about analyzing what he sees to create a portrait of the American mindset: what we learn—and more important, what we *don't* learn—from what surrounds us on TV. McKibben, who doesn't own a television himself, spends several months watching these video-tapes of a single day's television programming:

> I began spending eight- or ten-hour days in front of the VCR—I watched it all, more or less. A few programs repeat endlessly, with half-hour "infomercials" for DiDi 7 spot remover and Liquid Luster car wax leading the list at more than a dozen appearances apiece. Having decided that once or twice was enough to mine their meanings, I would fast-forward through them, though I always slowed down to enjoy the part where the car-wax guy sets fire to the hood of his car.

McKibben contrasts what one can learn from a day of television to what one can learn from a day in the woods, providing specific examples of each mode, and revealing his own personality at the same time.

All the moving image arts, especially in this age of digital delivery, can comment on our own lives and on the history surrounding them. They can also capture a cultural moment. Think of how at times movies such as *Thelma and Louise* or TV shows such as "Seinfeld" seem to speak for the feelings of large numbers of people in our society, generating catchphrases and images that become embedded in our collective consciousness.

Think about the moving image arts that form a backdrop to your own lives. For example, are there certain music videos that capture the emotion of your generation? Are there video games that contain the intricacies of visual art and storytelling for you and your peers? Are there television shows or films that become common meeting grounds for you and your friends? How can these arts add not only details and texture to your own personal story, but also help it become a more communal one?

Music

As we mentioned in Chapter 1, "The Body of Memory," music can key us into powerful memories that define the self. And music can also serve as a medium to channel some of the most vital issues of our time. We still look back at the 1960s antiwar movement by looking at the music that sprang out of it. Music is a vessel that holds the emotions of its time.

As an example, let's consider David Margolick and Hilton Als' book *Strange Fruit: The Biography of a Song*. "Strange Fruit," a song written for blues singer Billie Holiday, tells the horrendous story of Southern lynchings. Through the lens of this song Margolick and Als weave together the tales of Holiday's short, difficult, and heroin-addicted life, the white communist sympathizer who wrote the song, the struggle for civil rights, New York café society, even the history of lynching. This single song contains within it a story that branches out and out to speak of two extraordinary human beings as well as the thorniest problem in American history—race.

Another approach is to consider a type of music or a particular musician who has been influential to you at key moments in your life. For example, in her essay "The Pat Boone Fan Club," Sue William Silverman uses the occasion of the iconic musician Pat Boone coming to town for a concert to describe what this singer meant to her as a child and as a young woman. She remembers lying on her bed, magnifying glass in hand, as she studied his picture in *Life* magazine:

> I was particularly drawn to the whiteness in the photos. Pat Boone's white-white teeth beamed at me, his white bucks spotless. I savored each cell of his being as I traced my finger across his magnified image. . . . I fantasized living inside this black-and-white print, unreachable. This immaculate universe was safe, far away from my father's all-too-real hands, hands that hurt me at night.

The essay then travels through time to give us other memories of Pat Boone and meditations on the inherent contradictions at play in the narrator's life and that of Pat Boone's, always using that present-day concert as an anchoring thread.

Literature: The "Reading Narrative"

A "reading narrative" shows the author reading another piece of literature and using it as a springboard for actions and reflections. Like writers who use the visual arts, authors of reading narratives are somehow grappling with another artist's aesthetics as a means of probing deeper into their own. Phyllis Rose's book *The Year of Reading Proust: A Memoir in Real Time* is an excellent example, as the author reads all of Proust's *Remembrance of Things Past* while using it as a means to chronicle her own life, comparing her Key West to Proust's Balbec, the characters inhabiting her life to those in his.

Another fascinating example of a reading narrative is Jennifer Sinor's *Letters Like the Day: On Reading Georgia O'Keeffe*. This book focuses on the artist O'Keeffe's letters, primarily the nearly two thousand letters she wrote to her husband, the photographer Alfred Stieglitz. Sinor uses O'Keeffe's letters to meditate on the artist's life and work, and on her own. Sinor is personally present in the book, telling stories of relationships in her life defined by letters, giving us glimpses into her history and her family. Sinor also probes the nature of letters themselves: letters "give us something more than information . . . they most especially document a self who is becoming—a self stitching together, word by word, a version of who she thinks she is."

As Sinor reads O'Keeffe's letters, she notices how much both the content of the letters and their appearance, with exuberant "waves" of handwriting, reflect O'Keeffe's art. O'Keeffe's artistic habits, including her practice of returning to a subject again and again looking for its emotional center, become the book's aesthetic. Sinor describes her book as "nine essays that attempt to push words on the page as O'Keeffe pushed paint on her canvas."

Most of us can remember at least one "eureka" reading moment. That moment may give us permission to do things differently in our own work: use a new voice, dig deeper, or consider new subject matter as potentially ours. These "eureka" writers are our literary mentors, whether we realize that or not. And what we read may spur us on in many different ways—other authors inspire us, give us permission, and also irritate us in ways that stimulate us to try something new.

TRY IT

1. For each of the Arts categories described in this chapter—Visual Arts, Moving Image Arts, Music, and Literature—brainstorm a list of the works that have been part of your own life. Spend about three minutes with each category, not worrying about whether something fits or not. You can expand beyond what we have identified in each category; for example, is fashion, for you, a visual art? or Instagram? Allow your mind to roam widely.

Go back and look over your complete list. How do these works, on their own, form a picture of your life and the life of your generation? You can use this list as a resource for future writing.

For now, choose just one item on your list and write a scene of your interaction or encounter with this artwork. What themes arise? How does the artwork enable you to access certain memories or issues?

2. Begin an essay by describing a piece of visual art that has always intrigued you. Feel free to interpret the details, creating a speculative narrative about what is happening in the painting or what was going through the painter's mind. Find other interpretations from art scholars and begin to create an essay that approaches this artwork from several different angles.

3. Begin an essay by describing a particular artwork in vivid, active detail. Allow your mind to then make associations to personal memories.

   VARIATION: Parallel your interpretation of a particular artwork or artist with events going on in the world around you or with events unfolding in your own life.

4. Think about a film that you love, or a YouTube video, or a music video, that you could watch any number of times. Look closely at the conventions and physical experience of film or video, and question your obsession. Can you borrow the visual style of the work in question? Can you write an essay that you model on scenes in the work you've viewed? Where did you first see the film or video, and what has it represented to the larger culture?

5. Think about television commercials that stick with you. How do they define the eras they appear in? How have they shaped you, perhaps in terms of social relationships, signs of status, body image?

6. Write an essay that uses popular television or radio shows to establish the time and place of your piece. What were the shows you watched as a child? How did they establish the routine of your day? Why do you think those particular shows hooked you?

7. Are you into video games? Do you play them or watch others play them? Try to describe a particular video game for its aesthetic appeal. Why do you think you and others are drawn to it? What does it reflect about your lives?

8. This prompt expands on uses of music presented in Chapter 1. Identify the piece of music that's been most important to you in your life. First, try to write down why it means so much to you, and when and where you can remember hearing it. If there are lyrics, write down all you can remember, and list adjectives that describe the melody.

   Now try tracing all of the cultural connections of the song, as the authors of *Strange Fruit* did. This may or may not take a little bit of research.

9. Try to imagine your way into the head of a musician you love. Create a speculative narrative that combines fact and fiction to bring that person's music to life on the page.

10. Think about your reading life. What piece of writing has "taken the top of your head off," to use Emily Dickinson's phrase? Write a reading narrative in which you enter into dialogue with this writing—feel free to quote it. How has this reading experience changed you and helped you redefine your life and your mission as a writer?

11. Write a history of your life through the books you've read. What was your favorite book at age five? Age ten? Age sixteen? Age twenty? Write these out in sections, rendering in specific, sensory detail the memories these books inspire in you.

FOR FURTHER READING

In Our Anthology
- "On Touching Ground" by Jericho Parms
- "The Night My Mother Met Bruce Lee" by Paisley Rekdal

RESOURCES AVAILABLE ONLINE
- "Inventing Peace" by Lawrence Wechsler

Print Resources
- *Strange Fruit: The Biography of a Song* by David Margolick and Hilton Als
- *The Age of Missing Information* by Bill McKibben
- *The Year of Reading Proust: A Memoir in Real Time* by Phyllis Rose
- *The Pat Boone Fan Club* by Sue William Silverman
- *Letters Like the Day: On Reading Georgia O'Keeffe* by Jennifer Sinor
- *A Postcard Memoir* by Lawrence Sutin

7

Glorious Facts:
Research and the Research Essay

Facts in all their glorious complexity make possible creativity. The best nonfiction writers are first-rate reporters, reliable eyewitnesses focused on the world, not themselves, and relentless researchers with the imagination to understand the implications of their discoveries.

—Philip Gerard

Working on a book that combined memoir with environmental writing, I found in many areas I was overwhelmed with information. Pesticide research, industrial waste, radiation, and the course of the Cold War: books, papers, old newspapers piled up and slid off my desk, defying all attempts at organization. In other ways, though, I found questions that had no answers: questions about the root causes of environmentally related disease, family stories that were irreconcilably different in everyone's telling.

It was an enormous relief to sit at my desk one day and realize that the lack of answers—the evasions, the uncertainties, the whole process—was a story in itself. I continued to research as doggedly as I could, but when I came up blank again and again, I began asking that emptiness whether it had a story to tell. One day I conclude the tale of a particularly frustrating phone call with these words: "I make telephone calls, hour after hour. Mostly I listen to message machines. EPA sends me to DEP, which sends me to ATSDR, which sends me to the County Board of Health, which says it has no records."

By the time I wrote this passage, I had tried to write around what I couldn't uncover, in many awkward and unsuccessful ways. I avoided subjects I needed to confront, or I tried to fake a knowledge I didn't have. I finally realized—with a liberating shock—that the reader needed to confront my own frustrations and uncertainties just as I had, to understand this story. The reader needed to hear and see the whole inquiry, even the phone calls that petered out into more avenues of possibility without certainty.

—SUZANNE

The Myriad Things Around Us

Can you imagine writing an entire book about four plants? One exhibit in a quirky museum? Sand? Lovely, profound, and popular books have been published in the last few years about such things. We call this genre *topical nonfiction*—essays that draw from specific, concrete topics. New journalism, a mode of journalism identified in the 1970s, led the way to topical nonfiction, as journalists like Tom Wolfe insisted the teller of the story must always be considered an active and subjective presence in the work.

Michael Pollan, in the *Botany of Desire: A Plant's-Eye View of the World*, chose as a subject four plants—marijuana, the app'le, the tulip, and the potato—weaving into their histories stories of cultural shifts, the drive for intoxication, and how we humans adapt to our plants as much as they adapt to us. Pollan's own garden and experiences with these plants provide a memoiristic thread.

Another research-oriented nonfiction writer, Atul Gawande, is a surgeon. His books have covered medical topics such as how we handle the end of life, but also more apparently mundane subjects, such as checklists. Gawande's *The Checklist Manifesto: How to Get Things Right,* offers a fascinating look at human decision-making, and what happens in the process of making mistakes.

Finally, Mary Cappello's *Swallow: Foreign Bodies, Their Ingestion, Inspiration, and the Curious Doctor Who Extracted Them* is a terrific example of how research can unlock new obsessions. With a spare afternoon in a strange (to her) city, she wandered into Philadelphia's Mutter Museum, a museum of the history of medicine and medical anomalies. There, she found herself drawn to a collection of strange objects humans had swallowed, amassed by a doctor named Chevalier Jackson. Cappello made many more visits to the museum to write her book, which encompasses Jackson's biography along with deeper questions of why people, whether patients or healers, feel compelled to do what they do.

Eastern religions speak reverently of "Indra's net"—a web of interconnectedness with a jewel at each intersection that can be used to embody the interconnectedness of the world. Gifted writers find the "webs" attached to the subjects that draw them—the deeper implications of an intoxicating plant or a compulsive, yet destructive, behavior.

As a writer, once you begin to look closely at what's around you—recognizing both the closest details and the larger ways each thing fits into the "Indra's net" that holds us all together—nothing will seem less than a fruitful subject for your writing.

Porosity

Perhaps we can equate openness to research with openness to incorporating the world around us and its events into our own life meditations, a kind of artistic *porosity* to the world around us. Porous materials, such as fabrics, absorb what comes in contact with them. The best nonfiction writers have a special porosity to what is around them; they're unable to ignore even a moth they happen to notice.

Not everyone will want to do full-blown investigative journalism. It's worth remembering that sometimes the best research we can do involves going somewhere we wouldn't normally go and talking to people we wouldn't normally talk to—and of course, really listening. Are you writing an essay about someone who lifts weights? Get a day pass to a gym and absorb the culture of weight lifting—how lifters push themselves, how muscle curves out of itself when flexed. Imaginatively, see your subject there.

Be open and interested. If you want to write about your childhood, don't settle for your memories, but look at the inventions, history, and popular culture that shaped your world at the time. Look up timelines of scientific breakthroughs, hit movies and songs, and key events from the period. (Many online sites provide such timelines.) Do the same for family members you write about. Create an inner sketch of the tastes, politics, and social standards of their worlds. What messages were they hearing? How did those messages help shape them into the people they became—the people you know?

Using Fact as Metaphor

Factual research will most often be used for what it is: fact. Water may contain a certain complex of chemicals; weight lifting may have such-and-such effects on the body. These facts can become the basis of an essay that explores the physical wonders and limitations of our world. At times, however, fact will also function as metaphor, informing the essay both on its own terms—information about the physical world the reader may need or find interesting—and as a basis for comparison for a more intangible part of the piece.

One writer, Jen Whetham, wrote an essay, "Swimming Pool Hedonist," chronicling how swimming and swimming pools have defined her and held her milestones: learning to trust, early sports success, even a first sexual encounter. The first draft of the essay began by saying, "My earliest memory is at a swimming pool," and included a passing reference to the odor of chlorine. That odor turned up again and again, and so Jen researched the chemistry of chlorine; she came up with this section in her final version:

> My skin has always smelled like chlorine. . . .
>
> Chlorine is missing one electron from its outer shell: this makes it highly attractive to other molecules. Chlorine's extreme reactivity makes it a powerful disinfectant: it bonds with the outer surfaces of bacteria and viruses and destroys them. When it kills the natural flora on human skin, the reaction creates the stuffy, cloudy smell we associate with chlorine.
>
> Chlorine marks us in ways we cannot see.

The essay goes on to use the touchstone of chlorine—odorless, changing forever what it contacts—as a metaphor for all the invisible ways life touches and changes us, and how we touch and change one another. It is a subtle and nuanced use of fact as fact, and fact as metaphor.

Researching a Key Piece of a Story

In Terry Tempest Williams's "The Clan of One-Breasted Women," the close of her book *Refuge: An Unnatural History of Family and Place*, Williams begins to examine the larger forces that may be contributing to her family's high breast cancer rate. In the following excerpt, you can see her seamless and organic movement from personal history into researched analysis. She has, as this dialogue begins, told her father of a recurring dream she has of a flash of light in the desert.

"You did see it," he said.

"Saw what?"

"The bomb. The cloud. We were driving home from Riverside, California. You were sitting on Diane's lap. She was pregnant. . . . We pulled over and suddenly, rising from the desert floor, we saw it, clearly, this golden-stemmed cloud, the mushroom. The sky seemed to vibrate with an eerie pink glow. Within a few minutes, a light ash was raining on the car."

Williams goes on to tell us that "above ground atomic testing in Nevada took place from January 27, 1951, through July 11, 1962." Williams provides an analysis of the political climate of the period—the growth of McCarthyism and the Korean War—summarizes litigation stemming from the tests, and returns seamlessly to her own story. She clearly researches the dates of the bomb testing as well as the wind patterns during those years, but she weaves those facts unobtrusively into her own narrative.

Launching (and Loving) the Research Essay

Sometimes, maybe much of the time for certain writers, we use research just to expand on a key detail in a piece. When did a family member arrive in the United States? What is the science behind an eclipse you watched? When those crucial "moments of being" occur in your nonfiction, you want to make sure you fully understand their components.

Even in a more researched essay, one perfect fact can keep readers tied emotionally to your story. In Barbara Hurd's *Listening to the Savage: River Notes and Half-Heard Melodies*, the author spends a period of many months simply observing the terrain of the Savage River, near her home. In her essay from that book, "To Keep an Ear to the Ground" (see Anthology), Hurd begins her exploration of listening with a gripping piece of history:

> In China long ago, people hid drums inside holes they'd dug along ancient roadways. To put an ear to the ground was to bend down, miles, maybe days, later and listen for the deep percussion of the enemy's boots approaching.

China and its history do not recur in this essay, but the concept of listening as vital to survival does, as the author, a naturalist, attempts to connect with her home landscape through sound.

The research-driven essay, one that begins with a subject and builds its narrative on the quest to learn about it, is one every writer should try. We think you'll want to keep research writing in your repertoire—doing original research and connecting it to your obsessions can be exhilarating. You get to challenge yourself to understand your own fascinations and draw readers into them as well.

Emily Dickinson calls those subjects that dwell in our minds and form our obsessions our *flood subjects*. Like Cappello visiting that swallowing collection at the Mutter Museum, we keep returning to our flood subjects. We can't help ourselves. We want, even *need,* to know more.

A powerful way to begin a research essay is by freewriting on a flood subject. When did you first learn about, or encounter, this subject? Why does it obsess you? What was your version of that fateful turn into the Mutter Museum? Consider what you do know about your flood subject, what you don't, and what you most want to learn.

As you write, list questions. Create "research challenges" for yourself. If you want to understand why physicists believe time may be only a limited construct, or why birds migrate, or why your grandparents won't talk about the country they emigrated from, write down all the questions you have, with provisional ideas for answering them. Write the simple, factual questions first and proceed to the more complex and conceptual ones. Don't stop yourself because you think you cannot answer the question. Often, if you consider your options—participatory research, primary sources, interviews—you'll find the impossible becomes possible. Research plans should always be ambitious.

As we freewrite about a research subject, deeper, metaphorical, even philosophical questions often emerge. Scratch the surface of a fact and it may suggest something profound about what it means to exist in this world. To continue the grandparent example, this progression from straightforward to more complex questions might look like this: "I wonder if I could learn details of the political situation at the time they left," to "What does it mean for family trust when stories are kept secret?"

Science and Other Technical Research

Albert Einstein wrote, in his essay "The World as I See It": "The most beautiful experience we can have is the mysterious. It is the fundamental emotion that stands at the cradle of true art and true science. Whoever does not know it and can no longer wonder, no longer marvel, is as good as dead, and his eyes are dimmed." This sense of the mysterious can visit us daily, if we're open to it. A friend said recently that every time he reads the news, he finds something that shakes up his view of the world: Stephen Hawking has pronounced we must colonize other planets and should fear computer intelligence; there may be infinite parallel universes; smart homes may soon make more decisions about our lives than we do.

When you write about science in creative nonfiction, it becomes much more than a recitation or analysis of facts: it is a means of probing the deepest levels of our common existence. Right now, we live steeped in startling scientific and technological advances. These changes signal more than quirky facts. They speak to our deepest assumptions about who we are.

It can be intimidating to draft an essay about a field in which we don't have expert training, whether it's medicine, science, technology, or another area. But many successful writers, including Annie Dillard and Mary Roach, show us how an interested layperson can bring plenty of insight to such essays. These writers do their homework, using reading, immersion, and interviews. They also bring their vulnerable selves to their subjects. In the essay "Total Eclipse," Dillard writes, "The sun was going, and the world was wrong." Later she tells us "the Crab Nebula, in the constellation Taurus, looks, through binoculars, like a smoke ring. It is a star in the process of exploding. Light from its explosion first reached the earth in 1054." Dillard lets us see the sky with her subjective vision before giving us astronomical history.

Of course, in areas in which you have training and expertise, use them! Just remember that your readers will always need your personal voice to guide them through an unfamiliar topic, as the image of something as temporary as a smoke ring makes the millennia contained in the nebula's light hit home.

Participatory Research

Working with Immersion

Immersion refers to the technique of actually living an experience, typically briefly, to write about it. The late George Plimpton, who was a writer and editor of the *Paris Review*, lived as a football player to research the book *Paper Lion*. Lee Gutkind, a writer and editor of the journal *Creative Nonfiction*, has done a great deal of immersion writing: he has lived as a circus clown and has followed transplant doctors and umpires on their rounds.

Writers differ in their approaches to immersion research. Gutkind writes of the author's need to become invisible, almost a piece of furniture in the room with the subject(s): "I like to compare myself to a rather undistinguished and utilitarian end table." Joan Didion, on the other hand, is always a presence in her research, one whose shy and questioning self forms another character in the piece.

The writer Mary Roach's books are remarkable for the zeal with which she tackles immersion. Funny and deeply informative, Roach's books offer readers a chance to share experiences we'll probably never have. Her fumbling around in odd situations makes her books funny and approachable. In *Packing for Mars: The Curious Science of Life in the Void*, for example, she experiences as much as she can of space simulations. Roach "Supermans it," as she puts it, around a capsule in zero gravity, examining how simple bodily functions can become ludicrously difficult in that environment.

Immersion provides readers with a real-time experience they would likely never have. At the same time, immersion exposes you, the author, in a profound way. You are the reader's surrogate, with both your curiosities and your uncertainties illuminated by this new act. Your sense of yourself, your self-confidence, and your assumptions will probably be pushed and probed. When we're in unfamiliar territory, it outlines who we are—both before and after the experience.

Suzanne once, for a book, learned simple sign language and conversed with an orangutan named Chantek, who had been raised signing. The gravity of the orangutan's responses, the sense of him as a present, sentient being, revealed a great deal about animal intelligence. It also challenged Suzanne's sense of what it means to be human and revealed her nervous presence, as she attempted to converse with a creature so seemingly different, one caged in a zoo.

What experiences would enhance your research? Keep this question in mind as you plan, laying out research challenges for yourself. Our students have practiced tantric yoga, interviewed therapists, spent time in sensory deprivation tanks. Again and again we hear comments like, "I couldn't believe they let me do this," and "I couldn't believe how open they were." Don't write off any possible experience. Most people love introducing someone to things they are passionate about. One deep immersion can make an essay or even a book.

Place-Based Research

Place-based research may overlap with immersion, but it invokes a greater sense of observation. It is experiential, but in a less participatory sense. In place-based research, we work on uncovering and meditating on the meaning of a place—the layers of geography, history, even human desire that have made it what it is. And part of this story of place is our story—our need to be there, our fascination with the place, and often our drive to put our own mark on it. It differs from the approach to place writing described in Chapter 3, "Taking Place," in that here, the place itself becomes the subject.

In place-based research, you might choose a place that interests you but that you don't know well. Or you may decide to sink yourself into a place you already know. Orhan Pamuk, in *Istanbul: Memories and the City*, meditates on the city of his childhood, its history, its neighborhoods, its faults, and its triumphs. It is his intimacy with Istanbul that propels the book, a connection he describes this way:

> My imagination, however, requires that I stay in the same city, on the same street, in the same house, gazing at the same view. Istanbul's fate is my fate. I am attached to this city because it has made me who I am.

In "To Keep an Ear to the Ground" (see Anthology), Barbara Hurd, along with her granddaughter Samantha, chooses to connect with this land through listening, like the Chinese peoples she references at the start. She goes out to the river with a game plan: "Sometimes when I put my ear to the ground, I make my own arbitrary rules: No listening for anything that has a plan for me. No listening to anything that knows I'm listening." Along with her granddaughter, the author puts her ear to the ground—literally!—and hears the "whish of ferns," a sound that leads her to a meditation on these plants, at once both so prevalent and so primeval, and their role in this place she is observing.

Marjorie Rose Hakala, in "Jumping the Fence" (see Anthology), offers a meditation on a *type* of place: zoos. She focuses on the significance of places where animals exist to be seen, live in confinement, and only capture the public's attention when "(1) An animal was born. (2) An animal died. (3) The barriers broke down. Something got out of the zoo, or someone got in." Her piece focuses on times when creatures escape their enclosures, or when humans break in, and the implications: A cobra escapes its glass case, but after a long period of searching, is found still in its World of Reptiles building. A tipsy dental student jumps into an ostrich enclosure and steals an egg. Ultimately, Hakala considers the yearnings of both humans and animals, as these are captured in the physical places of zoos:

> Building a fence and tearing one down are both acts of violence against the ideal of peaceful freedom, an ideal that could never be realized unless we redesigned the whole menagerie of earth. We build an illusion of that world instead and gaze in, our hands against the glass, hoping the barrier will hold, wondering if today is the day when it will break.

Focusing in on a place through research, striving to understand it, is deeply rewarding. What places feel essential to you, your family, your history? Or conversely, what places seem to hold secrets you would love to unlock? As you plan your research, make note of the places that inform your story or capture your imagination. Stay attentive to what wonders observation can unfold.

The Interview

You'll find as many interview styles as there are writers in this world. One of the great interviewers of the late twentieth and early twenty-first centuries was Italian writer Oriana Fallaci. Fallaci was more than a questioning presence at her interviews: she was an active listener and provocateur, one whose presence often became the interview. When the Ayatollah Khomeini told Fallaci he did not force women to cover themselves, she removed her head covering. (He left the room.) She also asked the Shah of Iran if he would arrest a journalist like her if she were Iranian. (He would.)

Regardless of your style, here are some tips that will help any interview go more productively. Most researchers ask a few "throw-off" questions—those with simple and less important answers—to relax their subjects before moving on to more difficult questions. And, as far as that goes, the toughest questions should be saved for last. If someone shuts down because you ask her about her silence around her first marriage, you don't want that uneasiness to ruin the whole interview. Begin with the simplest and least emotional information, and move forward from there.

Always begin an interview with a list of questions you want to ask; a prepared list will prevent you from forgetting to ask something important because of nerves or simple absentmindedness. Also, end interviews with an open-ended question that will direct you to your next research source. Finally, ask your subject what questions that person thinks you should ask. It's surprising how much insight and new information emerges through this method.

Be respectful, always, with the people who grant you an interview. And with everyone who appears in your writing, for that matter. Always ask people how they wish to be designated—pronouns, titles, and how they'd like their names to appear.

Developing Print Research Skills

Here we'll explore three commonly used and easily accessed print research sources—the library, the internet, and primary sources, such as legal documents and letters.

The Library

Libraries, even in the age of the internet, remain a powerful resource. They are home to books we need, along with archives, special collections, and research librarians. Library websites have become more and more helpful, as the last few decades have seen a rush of digitizing library collections. The

New York Public Library, one of our country's premier libraries, has digitized three-quarters of a million documents, photos, and other media.

Library collections differ greatly, and it helps to get to know the libraries you have access to. Cities like New York have an astonishing number of libraries. Major universities alone may have upward of a dozen. Identify before you go what books or other materials will help you along.

For library browsing, reference librarians are every library's secret treasure. They are there to help you find the resources you need for your work, and they will know their library's collections well. Western Washington University's reference librarian Paul Piper suggests you develop a relationship with the research librarians at any library you regularly use. Let them know what your projects are—they will get a sense of what you want and keep a lookout for it.

Libraries often house special collections and archives within their walls. These hold rare books and manuscripts and other original materials: videos, photos, diaries, to name a few possibilities. Often the papers of notable people, such as letters, handwritten poems or stories, sketches, and the like, are housed in libraries. Library archives, too, hold original documents and other historical works. Some archived material may be available online in digital form. But much will not, and we encourage you to carefully search library holdings. Seeing and holding original documents related to your passions is a once-in-a-lifetime experience.

Special collections can be regional. The Center for Pacific Northwest Studies at our Western Washington University library houses an in-depth collection of materials involving the Northwest. It includes letters, photos, old newspapers, maps, and rare books. These collections are treasure troves. Even if you're not certain what you're looking for, if an archive or special collection dovetails with your interests, it will richly reward your time.

The Internet

An enormous amount of material is posted on the web in its entirety—Environmental Protection Agency reports, NASA photographs, the records of ships carrying immigrants who arrived at Ellis Island. And so much more. Numerous databases can put you in touch with books and articles on particular topics—PubMed for medical research, and JSTOR, which is a wealth of books, primary sources, and journal articles, to name just two. JSTOR alone allows full-text searches from nearly two thousand journals. There are thousands of quality databases out there.

It is an exciting and a bewildering time to do internet research. In addition to text-based search possibilities, there are videos, photos, podcasts. There are several thousand TED talks available online, talks by experts on an enormous variety of topics. The Khan Academy offers quality, free online courses on everything from literature to computing, geared to all levels of learners. Other institutions offer free online courses as well. We strongly urge you to go beyond looking for specific answers to your research questions and cast a wider net to see what's out there.

If you can think of an institution that would house information you need, consider checking its website. Museums, libraries, government organizations, private groups, all offer immense amounts of information on the web.

Primary Sources

One writer we know wanted to research a point in family history about which he'd heard conflicting stories—his grandparents' marriage and the birth of his mother. Visiting the courthouse in the county where the marriage took place, he requested his grandmother's marriage license and was handed a license to a marriage other than the one to his grandfather. Intrigued, he recovered copies of both marriage licenses, wedding announcements that ran in the newspapers of the time, and his mother's birth certificate—and discovered his grandmother had been pregnant and just divorcing when she married his grandfather. Back in the 1930s both events would have prompted a great deal of scandal. Tensions in family relationships suddenly fell into place.

You may not discover anything quite so interesting, or you may find something far more interesting, but the fact is, courthouses keep records of births, adoptions, marriages, divorces, deaths, and more. Anyone can request copies; you visit the courthouse in the proper town or county, ask to see the directory of records, and request copies of what you want. Or you can register with an online service like Courtlink, which, for a fairly low fee, can generally obtain legal documents on file anywhere in the country. If you're researching a topic in a particular town, you might want to try the historical society; most towns have them, and they keep all sorts of documents, including deeds of sale, photographs, and frequently, diaries and old publications. Old newspapers, too, teem with information and are often kept in local libraries on microfilm. You may want to back up your family interviews with research into what really happened.

There are so many other print sources of information they're hard to list here. The Government Printing Office, for example, has reports and statistics available on everything imaginable, from congressional testimony to government-sponsored research. Of course, many primary sources are now available on the web. You can find some of these on your own. Ancestry record services can unlock more: you can pay to sign up, if you want to do significant family research, or see what you can glean in the free-trial period, if there is one. It is a mistake, though, to try to find records online and give up if you cannot. Places like courthouses and city halls hold marriage certificates, old deeds, and trial transcripts that provide firsthand information you cannot get anywhere else. Visit them, look carefully, and see if you find the kinds of facts that give surprise and energy to your story. (See "The Coroner's Photographs" by Brent Staples in our Anthology for an example of how to use primary sources as the basis for an essay.)

Finally, primary sources include documents held by individuals—their letters, journals, photographs, and so on. We know writers who have gained a new understanding of an ancestor by finding the notes she put on the pages of an old cookbook. Do not assume people you are interested in learning about won't share their private papers. Ask. Sometimes people are surprisingly willing to share their histories with you. Remember, most of your subjects won't object to the fact of you writing about them, but will simply want to feel understood.

The Research Map

It is nearly always the case that research begets more research. Our initial questions suggest other questions, and as we go, we refine the true nature of our curiosities. Sometimes our starting point turns out to hold just a kernel of what really captures our imagination.

Our student, writer Zoe Ballering, began a research essay by freewriting about her fascination with naked mole rats. She had seen them at a science museum—hairless, blind mammals that live in colonies like ants. She realized as she freewrote that she was most fascinated by the mole rats' inability to feel pain. As Zoe considered her questions, she realized pain itself was what intrigued her. In the process of researching the mole rats, she learned about a rare medical syndrome: a congenital absence of ability to feel pain. Then she discovered associated research on the relationship between physical pain and the capacity for empathy. Zoe finished her research process with an essay rich in detail and profundity, addressing empathy, embodiment, how pain is experienced and measured. She never returned to her naked mole rats!

Research can be overwhelming. You have material from each stage of the journey building on your desk and in your computer files, and often a less-than-coherent sense, as time goes by, of how you got there. You may have pages of your own notes, piles of books, articles, copies of deeds, and so forth. How do you keep these pieces together?

We suggest, for a research-driven piece, building a "research map." It will allow you to track where you have been and where you are going in your research, generate new questions, and continually note the connections you make. Some writers take construction paper or a whiteboard and use a Sharpie or pen for their map. Another writer might create an online document in a presentation platform; another might choose a large notebook. What works for you may be wholly unique to you. The point is to create a space in which you can map the progression of your research, your ideas, and the questions and answers bubbling out of both.

Make a circle or other point on your research map in the place you started, with the questions you first raised. Make notes on what interested you. Then map each move with another circle or point each time your research changes or expands. Write down new questions raised by each move; freewrite a paragraph. Note your sources. Zoe's research map began with naked mole rats, but her next circle concerned what it would mean not to feel pain. You can update your research map as you go or set a time—maybe once a week—to check in with yourself. It's a wonderful activity for a group or a class.

The research map is a way of mapping your curiosities. It also enables you to keep your research material organized as you plot new courses—you can label each circle on your map by letter, A, B, C, and so on, using these letters as a sorting or labeling device for your notes and documents. You can begin your research with a provisional research map. Just be open to the many diversions, zigzags, and fruitful detours that will come your way.

Finally, the research map offers useful structure to draw on for your final essay. You can see where you began and what you were curious about at that time—material you may draw from to start. The you who began the journey of the research essay is always partially the person you were before you learned more. Your transitions between the research threads of your essay will be outlined for you, to draw on in drafting and revision. The map provides a tool for understanding your research progress, and for going back and recreating those moments when a casual remark, or a few sentences of text, changed the course of your essay. Those twists generate the kind of excitement that makes an essay sing.

Try It

1. Create research challenges for yourself, or do this with a group. List types of research—primary source, immersion, the interview—and write out for yourself how each one could add to your project. Who could you interview? What historic documents might help? Where could you go to be part of an experience related to your search? Also write questions this research might answer, and commit yourself to a time frame for each challenge. If you do this with a class or a group, report in once a week or so on your progress.

2. The poet Kimiko Hahn wrote her book *Brain Fever* by clipping neuroscience articles from newspapers like the *New York Times*. She used language from these articles in her poems as well as facts, melding them into meditations that are often deeply personal. From an article on the millions of miles of wiring in the human brain, Hahn moves in one poem to her young child, eating a bowl of spaghetti. Spend time reading top-notch science reporting. What in your life feels connected to the research, as Hahn's child eating pasta does with her developing brain filaments? Write an essay that brings these facts together with the richness of your own experience.

3. Chances are you've already had at least one terrific immersion experience, even if you didn't call it that: maybe it was a summer working at a ranch. Maybe it was the time your uncle dragged you along to a meeting of the local Elks Club. Fascinating immersion experiences exist all over. Do you live near a hospital? A casino? A Society for Creative Anachronism? Ask folks if they would mind you observing them a while for an essay. Keep notes, use a recorder, or both.

Decide, before you begin your immersion experience, how you see your role. Will you take the approach of Didion and acknowledge your presence in the events you write about, or like Gutkind, try to keep yourself out of the narrative? Adjust your presence accordingly.

4. Consider a place that is meaningful to you, as Hurd considers the Savage River. Or like Hakala, choose a type of place that fascinates you. Spend time at this place, or places, with a notebook and an open mind. Don't make judgments ahead of time about what might prove worth writing about. Experience the place, its inhabitants, note its rhythms and cultural assumptions.

5. To hone your interview skills and create a body of information you'll almost certainly want to come back to, try family interviews. These interviews are generally far less intimidating than tracking down your local physicist to ask questions about the implications of the Big Bang (if they are even more intimidating, write about that!). Start with a question you have always wanted to get an answer, or a clearer answer, to. It may be the life story of the family scapegrace, an immigration story, or a detailed picture of a parent's early years. Make a list of questions; keep them fairly simple.

Ask your questions of two or three different family members—preferably several generations, such as a cousin, a parent, a grandparent—and make note of the discrepancies between their versions of events. This will tell you a lot about the structure of your family. Typically, families have keepers-of-the-family-name types, as well as "tell-all" types. You may want to meditate on who plays these roles in your family (does the answer surprise you?) and, of course, who you are in the hierarchy of things.

6. List all the "flood subjects" you can think of. Freewrite on each: When did this subject begin to interest you, and why? What is your personal connection to each? Create clear connections between these questions and episodes from your life, as Pamuk does in *Istanbul*. Write a short and concise question that each of these subjects raises for you. Use each question as a title, do some research, and see how your question pushes your integration of what you learn and what generated your wonder in the first place.

7. Begin a research map, starting with initial questions and freewriting at least a paragraph about how these questions inform your sense of the world. Create tentative new points on your map. Give yourself a deadline for each piece of research and include at each stop on the way a freewrite on how this knowledge changed your thinking. Who was the early you of this research? How does a more informed you now emerge, and how do these voices differ?

8. Write, perhaps after doing some initial research for your essay, all the aspects of your research questions that must remain unknowable. For instance, we can know how possible it is that we humans will colonize other planets. We cannot know if we actually will. Freewrite on these unanswerable questions. Describe how it feels to acknowledge the limits of your research. We sometimes forget the fascination of what cannot be known.

9. Look for experts whose work dovetails with your interests. If you are at a college or university, you will have access to physics departments, advanced computing and technology, possibly schools of medicine, to name a few possibilities. Identify what expertise you can find locally. Then consider other experts you may be able to reach by email or phone. Ask to conduct quick interviews, including distance interviews, and see what you can learn. It's useful to check whether there is an experiment or other experience related to this person that you can witness.

10. Check your local libraries for archives and special collections. Again, you limit yourself if you have an overly narrow sense of your interests. Even if the collections don't immediately speak to a subject at hand, make an appointment to visit (many of these library collections, though not all, will be available by appointment). Ask the librarians who work in these areas to tell you what they think the most interesting pieces of the collection are. See if any piece of this archived material sparks an essay.

For Further Reading

In Our Anthology
- "Jumping the Fence" by Majorie Rose Hakala
- "To Keep an Ear to the Ground" by Barbara Hurd
- "Leap" by Brian Doyle
- "The Coroner's Photographs" by Brent Staples

Resources Available Online

- "Marrying Absurd" by Joan Didion
- "Total Eclipse" by Annie Dillard
- "The World as I See It" by Albert Einstein

Print Resources

- *A Mind Apart: Travels in a Neurodiverse World* by S. (Paola) Antonetta
- *Body Toxic: An Environmental Memoir* by S. (Paola) Antonetta
- *Swallow: Foreign Bodies, Their Ingestion, Inspiration, and the Curious Doctor Who Extracted Them* by Mary Cappello
- *Pilgrim at Tinker Creek* by Annie Dillard
- *Istanbul: Memories and the City* by Orhan Pamuk
- *Paper Lion* by George Plimpton
- *The Botany of Desire: A Plants'- Eye View of the World* by Michael Pollan
- *Packing for Mars: The Curious Science of Life in the Void* by Mary Roach
- *The Immortal Life of Henrietta Lacks* by Rebecca Skloot
- *Refuge: An Unnatural History of Family and Place* by Terry Tempest Williams

PART II

THE MANY FORMS OF CREATIVE NONFICTION

The best work speaks intimately to you even though it has been consciously made to speak intimately to thousands of others. The bad writer believes that sincerity of feeling will be enough, and pins her faith on the power of experience. The true writer knows that feeling must give way to form. It is through the form, not in spite of, or accidental to it, that the most powerful emotions are let loose over the greatest number of people.

—JEANETTE WINTERSON

8

The Tradition of the Personal Essay

After a time, some of us learn (and some more slowly than others)
that life comes down to some simple things. How we love, how alert
we are, how curious we are. Love, attention, curiosity. . . . One way
we learn this lesson is by listening to others tell us true stories of their
own struggles to come to a way of understanding. It is sometimes
comforting to know that others seem to fail as often and as oddly as
we do. . . . And it is even more comforting to have such stories told to
us with *style*, the way a writer has found to an individual expression
of a personal truth.

—Scott Walker

I am a young woman in college, beginning to write. One day I pick up
Annie Dillard's book *Pilgrim at Tinker Creek*. A book-length, meditative
personal essay, *Pilgrim* documents the speaker's observations of the natural
world around her home in Virginia. It is at once deeply individual, as she
looks at the "rosy, complex" light that fills her kitchen in June, and deeply
philosophical, as she draws everything into relationship with the galaxy that
is "careening" around her. It is a bold book, drawing on the seemingly small
to embrace the entire world. More important to me at the time, the speaker
is a young woman in her twenties, the author herself. She's not speaking
with the authoritative male voice I have come to associate with the essay.
She speaks as Annie Dillard, with only the authority of our shared human
experience.

I was fascinated to learn later that Annie Dillard originally began *Pilgrim
at Tinker Creek* in the voice of a middle-aged male academic, a metaphysician.

101

She didn't trust her own young woman's voice to engage and convince her audience. Other writers persuaded her to trust her voice and abandon the constructed one, and the book won the Pulitzer Prize, proving that the personal essay form is a broad one. It only requires that you be alert, perceptive, and human.

—SUZANNE

Find Your Form—Find Your Slant

We began this book with a nod to Emily Dickinson and her mandate to "tell all the truth but tell it slant." Part 1, we hope, has helped you find out just what kinds of "truths" you may have to offer. Now your job is to find a way to "tell it slant," to find the forms that will contain these truths in the most effective and interesting ways. As a writer of creative nonfiction, you must continually make artistic choices that will finesse life's experience into art that will have lasting meaning for others. As Theresa Warburton and Elissa Washuta put it in their anthology *Shapes of Native Nonfiction*:

> The basket. The body. The canoe. The page. Each of these vessels has a form, a shape to which its purpose is intimately related. Each carries, each holds, and each transports. However, none of these vessels can be defined solely by their contents; neither can their purpose be understood as strictly utilitarian. Rather, the craft involved in creating such a vessel, the care and knowledge it takes to create the structure and shape necessary to convey, is inseparable from the content that the vessel holds. To pay attention only to the contents would be to ignore the very relationships that such vessels sustain.

Through a careful attention to form, you will be able to create art out of your own experience. Understanding *how* we are structuring our experience forces us to be concrete and vivid. Ironically, the more particular you make your own experience—with sensory details, compelling metaphors, and luscious rhythms—the more fully a reader will feel the personal story along with you. By experiencing it, readers begin to *care* about it, because your experience has now become their own.

The Personal Essay Tradition

The personal essay is "the way a writer has found to an individual expression of a personal truth." When Scott Walker wrote those words in 1986—in his introduction to *The Graywolf Annual 3: Essays, Memoirs, and Reflections*—the personal essay was making a comeback. The reading public seemed hungry for a form that engages us the way fiction does, but that also teaches us something about the way real life works. While the phrase "creative nonfiction" had not yet come into popular use, "personal essay" seemed adequate to convey that sense of combining a personal voice with a factual story.

In the West, scholars often date the essay tradition back to the sixteenth-century French writer Michel de Montaigne. *Essays*, composed in Montaigne's retirement, lay much of the groundwork for what we now think of as the essay style: informal, frank (often bawdy), and associative. His book moves easily from a consideration of the classical author Virgil to pieces like "Of Smells" (see Anthology). His title *Essays*, playing on the French verb meaning "to try," gives us the term we now use routinely in nonfiction writing. The essay writer "tries out" various approaches to the subject, offering tentative forays into an arena where "truth" can be open for debate.

Phillip Lopate, editor of the historically astute anthology *The Art of the Personal Essay*, puts it this way: "The essayist attempts to surround a something—a subject, a mood, a problematic irritation—by coming at it from all angles, wheeling and diving like a hawk, each seemingly digressive spiral actually taking us closer to the heart of the matter."

Prior to Montaigne, as Lopate's anthology illustrates, plenty of writers worked in what we would now consider a personal essay mode. Just a few examples include Sei Shōnagon, a tenth-century Japanese courtesan who created elaborately detailed lists that revealed much about herself and her place in the Japanese court; the Japanese monk Kenkō's meditative ruminations translated as *Essays in Idleness*; or Roman emperor Marcus Aurelius, whose book *Meditations* embodies an aphoristic essay style, creating pithy "slogans" as advice to those who will succeed him. The Stoic philosopher Seneca the Younger and the Greek biographer Plutarch both wrote "essays in disguise" in the form of letters that ruminated on a range of subjects, from noise in the marketplace to the proper comportment to maintain in the face of grief.

After Montaigne, British essayists such as Charles Lamb and William Hazlitt made the essay form their own. According to Lopate, "it was the English, rather than Montaigne's own countrymen, who took up his challenge and extended, refined, and cultivated the essay." Both Lamb and Hazlitt wrote in the style of Montaigne, creating essays with titles such as "A Chapter on Ears" (Lamb) and "On the Pleasure of Hating" (Hazlitt). At the same time in America, Thoreau was writing his journals and *Walden*, works that would form the foundation of American nature writing taken up by writers such as Edward Abbey and Annie Dillard.

Women left an indelible mark on the essay too. Just a few examples include Maria Edgeworth, a memoirist and feminist from the Romantic period; Isabella Bird, a nineteenth-century travel writer who died in her seventies with her bags packed; and Nellie Bly, another nineteenth-century woman writer who pushed her way into the male world of journalism, famously practicing immersion in sweatshops and institutions.

As an essayist, you should take it upon yourself to study the tradition, not only for general knowledge but to situate yourself within that literary lineup. How does your own writing work with or against the stylistic tendencies of a Joan Didion, say, who in turn has a voice that emerges in direct dialogue with the voice of essayists such as George Orwell? Lopate's *The Art of the Personal Essay* is a good place to start, but also look at works of your contemporaries to see how the essay is evolving in your own generation. By reading widely, you will learn not only what is possible, but what has still to be discovered.

You may find, as Lopate has, that "at the core of the essay is the supposition that there is a certain unity to human experience." The personal essay carries the implication that the personal, properly rendered, is universally significant or should be. Montaigne echoes this: "Every man has within himself the entire human condition." At the same time, Lopate writes that "the hallmark of the personal essay is its intimacy. The writer seems to be speaking directly into your ear, confiding everything from gossip to wisdom." These two poles—intimacy of voice and universality of significance—go to the heart of the personal essay tradition. The essay speaks confidingly, as a whispering friend, and these whispers must be made meaningful in a larger context—capturing a piece of larger human experience within the amber of your own.

The Way Essays Work

What makes an essay an essay? How can you recognize one when you see it? When we study fiction writing or poetry, certain elements of form are easy enough to identify, such as plot or character development in short stories, or lineation and rhythm in poems. Essays can be analyzed the same way, but the task is complicated by the wide variety of styles and forms encompassed by the term *personal essay*. Many of these forms overlap with content, and perhaps you've already experienced several of them in the first section of this book. You've already been writing memoir, for example, when you focus on selected memories for a particular metaphorical or narrative effect. You've already started a nature essay when you described some aspect of the environment around you. Perhaps you've already tried the travel piece or a biographical sketch of someone close to you. All of these are forms defined more by content than craft.

When we turn our attention to craft, we can begin to see some stylistic qualities that help define the essay form. In his essay "A Boundary Zone," Douglas Hesse describes the difference between essays and short stories in terms of movement. In any narrative prose piece, some sense of forward movement emerges. Visualized horizontally, this line keeps the story moving forward. Some essays read almost like short stories, with clear plots, characters, dialogue, and so on, relying more on the horizontal movement. In contrast, a more essay-like narrative might have a stronger vertical line to it, going below the surface, using a reflective voice that comments upon the scenes it recreates. (See also Chapter 12, "The Basics of Good Writing in Any Form," for more discussion of forward movement in creative nonfiction.)

Once you begin seeing essays in terms of their movement, you can decide how your own work might fit or work against the categories of personal essay. At one extreme, we have the short-story style that engages us with plot, subplots, and scenes. At the other extreme is the analytic meditation that engages us through the power of the writer's interior voice. Where do you fall on this grid? How can you expand your talents and write essays that create their own definitions?

The "I" and the Eye: Framing Experience

The self inhabits the personal essay, whether or not you write directly about your own experiences. It is this "I" that picks and chooses among the facts. This "I" recreates those essential scenes and makes crucial decisions about what to include and what to exclude. The "I" decides on the opening line that will set up the voice of the piece, the essential themes and metaphors. The "I" gives the essay its *personality*, both literally and figuratively.

A useful way of looking at how creative nonfiction employs the "I" is to align the genre with photography. Both photography and creative nonfiction operate under the "sign of the real" (a phrase coined by literary theorist Hayden White); both operate *as though* the medium itself were transparent. In other words, when you look at a photograph, you are lulled into the illusion that you see the world as it is—looking through a window, as it were—but in reality you are being shown a highly manipulated version of that world. The same is true with creative nonfiction.

Both photography and creative nonfiction actually function just as subjectively as fiction and painting, because the personal "eye" is the mechanism for observation, and the inner "I" is the medium through which these observations are filtered. As Joan Didion puts it, "No matter how dutifully we record what we see around us, the common denominator of all we see is always, transparently, shamelessly, the implacable 'I.'"

The minute you begin to impose form on experience—no matter how dutifully you try to remain faithful to history or the world—you're immediately faced with a technical dilemma: How do you effectively frame this experience? What gets left outside the confines of this frame? Are some frames more "truthful" than others? And the way you decide to frame the world directly reflects the "I" and the "eye" that perform this act of construction.

Wallace Stegner, in his book *Where the Bluebird Sings to the Lemonade Springs*, posits that our task as writers is "to write a story, though ignorant or baffled. You take something that is important to you, something you have brooded about. You try to see it as clearly as you can, and to fix it in a transferable equivalent. All you want in the finished print is the clean statement of the lens, which is yourself, on the subject that has been absorbing your attention."

The Persona of the First-Person Narrator

Just as the details of the world and experience may be framed or constructed by a mediating "I," so too is that "I" a fabrication for the purposes of the essay. We are not the same on the page as we are in real life, and we must be aware that the "I" is just as much a tool—or a point of view or a character—that we manipulate for particular effects. The "I" on the page is really a fictional construction, reflecting certain parts of us, leaving others out, or exaggerating certain aspects for the purposes of the essay at hand.

In *The Situation and the Story*, memoirist Vivian Gornick writes about finding her voice in creative nonfiction. "I began to read the greats in essay writing—and it wasn't their confessing voices I was responding to, it was their truth-speaking personae," she writes. "I have created a persona who can find the story riding the tide that I, in my unmediated state, am otherwise going to drown in." The narrating "I," the persona you create, is the one who has the wherewithal to rescue experience from chaos and turn it into art.

Traditional Forms of the Personal Essay

Remember, most essays use several elements of different literary approaches. But for purposes of scrutinizing our own work and understanding our traditions, we can discuss nonfiction in terms of categories, bearing in mind all the while that we don't want to allow ourselves or the writers we admire to be limited by those categories.

Memoir

A nonfiction category strongly linked with the personal essay is memoir. *Memoir* comes from the French word for *memory*; to be memoir, the writing must derive its energy, its narrative drive, from exploration of the past. Its lens may be a lifetime, or it may be a few hours.

William Zinsser, who edited *Inventing the Truth: The Art and Craft of Memoir*, says, "Unlike autobiography, which moves in a dutiful line from birth to fame, memoir narrows the lens, focusing on a time in the writer's life that was unusually vivid, such as childhood or adolescence, or that was framed by war or travel or public service or some other special circumstance." In other words, memoirists need not have had fascinating lives, worth recounting in every detail. (Those kinds of books, as Zinsser notes, are generally considered autobiography.)

Remember those "shocks of memory" from Chapter 1, "The Body of Memory," and how those authors focused on small moments from their lives? These are great examples of how memoir works. The author is curious about a memory, then gradually finds a guiding, prevalent theme in that memory, leading to other connected experiences. Through this exploration, ideally, their writing not only describes the author's life, but helps us understand our own. As Adam Gopnik wrote in his introduction to *The Best American Essays 2008*: "Memoir essays move us not because they are self-indulgent, but because they are other-indulgent, and the other they indulge is us, with our own parallel inner stories of loss and confusion and mixed emotions."

In his essay "Backtalk," Richard Hoffman provides a defense of the surge of memoir as a corrective to a culture that has accepted the verb *to spin* to mean deliberate distortion of our news. "The ascendance of memoir . . . may be a kind of cultural corrective to the sheer amount of fictional distortion that has accumulated in [our] society." For those of you interested in the memoir form, Hoffman's words may provide a useful starting point; think of yourself as an "unspinner," a voice striving to undo some of the cultural distortion you see around you.

Literary or New Journalism

In 1972, for an article in *New York* magazine, Tom Wolfe announced "The Birth of the 'New Journalism.'" This new nonfiction form, Wolfe claimed, would supplant the novel. It allowed writers the luxury of a first-person voice and the use of literary devices—scene, imagery, and so forth—in the service of reporting. In other words, Wolfe's new journalism marries traditional journalism with the personal essay. Wolfe cited such new journalists as Hunter S. Thompson, then writing a first-person account of his travels among the Hells Angels.

Wolfe emerged as one of the leaders of New Journalism, along with other writers such as Joan Didion, Gay Talese, and Norman Mailer. Wolfe rode buses with LSD guru Ken Kesey and his Merry Pranksters to write *The Electric Kool-Aid Acid Test*, all the while using his first-person voice liberally and appearing in his trademark starched high collars and white suits, a character in his own right. Wolfe's insistence on the primacy of his own experience in the act of reporting comes through even in his titles, like this one of an essay about Las Vegas (surely one of the loudest cities in the country): "Las Vegas (What?) Las Vegas (Can't Hear You! Too Noisy) Las Vegas!!!!" New Journalism does stress the act of reporting; its practitioners have done some of the most intense reporting in the nonfiction world. But they also avail themselves of literary techniques and a personal voice.

As research becomes more crucial even to very personal nonfiction, such as Andrew Solomon's *The Noonday Demon* (a heavily researched but intimate look at depression), the lines between other forms of nonfiction and new journalism blur. And, in the age of instant information on the internet, traditional journalism becomes more interpretive and less formulaic. (See also Chapter 7, "Glorious Facts: Research and the Research Essay.")

David Foster Wallace, both a novelist and a nonfiction writer, once said, "Writing-wise, fiction is scarier but nonfiction is harder—because nonfiction's based in reality, and today's felt reality is overwhelmingly, circuit-blowingly huge and complex." He deals with this complexity through innovative uses of form: his writing often combines immersion research with a fiction writer's sensibility, and the resultant work exhibits his unique voice and playfulness. For example, in his essay "Consider the Lobster," he travels to the Maine Lobster Festival, where he observes:

> . . . lobster rolls, lobster turnovers, lobster sauté, Down East lobster salad, lobster bisque, lobster ravioli, and deep-fried lobster dumplings. . . . There are lobster T-shirts and lobster bobblehead dolls and inflatable lobster pool toys and clamp-on lobster hats with big scarlet claws that wobble on springs.

These list-like observations are a hallmark of Wallace's work, and he intersperses direct observation with in-depth information gleaned from many sources. Throughout the essay, footnotes give interesting "factoids" as well as his running commentary on what he is learning and observing about the humble lobster. These techniques let us learn a great deal about lobsters, certainly, but we also learn about Wallace and his own sensibilities. The essay ends up debating the moral issues involved with cooking live lobsters. "I am concerned," he writes, after bringing up these issues, "not to come off as shrill or preachy when what I really am is more like confused, uneasy." We probably wouldn't be all that interested in lobsters and the moral issues they raise if Wallace didn't show them to us with this self-revealing, and highly entertaining, voice.

The Meditative Essay

Composing his essays, Montaigne referred to himself as an "accidental philosopher." The term *essay* carries a double meaning of both *trying* and *proving* or *testing*. To essay an action means to attempt it; to assay a substance, particularly a metal, means to test it, weigh it, and try to determine its composition.

The essay form lends itself to tentative, meditative movement, and the meditative essay derives its power from careful deliberation on a subject, often but not always an abstract one. Some meditative essays announce their approach in their title, like Abraham Cowley's "Of Greatness." Montaigne is often a little more down-to-earth, with titles such as "Of Smells" (see Anthology) that announce their topic and the author's intent to mull on that topic for a while.

Often a meditative essay must still have some grounding element to make abstract thoughts more concrete. For example, in his essay "Hereafter in Fields," Robert Vivian meditates on the nature of hope, time, and the self—all within the confines of a long car ride through Nebraska. He begins the essay this way: "The way the sun shimmers in the long Nebraska grass just off the highway can make you feel hope again, like there's still time for lovelier, finer things." He uses the phrase "if only" throughout the essay to express his thoughts and longings, and he writes: "I am not the same person after this fifty-mile drive to and from. It doesn't matter who I am in either city, but who I am in between."

Take a look at Barbara Hurd's essay "To Keep an Ear to the Ground" (see Anthology). Note how she literally grounds us in scene—kneeling down in the dirt with her granddaughter—to begin an essay that will meditate and muse on more abstract topics such as listening and trying to understand the world.

The Object Essay

Many writers have found that focusing on a physical object first, no matter how mundane, can also be a way into an effective meditative essay. For example, Dinah Lenney organized an entire book, titled *The Object Parade,* around a wide variety of objects that spurred memory or rumination. She writes in the introduction: "Things, all kinds—ordinary, extraordinary— tether us, don't they, to place and people and the past, to feeling and thought, to each other and ourselves, to some admittedly elusive understanding of the passage of time." The essays in the book are spurred by such objects as a metronome, a chandelier, a spoon, and a flight jacket.

Fabio Morábito wrote a book called *Toolbox* in which he delves into heady ideas triggered by objects such as screws, files, sandpaper, and nails. You can find other examples in the "Object Lessons" series published by Bloomsbury Books. In this series, authors write an essay or an entire book with a focus on a single object, such as "Sock" or "Remote Control."

The Essay of Ideas

Strongly connected to the meditative essay is the essay of ideas. The essay has long been *the* form for exploring the workings of the human intellect. Running the gamut from argument to rumination, authors have always used the essay as a vehicle for both developing and expressing ideas, holding political debates, and delving into personal philosophy. Many of us have bad memories of writing "themes" in high school, the five-paragraph essay that rigidly prescribed the way an intellectual essay could work: thesis, three supporting paragraphs, and a tepid conclusion. Here, in the realm of creative nonfiction, you can redeem the essay of ideas and return it to its rightful place in the literary arts.

As with all good creative nonfiction, it's important to make the essay specific to you and your particular voice. Writing about abstract concepts does not need to be dull or dry; on the contrary, here is an opportunity for you to use the techniques of vivid writing to illuminate difficult and obscure topics. You will seek to uncover the scenes, the details, the images, and the metaphors that make for a memorable essay.

For example, in her book *The Empathy Exams*, Leslie Jamison first presents us with a personal frame: she's employed as an actor for a medical school, pretending to suffer from various illnesses and acting through medical visits, to help new doctors learn to empathize with their patients. The situation is intriguing, often awkward, and sometimes comical, as when she tells us that "one time a [medical] student forgets we are pretending and starts asking detailed questions about my fake hometown—which, as it happens, is his *real* hometown—and his questions lie beyond the purview of my script." The reader moves naturally from Jamison's odd line of work to a deeper examination of the idea of empathy.

> Empathy isn't just listening, it's asking the questions whose answers need to be listened to. Empathy requires inquiry as much as imagination. Empathy requires knowing you know nothing. Empathy means acknowledging a horizon of context that extends perpetually beyond what you can see: an old woman's gonorrhea is connected to her guilt is connected to her marriage is connected to her children is connected to the days when she was a child.

Here the book expands enormously from an account of a job, however interesting the job may be in itself. Jamison uses her work as a lens to try to understand what elements form the basis of human empathy—to understand the feeling of empathy, and consider how to enable it further in ourselves. As in any great essay of ideas, she holds the concept up to the light and probes deeply what her subject is and what it isn't: empathy is not just listening, but an unbiased inquiry into another person's place in the world.

Paradoxically, when you write about abstract concepts—ideas—it is even more important to pay attention to the concrete details that make such things comprehensible. It is the combination of a personal urgency with intellectual musings that makes the essay of ideas thrive. Remember "Notes of a Native Son" from Chapter 4? Baldwin focuses on the death of his father, but issues of race and violence pulse through the essay, creating a political argument much more effective than any pundit's analysis.

The Sketch or Portrait

One of the most popular essay forms of the nineteenth century, the sketch or portrait held ground partly because of the lack of other forms of communication—the average person traveled little and, even after the invention of photography, saw far fewer photos than we see today. Writers like Dickens stepped into the breach, offering verbal snapshots of cities, foreign countries, and people.

Today we have newspapers, TV, and the internet, but the power of language to provide not just verbal pictures but emotional ones keeps the portrait an important form. Immediately after the September 11 attacks on the World Trade Center and the Pentagon, the *New Yorker* magazine commissioned a handful of writers to capture that day in short verbal portraits. The editors realized something crucial about that world-changing event: photos may best hold the searing image of the buildings, but a writer can also capture the reality of, as Jonathan Franzen put it, "stumbling out of the smoke into a different world."

The character sketch is also an integral part of the portrait form. Originally a kind of verbal photograph, portraits still can capture individuals in a way visual forms cannot, using imagery and description to leap from someone's surface to their essence. Maxine Hong Kingston's "No Name Woman" forms at once a largely imaginary portrait of the author's disgraced aunt and a portrait of her very real mother:

> If I want to learn what clothes my aunt wore, whether flashy or ordinary, I would have to begin, "Remember Father's drowned-in-the-well sister?" I cannot ask that. My mother has told me once and for all the useful parts. She will add nothing unless powered by Necessity, a riverbank that guides her life. She plants vegetable gardens rather than lawns; she carries the odd-shaped tomatoes home from the fields and eats food left for the gods.

What a world of information is packed into this formidable portrait! We see Kingston's mother sketched before us in terms of telling actions—choosing the practical over the ornamental, refusing to waste food, even for presumably religious reasons. We're prepared by this sketch for the tension mother and daughter experience over the suppression of the aunt's story, and the way that story reflects their own uncommunicative relationship.

Radio Essay

The ancient art of oral storytelling underlies the impulse of much contemporary creative nonfiction. We once told stories as a way not only to pass the time, but also to pass along our familial and cultural heritage.

Radio shows have always embraced storytelling as a mainstay of their offerings; in the days when radio provided the primary form of entertainment, people gathered to listen intently to their favorite narratives spun out in familiar voices. These days, with so many entertainment options available to us, oral stories still have a powerful draw, and there are many ways to hear them and learn from them about how to tell our own stories.

Magazine-style radio shows, such as *This American Life* and *A Prairie Home Companion*, led the way in their field. Ira Glass, host of *This American Life*, chooses a theme for each week's show, and then several segments elucidate that theme through true stories. Sometimes the story may be a personal narrative, and often the stories are research pieces with a twist. For instance, in one wildly popular episode, called "Act V," the entire show follows the story of prison inmates in a high-security prison, many of them incarcerated for murder, as they prepare to perform Act V of *Hamlet*. The men—many of whom have little education—give startling insights into the Shakespearean characters they portray, while the narrator of the piece shows the complexities involved in putting on a show in the prison environment.

Some popular radio shows have more affinity with spoken word or slam poetry, as the narrators tell their true stories to an audience. For example, *The Moth: True Stories Told Live* broadcasts live performances from stages in New York and around the country, with the rule that the narrator cannot use notes, so the pieces have a quality of spontaneity and vibrant energy. Often these stories are funny, but just as often they are infused with powerful emotion. For instance in one show titled "It Wasn't Enough," Charlene Strong tells us what it was like to experience the death of her partner while not being allowed in her hospital room. She went on to become a gay rights activist who was instrumental in change.

Video Essay

Some writers have gone further and taken the essay off the page and onto the screen. *Triquarterly*, an online literary journal, has become a showcase for the video essay form; the curator of this section, John Bresland, publishes several video essays in every edition.

The video essay allows the creative nonfiction writer to bring in still images, moving images, music, animation—a panoply of tools that bring your work to life in new and unexpected ways. In "Dead Christ," for example, Brian Bouldrey can show us a painting—Hans Holbein's *The Body of the Dead Christ in the Tomb*—while we hear the author's voice describing the details of that painting. Our gaze pans the disturbing image with Bouldrey's voice as a guide, leading us to an emotional and stirring association of Bouldrey's experience with the death of his partner from AIDS. Such an experience—while powerful enough on the page—is enhanced by the multimedia Bouldrey is able to include in the video form. (See also Chapter 10, "Mixed-Media, Cross-Genre, Hybrid, and Digital Works," for a further discussion of using other media in your work.)

TRY IT

1. Write a short piece of memoir using a particular event. Write quickly and then examine the piece in light of the distinctions between the intimate and the universal. Where do you speak as though the reader is a friend, listening at your side? Do you need to reveal more of yourself, of your feelings? And where is the universality of your experience? You may want to trade with a partner to uncover the answers to these questions.

   VARIATION: With Richard Hoffman's comments in mind, write a memoir of an event that seeks to "unspin" some kind of official version of it.

2. Write a journalistic story, perhaps about a colorful place nearby or an event in your community (a protest? a festival?) that uses reportorial style to capture the story but also includes your own presence as a character. Use literary devices to describe the people you see; use metaphor to paint their lives. Take advantage of literary devices, while respecting the factuality of journalism.

3. Write a sketch of a person or a place. Focus on keeping your work vivid and simple—a language portrait. Think of it as being intended for someone who cannot meet this person or visit this area.

4. Write an essay titled "On _____." Fill in the blank yourself and use the title as a way to explore an abstract concept in a personal and concrete way. All of us have abstract questions we would secretly love to write about. Why are we here? What does it mean to love a child? Why does society exist in the form it does?

5. Write down the abstract question you would most like to explore. Then freewrite a group of events you somehow associate with that question: a brush with death, giving birth, living in a different culture. Meditate on the question, alternating your meditations with the actual event.

6. Choose an object. This choice can be random or deliberate. You could start by choosing something that's right in front of you: a pencil, a stapler, a picture frame. Or look at something outside your window, or *in* your window. For example, in Virginia Woolf's famous essay "The Death of the Moth," she notices a moth fluttering in the corner of her window, which leads to a somber meditation on mortality. Start by describing your object and then allow this object to lead you into a meditation on larger ideas.

7. Consider recording your stories to tell before an audience and see how that process affects your structure, your content, and your written voice. Look at websites for storytelling shows and give yourself a goal of submitting a story to them.

8. Consider exploring how one of your essays could be expressed in video form. What kind of music could provide a soundtrack? What kind of images might you include?

FOR FURTHER READING

In Our Anthology
- "Of Smells" by Michel de Montaigne
- "First" by Ryan Van Meter
- "To Keep an Ear to the Ground" by Barbara Hurd

Resources Available Online

- "On Keeping a Notebook" by Joan Didion
- "Total Eclipse" by Annie Dillard
- "Backtalk: Notes Toward an Essay on Memoir" by Richard Hoffman
- "Consider the Lobster" by David Foster Wallace
- "The Birth of the 'New Journalism': Eyewitness Report" by Tom Wolfe
- "The Death of the Moth" by Virginia Woolf
- *This American Life* (radio show/podcast)
- *Modern Love* (radio show/podcast)
- *Quotidiana*, curated by Patrick Madden (public domain essays)
- *Snap Judgment* (radio show/podcast)
- *Triquarterly* (video essays)

Print Resources

- *Meditations* by Marcus Aurelius
- *Notes of a Native Son* by James Baldwin
- *Fun Home* by Alison Bechdel
- *Slouching Towards Bethlehem* by Joan Didion
- *Pilgrim at Tinker Creek* by Annie Dillard
- "A Boundary Zone: First-Person Short Stories and Narrative Essays" by Douglas Hesse in *Short Story Theory at a Crossroads*
- *Half the House* by Richard Hoffman
- *The Empathy Exams: Essays* by Leslie Jamison
- *The Object Parade* by Dinah Lenney
- *The Art of the Personal Essay: An Anthology from the Classical Era to the Present,* edited by Phillip Lopate
- *Toolbox* by Fabio Morábito
- *Cold Snap as Yearning* by Robert Vivian
- *The Graywolf Annual 3: Essays, Memoirs, and Reflections,* edited by Scott Walker
- *Shapes of Native Nonfiction: Collected Essays by Contemporary Writers,* edited by Theresa Warburton and Elissa Washuta
- *Inventing the Truth: The Art and Craft of Memoir,* edited by William Zinsser

9

Innovative Forms: The Wide Variety of Creative Nonfiction

I go out of my way, but rather by license than carelessness. My ideas follow one another, but sometimes it is from a distance, and look at each other, but with a sidelong glance . . . I love the poetic gait, by leaps and gambols.

—Michel de Montaigne

I find myself thumbing through an encyclopedia of Jewish religion I happened to pick up at the library. As I turn the pages of this marvelous book, I'm struck by how little I, a Jewish woman who went to Hebrew school for most of my formative years, know about my own religion. I start writing down the quotes that interest me most, facts about the Kabbalah and ritual baths and dybbuks and the Tree of Life. I've also started noodling around with some other stories: a recent trip to Portugal and the news I received there of my mother's emergency hysterectomy; notes on the volunteer work I perform at the local children's hospital; and musings about my on-again, off-again yoga practice. As I keep all these windows open on my computer, the voice of the encyclopedia emerges as an odd, binding thread, holding together these disparate stories in a way that seems organic. I begin to fragment the stories and to move these fragments around, finding the images that resonate against one another in juxtaposition.

I feel like a poet, creating stanzas and listening for the rhythms of the sentence, using white space, reading aloud to determine when another quote from the encyclopedia is necessary to balance out my personal story. Sometimes I have to throw out whole sections that no longer fit, but this editing leaves room for new segments, new phrases, new images that build and transform over the course of the essay, weaving in and out, but always grounded on the thread of prayer and the body. It takes some time, this shuffling gait, but finally I have an essay, "Basha Leah": a spiritual self-portrait in the form of a complex braid.

This lyric essay allows for the moments of pause, the gaps, the silence. The fragmentation feels correct to the piece: it allows for the moments of "not knowing," the unspoken words that seem truer than anything I could ever say aloud.

—BRENDA

Creative nonfiction has seen an explosion of experimentation in the last two decades, along with attempts to define what these new modes can accomplish. Of course, forms are rarely truly new. What we see now is greater formal diversity, and a reaching for language with which to discuss it. As we identify modes like flash nonfiction, collage, and the hermit crab essay, we teach ourselves how to understand texts we love, and how to use those formal innovations to enhance our own work.

However, these categories are not clear-cut. A critic could argue, rightly, that the lyric essay is inherently a hybrid form. Cross-genre, hybrid, and other categories overlap, and one person's hybrid might be another's collage. The experimentation behind all these categories is rich and exciting. We hope to give you the tools to create your own innovative works.

What Is the Lyric Essay?

Lyric. Essay. How do these two terms fit together? At first these words may seem diametrically opposed. *Lyric* implies a poetic sensibility concerned more with language, imagery, sound, and rhythm over the more linear demands of narrative. *Essay,* on the other hand, implies a more logical frame of mind, one concerned with a well-wrought story or a finely tuned argument, over the demands of language. When we put the two together, we come up with a hybrid form that allows for the best of both genres.

To put it simply, lyric essays do not necessarily follow a straight narrative line. The root of the word *lyric* is the lyre, a musical instrument that accompanied ancient song. Lyric poetry and essays are songlike in that they hinge on the inherent rhythms of language and sound. Lyric essays favor fragmentation and imagery; they use white space and juxtaposition as structural elements. They are as attuned to silences as they are to utterance. In its thirtieth-anniversary issue devoted to lyric essays, *Seneca Review* characterized them as having "this built-in mechanism for provoking meditation. They require us to complete their meaning."

The writer of the lyric essay brings the reader into an arena where questions are asked; it is up to the reader to piece together possible answers and interpretations. Fragmentation allows for this type of reader interaction because the writer, by surrendering to the fragmented form, declines a foregone conclusion. Writer and literary theorist Rebecca Faery notes, "In the essays that have in recent years compelled me most, I am summoned, called upon. These essays are choral, polyphonic; there are pauses, rests. . . . The rests in these essays are spaces inviting me in, inviting response."

The lyric essay requires an allegiance to intuition. Because we are no longer tied to a logical, linear narrative or argument, we must surrender to the writing process itself to show us the essay's intent. In so doing, we reveal ourselves in a roundabout way. When we write in the mode of the lyric essay, we create not only prose pieces but a portrait of our subconscious selves, the part of us that speaks in riddles or in brief, imagistic flashes.

Part of the fun of the lyric essay will be making up your own form as you go along. But for the sake of argument, we will break the lyric essay down into categories that seem to encapsulate the lyric essays we see most often: flash nonfiction (with a subset we call the micro essay), collage, the braided essay, the "hermit crab" essay, and a structure we're calling the "nonce" form.

Flash Nonfiction

William Wordsworth's poem "Nuns Fret Not at Their Convent's Narrow Room" celebrates the joys of the sonnet form, which he describes as the joys of working in small spaces—a sonnet has just fourteen lines. Such compression offers a relief from the heavy lifting required by a longer work, which Wordsworth describes as "the weight of too much liberty."

Flash nonfiction is a brief essay—usually a thousand words or less—that illuminates in a quick flash of light. It is tightly focused with no extraneous words, and it mines its images in ways that create metaphorical significance. The language is fresh, surprising, hinged on the workings of the imagination.

This form is a wonderful challenge to both write and read. The popular online magazine *Brevity* "publishes concise literary nonfiction of 750 words or fewer focusing on detail and scene over thought and opinion." This journal is an excellent place to find scores of diverse examples of the flash form—some that read like compressed narrative, and others that blur the line between prose and poetry. One such piece is A. Papatya Bucak's very short essay "I Cannot Explain My Fear." In it, Bucak lists fears, sometimes expanding for a line or two, but remaining in the rhythm of a list. It begins:

> Fear of bears, fear of ladders, fear of freezing. Once, in the Sonoran Desert, I woke with ice on my sleeping bag. Fear of a cancerous thyroid; fear of eating poisonous fish from Japan; fear of sharks, overly large seals and sea lice, too. Fear that my glasses are radioactive because the first time I had a nuclear scan the technician didn't tell me to remove them, but the second time he did. Fear of swimming to the bottom of the pool because people get suctioned to the filter and drown.

Bucak continues in this rhythm until the end, as the piece slows down, takes some breaths, begins new ways of listing, and approaches things the narrator does *not* fear:

> Once I saw a coyote standing on the stump of a tree in a farmer's field. Once I saw three bald eagles at once. Once I saw a snake with the leg of a frog sticking out of its mouth.

In this short piece, Bucak manages to create an inner self-portrait that relies wholly on imagery. Like a poem, this essay asks us to enter this world and make our own meanings.

Of course, success within a few pages will not look like success at a dozen pages. Strong flash nonfiction depends on recognizing the demands of this form. Lengthy description, exquisite scene-setting, and lots of backstory will quickly take you past your word count. Here are some tips for working effectively in brief nonfiction.

- *A strong title.* Your title needs to be powerful on its own and to add something substantial to your piece. Don't use a title that just sums up what the rest of the piece will do. Find one that adds to the reader's experience of the essay and gives its own spark of illumination.
- *As you go small, think smaller.* As with a poem, every word and every image needs to earn its space in flash. A single metaphor can make or break a brief essay. Wordplay becomes crucial in shorter spaces, and, surprisingly, shorter works can often bear more repetition than longer ones, as Bucak's "fear" recurs and becomes almost a poem or a chant.
- *Stay close.* You generally can't wander far from one thought or one scene in a flash essay.
- *Let your ending pack a punch.* With shorter work, we have a tendency to "read forward." We want to see where this quick ride will take us, rather than sinking into the movements of it, as we do in longer essays. Be sure your ending reflects powerfully on what has come before.

The Micro Essay

The micro essay is even shorter than traditional flash. At its best, the micro essay provides the crack of illumination certain phrases do, such as Franklin Roosevelt's "the only thing we have to fear is fear itself," or John Kennedy's "ask not what your country can do for you—ask what you can do for your country." Most of us can't forget these words, even if we don't recall their historical context. A strong short piece can glow with the same brightness.

The field of the micro essay grows, with more and more identified lengths—and names for them—popping up. Nanos are three hundred words; drabbles, one hundred; dribbles, fifty. The online journal *Six-Word Memoirs* publishes just that: six-word nonfictions that contain a meaningful nugget of narrative. (The inspiration for the six-word memoir comes from Ernest Hemingway's six-word story, "For sale: baby shoes, never worn.") An example of this tiny form, from *Six-Word*: "He called me goddess, then, Gladys."

To succeed, the micro essay must do what the flash piece does, with even more compression. That verbal lightning has just seconds to reveal its world. Look at Michelle Ross's "Cubist Mother," a micro essay clocking in at just one hundred words. Eight sentences long, "Cubist Mother" focuses on a vivid scene.

When I found my mother throwing dishes at the mortar wall behind our house, she said only, "I forgot these once belonged to my mother." In her hand was the pale blue dish, speckled like a bird's egg. Once upon a time, I'd stamped my feet if anyone else ate from it. Watching my mother hurl that dish, I thought of that Duchamp painting, *Nude Descending a Staircase, No. 2*. The curves of the figure's hips and buttocks, the metronomic swing of her legs and arms—all multiplied. Or is she disassembled? Shattered like a dish thrown against a wall.

Note how careful this writing is. The first sentences begin with introductory clauses. "When," "In," "Once," and "Watching" lead into sentences that land hard on crucial details: the dishes the mother smashes were her own mother's; they are like eggs, and therefore delicate; the figure of her mother reminds the speaker of a Cubist painting, a disrupted body. The last three sentences change the pattern, with an abrupt dash clause, a question, and finally a sentence fragment, as if the prose enacts the mother's falling apart (see Chapter 12, "The Basics of Good Writing in Any Form," for more on performative sentences). The title connects the mother's identity with the painting, and the ending ties the fate of the dishes with that of the mother.

Collage

Do you remember, as a child, making collages out of photographs, images cut from magazines, bits and pieces of text gathered from ticket stubs, documents, or newspaper headlines? Often, these mosaics represented the self in a way that no other form could quite accomplish.

The collage essay works in the same way. It brings together many different fragments and assembles them so they create something wholly new. *Juxtaposition* becomes the key craft element here. One cannot simply throw these pieces down haphazardly; they must be carefully selected because of how they will resonate off one another. You must listen for the echoes, the repetitions, the way one image organically suggests the next.

The writer must also provide some kind of grounding structure for the reader to hold on to. Going back to those collages you made as a child, they would be useless collections of fragments without the poster board and glue used to hold the pieces in place. The supporting architecture for a collage essay can take the form of numbered sections, or it can be subtitles that guide the reader along. Or the structure may be as subtle as asterisks delineating the white space between sections. The title, subtitles, or an epigraph (opening quote) can all provide a hint of direction for the reader.

For example, in her famous essay about the sixties, "Slouching Towards Bethlehem," Joan Didion uses a collage structure to mimic the disorienting atmosphere of that era in San Francisco. Alluding to the Yeats poem "The Second Coming," from which her title derives, she begins:

> The center was not holding. It was a country of bankruptcy notices and public-auction announcements and commonplace reports of casual killings and misplaced children and abandoned homes and vandals who misspelled even the four-letter words they scrawled. . . . People were missing. Children were missing. Parents were missing. Those who were left behind filed desultory missing-persons reports, then moved on themselves.

Starting off with a declarative sentence that telegraphs both theme and form, the essay then proceeds in many sections separated by white space. The structure employs posters seen on the streets, casual conversations, immersion in an apartment where a group is dropping LSD, and so on. Didion, after this first introductory section, does not directly comment upon anything she sees; her point of view is evident from what she chooses to include and how she juxtaposes the sections. The reader puts it all together.

A collage can also be done within a single short essay, without the use of white space, numbers, or other sectioning devices. Take a look at Ira Sukrungruang's short essay "Because, the Ferguson Verdict" (see Anthology). He uses a repeating word, *because* (this kind of move is called *anaphora*), to list the ways he is personally affected by events occurring in the larger world.

Collage can also extend beyond the essay into book-length forms. For example, *Bluets,* by Maggie Nelson, is an extended meditation on the color blue structured by short, numbered sections, small snippets that move in an associative way from one to the next. It begins:

> 1. Suppose I were to begin by saying that I had fallen in love with a color. Suppose I were to speak this as though it were a confession; suppose I shredded my napkin as we spoke. . . .

2. And so I fell in love with a color—in this case, the color blue—as if falling under a spell, a spell I fought to stay under and get out from under, in turns.

This book begins in supposition ("Suppose . . .") then proceeds to meditate on this premise for 240 sections, using her own words, words from correspondence, quotes from research, and so on. Nelson ends the book with dates, "(2003–2006)," indicating the way she allowed plenty of time and space for this collage to fall into place.

Another word for a collage essay is the "paratactic" essay, which means to place things side by side. Carl Klaus, in his book *The Made-Up Self: Impersonation in the Personal Essay,* describes paratactic as "juxtaposing discrete sentences, paragraphs, and larger units of discourse." He reminds us that this type of rhetorical style is nothing new; authors from Montaigne, to George Orwell, to E. B. White often used this structure to great effect.

The Braided Essay

On the Jewish Sabbath, we eat a bread called challah, a braided egg bread that gleams on its special platter. The braided strands weave in and out of one another, creating a pattern that is both beautiful and appetizing. We eat a special bread on the Sabbath because this day has been set aside as sacred; the smallest acts must be differentiated from everyday motions.

The braided challah is a fitting symbol for an essay form closely allied with collage: the braided essay. In this form, you fragment your piece into separate strands that repeat and continue throughout the essay. There is a sense of weaving about it—of interruption and continuation—like the braiding of bread or of hair. (See "A Braided Heart: Shaping the Lyric Essay" by Brenda Miller on the *Tell It Slant* website.)

For example, take a look at "On Touching Ground" by Jericho Parms (see Anthology). She braids several different strands: her experience in the gallery at the Metropolitan Museum of Art, looking at a horse sculpture by Degas; memories of horses, especially with her grandfather; research on wild mustangs and on the way horses run; research on another artist, Eadweard Muybridge; memories of home; and observations and research on other works by Degas. The structure works a bit differently than a collage essay, because these threads reappear in substantial sections, echoing one another.

As you see in this essay, the braided form allows a way for research and outside voices to intertwine with one's own voice and experience. When you write a braided essay, find at least one outside voice that will shadow your own; in this way the essay gains texture and substance.

Another well-known example is "The Fourth State of Matter" by Jo Ann Beard. Spurred by her experience of a mass shooting at her workplace, the essay is anchored by this central, narrative plot line. But three other strands also propel the essay forward: her dying collie, her recent divorce, and squirrels inhabiting her attic. All these stories weave and intersect; while we might not understand *how* they're all connected at first, the essay uses strong scenes, imagery, and metaphor to bring them all together in the end. It becomes a heartbreaking piece about loss of all kinds, something that would have been more difficult to do if she had focused solely on the unfolding tragedy.

The "Hermit Crab" Essay

Where we—Suzanne and Brenda—live, in the Pacific Northwest, there's a beautiful place called Deception Pass. Deception Pass is prone to extreme tides, and in the tide pools you can often find hermit crabs skulking about. They look a little like cartoon characters, hiding inside a shell, lifting up that shell to take it with them when they go for cover. They move a few inches, then crouch down and stop, becoming only a shell again.

A hermit crab is a strange animal, born without the armor to protect its soft, exposed abdomen. And so it spends its life occupying the empty, often beautiful, shells left behind by snails or other mollusks. It reanimates these shells, making of them a strange, new hybrid creature that has its own particular beauty, its own way of moving through the tide pools and among the rocks. Each one will be slightly different, depending on the type of shell it decides to inhabit.

In honor of these wonderful creatures, we've dubbed a particular form of lyric essay the "hermit crab" essay. This kind of essay appropriates existing forms as an outer covering, to protect its soft, vulnerable underbelly. It is an essay that deals with material that seems born without its own carapace—material that is soft, exposed, and tender, and must look elsewhere to find the form that will best contain it.

The "shells" come where you can find them, anywhere out in the world. They may borrow from fiction and poetry, but they also don't hesitate to armor themselves in more mundane structures, such as the descriptions in a mail-order catalog or the entries in a checkbook register.

For example, in her short story "How to Become a Writer," Lorrie Moore appropriates the form of the how-to article to tell a personal narrative. The voice of the narrator catches the cadence of instructional manuals, but at the same time winks at the reader. Of course these are not impersonal instructions but a way of telling her own story. And by using the literary second person, the reader is unwittingly drawn along into the place of the narrator and a natural interaction develops:

> First, try to be something, anything, else. A movie star/astronaut. A movie star/missionary. A movie star/kindergarten teacher. President of the World. Fail miserably. It is best if you fail at an early age—say, fourteen. Early, critical disillusionment is necessary so that at fifteen you can write long haiku sequences about thwarted desire.

Though "How to Become a Writer" is presented as fiction, the story can act as a fine model for innovative lyric essays in the how-to mode. What are the aspects of your life that you could render in how-to form? How will the second-person address enable you to achieve some distance from the material and thus some perspective? These types of essays can be quite fun to write; the voice takes over and creates its own momentum.

Take a look at "Math 1619" by Gwendolyn Wallace (see Anthology). Wallace wrote this essay while still a senior in high school, and by appropriating the form of math problems, she is able to tell a powerful story about what it is like to be a marginalized student. She sets up the form with a voice we'd expect to hear, and then quickly deviates from that voice to show that she is telling her own story. The essay begins:

> Show all of your work clearly and thoroughly. You may use an approved calculator, but the use of a tablet is not permitted. Once you have completed the problems, hand your test to the white man seated at the front of the classroom.

Note how the essay pretends to be a standard math test in the first two lines, using the objective, bland voice of instructions. But by the time we reach the end of the third line, we are cued in to the fact that this essay will unfold as a personal story centered on race. The essay then proceeds in a series of math test problems, including the forms of multiple choice, graphs, and word problems, all telling specific stories about Wallace's experiences. By containing her personal story in this quiz form, Wallace not only creates a unique essay that effectively conveys difficult content, she also shows that this subject does not come with easy answers.

In a hermit crab essay, you can decide how deeply you want to use the form. On one end of the spectrum, you can fully inhabit the voice of the form, as Wallace does in her essay, or you could simply use the form as a way to structure your piece (a more formal way of making a collage or braided essay). For example, in her essay "The Pain Scale," Eula Biss uses the form of the pain scale—which attempts to measure one's pain on a scale of 0 to 10— as a way to structure a highly complex piece that explores not only the nature of pain, but the many different ways we try to measure the immeasurable.

Often when you write in these forms, you'll find yourself writing about memories and topics you never thought you would approach. It can often be a way to break through resistance, because your conscious mind will be occupied with the form itself. The form can then lead to what we like to call "inadvertent revelations," where it seems as though the *essay* is revealing unexpected insights, not the writer.

For example, one of our students had trouble writing about growing up with a mother who suffered from a hoarding disorder. This student grew up in complete chaos, and her writing had been too chaotic to make sense. When she decided to write her story in the form of a real estate ad—with the chipper voice of the ad revealing the horrifying state of the house—she created a powerful story with a great deal of compassionate perspective.

Some writers have successfully extended the hermit crab essay into book-length form. In 2005, Amy Krouse Rosenthal published *Encyclopedia of an Ordinary Life* in the alphabetical form of an encyclopedia, and followed up years later with *Textbook,* which is sectioned into various school topics, such as Social Studies, Geography, Midterm Exam, and so on. Within these sections she uses assessments, graphs, visual images, and even a literal texting component: she invites readers to text her with different comments or pictures along the way. In this way, her form highlights the interactive nature of these innovative works.

As you try your own hermit crab forms, you may find the process quite fun; a spirit of playfulness can underlie even the most serious of these essays. But it can also be difficult to know how to pull off a successful hermit crab essay without it becoming mere gimmick. Here are some areas to pay partic-ular attention to in these forms:

- *Beginnings*: How can you announce the form early on, and create a strong introduction? How can you start small and build intensity from there?
- *Specific scenes*: How can you allow your own story to unfold within the form? How can you choose and suspend key moments that will deepen the essay? Where should those moments come?
- *Find the bigger theme*: How can the essay transcend your personal expe-rience and express a larger idea or universal emotion?
- *Endings*: Many people have trouble ending their essays. Allow the form to give you a natural endpoint, if possible. Or keep in mind the main theme you want to express; how can the ending scene bring forth that theme most strongly?

The Nonce Form

More than one thousand years ago, a Japanese writer and member of the court, Sei Shōnagon, began to write her experiences in the form of lists. Shōnagon was not a narrative writer. She did not tell stories, though her lists hint at them. Mostly, Shōnagon thought in categories, such as "Hateful Things," "Adorable Things," and so on: she had many list headings, and these guided her content. At times we love Shōnagon for cracking open with preci-sion a different era, as in "Hateful Things," when she complains about a hair "rubbing one's inkstick . . . making a nasty, grating sound." Often Shōnagon is timeless, as when she complains of someone who "discusses all sorts of subjects at random as though he knew everything."

Shōnagon's lists, with their guiding titles, give us an example of a writer innovating a form to best accommodate her particular gift. In poetry, such a creation is called a *nonce* form. Authors create nonce forms for a specific work, though subsequent writers may borrow and adapt the form, as many writers have built on Shōnagon's lists. We are taking this term from poetry and introducing the nonce essay.

Nonce forms overlap at times with hermit crabs, but with the difference that in the nonce form, the author is not mining a pre-existing form, like the pain scale, for its inherent meaning. Rather, the nonce author tries to find the perfect formal vehicle, as Shōnagon used lists to capture her associative thinking.

In his essay "Michael Martone's Leftover Water," Patrick Madden nabs a bottle of Dasani water partially drunk by the writer Michael Martone and auctions it off on eBay. He encourages others to use the "Ask the Seller" function to pose questions during the sale, and uses the questions and answers as a structure:

Q: I'd like to inquire about the safety of this product . . . ? Apr-01-09
A: You are hoping, perhaps, to catch some of what he has? Some of that "benign neurosis" (to borrow a phrase from George Higgins) called "writing"?

This essay uses eBay—and the long piece of narrative leading up to it—not as a borrowed form, but as a nonce vehicle: to generate random questions for the author to answer, to perform the provocation of selling a well-known writer's used water bottle (it sells for around $20). The form becomes a commentary on fame and the possibilities of "catching" literary talent.

Graphic Memoir

Writers create these memoirs, also called "autobiographical comics," in comic book panels, a form that allows us to read on many different levels. The visual story often complements the written story, but can also contradict it or comment upon it in original ways. Take a look at "Perdition" by Kristen Radtke (see Anthology). In this short graphic memoir, the style of the images, the shading, the framing all contribute to the feeling we get from this autobiographical piece.

The Pulitzer Prize–winning books *Maus I* and *Maus II*, by Art Spiegelman, took on the challenging material of Holocaust survival and framed it in the images of Jews as mice, Germans as cats, and Poles as pigs. Throughout, we see the narrator, Artie, struggling with how to portray his father's story as a Holocaust survivor, while at the same time telling his own story of what it's like to be the child of a survivor. This "meta" narrative—the writing behind the writing—threads throughout the books, with images breaking through their frames, being erased and reenvisioned as new information comes to light.

Alison Bechdel's *Fun Home: A Family Tragicomic* tells the story of the author's complex relationship to her father, a relationship that was mired in secrets. *Salon* magazine said: "Bechdel's years of drawing a serial comic strip have honed her ability to convey oceans of feeling in a single image, and the feelings are never simple; *Fun Home* shimmers with regret, compassion, annoyance, frustration, pity and love." The graphic elements become crucial in understanding not only the story, but the narrator's evolving perspective and point of view.

While we don't all have the talent and training to write a graphic memoir, it could be useful to look to this form as a model for how we might be able to "convey an ocean of feeling in a single image." You could envision a traditional narrative as a comic strip and allow this visualization to help you home in on the key details, scenes, and gestures that are necessary to bring your story to life. Or you might collaborate with a talented artist who could envision even a small part of your work in the complexities of visual language.

TRY IT

1. Write an essay that has fewer than five hundred words. Give yourself a time limit—a half hour, say—and write about one image that comes to mind or an image that has stayed in your memory from the last couple of days. Use vivid, concrete details. Do not explain the image to us but allow it to evolve into metaphor. If you are stuck, open a book of poetry and write down the first line you see as an epigraph (an opening quote). Write an essay using the epigraph as a starting point for either form or content or imagery. If you write more than five hundred words (about two pages), you must trim and cut to stay under the limit. Find what is essential.

    VARIATION FOR A GROUP: Each person brings in a line of poetry as an epigraph and offers it to a partner. Write for fifteen minutes, and then pass this epigraph to the next person. Write again for fifteen minutes. Continue this process for as long as you like. Try shaping one of these experiments into a complete essay of fewer than five hundred words.

2. Choose an even more limited word count—fifty, one hundred, three hundred words—and force yourself to write to that exact number. It's remarkable how, as Wordsworth noted, restrictions can become liberating. Aim your piece at a specific journal. Publishing venues for the micro essay continue to grow. The journal *Nano* publishes, guessably, nanos. *Creative Nonfiction*, one of the first journals to focus on literary nonfiction, publishes essays called Tiny Truths, delivered on the platforms of Twitter or Instagram. There are many other publications open to or specializing in micro essays.

3. Begin a piece by imitating Bucak's "I Cannot Explain My Fear." You can list fears, or loves, or jealousies, or any kind of emotion at all, transforming that emotion into a concrete list that reveals some narrative about your life. Try to do this in three hundred words.

4. If you have an essay you feel may be overly wordy, force yourself to remove half of the word count, distilling each part of it down to its essential elements. Then do this refining again. It's surprising how much verbal padding we can remove, reducing that essay to its molten core. See if you can incorporate this distillation into a revision.

5. Look at a book that operates through micro-essay lengths, such as Maggie Nelson's *Bluets*. List the connections between the pieces of her book, as well as the leaps she makes between segments. Take an essay you are unhappy with and try this strategy of creating micro length building blocks, loosely associated, and forming out of them a whole.

6. Go back to one of your own pieces and turn it into fragments. Take a pair of scissors to it and cut it up into at least three different sections. Move these around, eliminating what no longer fits, juxtaposing the different sections in various ways. How can you make use of white space? How can you let the images do the talking for you?

7. Wander the streets of your town looking for random objects. Gather as many of these as you like, then bring them back to your desk and start arranging them in a way that is artistically pleasing. Then write for several minutes on each object

and see if you can create a fragmented essay that juxtaposes these elements in the same way.

> **VARIATION FOR A GROUP:** Go out and gather objects individually, but come back together as a group to sift through the pile. Use each other's objects to create three-dimensional collages. Then write for one hour to create a collage essay using these objects as a guide.

8. Experiment with transitions and juxtaposition. Find one image to repeat in the essay from start to finish, but transform this image in some way so that it has taken on new characteristics by the end of the collage essay.

9. Go back to an essay that's been giving you problems. Look for the one image that seems to encapsulate the abstract ideas or concepts you're trying to develop. Find at least one outside source that will provide new information and details for you. Explode the essay into at least three different strands, each focused on different aspects of that image, and begin weaving.

10. Write an essay in the form of a how-to guide using the second-person voice. You can turn anything into a how-to. In Lorrie Moore's book *Self-Help*, she has stories titled "How to Talk to Your Mother" and "How to Be the Other Woman."

11. Brainstorm a list of all the forms in the outer world that you could use as a hermit crab essay model. The possibilities are endless. Choose one of these forms and begin writing content *suggested by the form*. For example, Brenda wrote a hermit crab essay called "We Regret to Inform You" using the form of the standard rejection note as her shell. The form suggested the content, not the other way around. Let the word choices and tone of your shell dictate your approach to the topic.

12. Write a list of the topics/issues in your life that are "forbidden," the things you could never write about. You could write a list using a repeating phrase such as: "I could never write about . . ." or "I'm afraid to write about. . . ." Choose one of these, and then begin to contain it in a hermit crab form. (Or maybe the list, itself, will create its own lyric essay!)

13. Create a nonce form. Consider using forms from poetry, like the villanelle, or other arts (Desirae Matherly's "Solo" uses sections of one hundred and thirty words to match the number of Bach's measures in the musical form called the

fugue.) Consider how your essay wants to move, whether associatively, through questions and answers, and so on, and look for forms that might contain this movement.

FOR FURTHER READING

In Our Anthology
- "Of Smells" by Michel de Montaigne
- "On Touching Ground" by Jericho Parms
- "Perdition" by Kristen Radtke
- "Because, the Ferguson Verdict" by Ira Sukrungruang
- "Math 1619" by Gwendolyn Wallace

Resources Available Online
- "The Fourth State of Matter" by Jo Ann Beard
- *Brevity: A Journal of Concise Literary Nonfiction*
- "I Cannot Explain My Fear" by A. Papatya Bucak
- "Slouching Towards Bethlehem" by Joan Didion
- "Michael Martone's Leftover Water" by Patrick Madden
- "A Braided Heart" by Brenda Miller
- "Cubist Mother" by Michelle Ross
- *Six-Word Memoirs*
- *Tiny Truths* in *Creative Nonfiction*

Print Resources
- *The Shell Game: Writers Play with Borrowed Forms,* edited by Kim Adrian
- *Fun Home: A Family Tragicomic* by Alison Bechdel
- *The Spirit of Disruption: Landmark Essays from* The Normal School, edited by Steven Church
- *The Next American Essay,* edited by John D'Agata
- *We Might as Well Call It the Lyric Essay,* edited by John D'Agata
- *Encyclopedia of an Ordinary Life* by Amy Krouse Rosenthal
- *Textbook* by Amy Krouse Rosenthal
- "Basha Leah" by Brenda Miller in *Season of the Body*
- "We Regret to Inform You" by Brenda Miller in *An Earlier Life*
- *Bluets* by Maggie Nelson

- *Between Song and Story: Essays from the Twenty-First Century,* edited by Sheryl St. Germain and Margaret Whitford
- *Bending Genre: Essays on Creative Nonfiction,* edited by Margot Singer and Nicole Walker
- *Maus I: A Survivor's Tale—My Father Bleeds History* and *Maus II: A Survivor's Tale—And Here My Troubles Began* by Art Spiegelman

10

Mixed-Media, Cross-Genre, Hybrid, and Digital Works

The interplay of text and images was very important, and I think it allows the reader to jump off to consider their own lives because the images are sort of shared islands between us.

—LAWRENCE SUTIN

When I was young, I saw a movie called *Earthquake*, a movie announced as a new cinematic experience. It used Sensurround, a technology that sent out low frequency sound waves felt in the body more than heard, creating a physical addition to the screen that reflected the film's quakes, temblors, and general mayhem. Earlier movies used a technology dubbed Smell-O-Vision, a system that released scents into the theater. Though Sensurround never quite caught on, I remember the excitement of sitting in that theater, feeling as well as seeing the events depicted on the screen. The rocks and rumblings felt through the seats made the experience even more immersive.

Sometimes the wonder of a work that is words on the page is exactly what we want. I would have hated anyone adding more to my experience of my favorite book, *Jane Eyre*, with Sensurround or Smell-O-Vision! I wanted to keep that world in my mind, to fill it with my own inventions.

Later in life, I fell in love with the kind of digital literature I found in online journals like *The New River: A Journal of Digital Writing & Art*— beautiful works that might use bird calls, the Jewish Midrash, mystery stories with navigable settings. I still never miss an issue; sometimes it's exciting for more than one of our senses to be engaged in a text-based work. And sometimes we want navigation options that create our own reading and viewing experiences. Still, great literature is great literature. As the editors of *The New River* put it, "we cannot help but love stories and puzzles. We just find new packages for them."

—SUZANNE

New Packages

Sometimes we want what Suzanne wanted with a favorite book—words on the page, a story told through one literary medium, ready for the readers' imaginations. But sometimes adding a poem or a speculative narrative that partakes of fiction is what we need to fully plumb our stories. At other times we feel called upon to add art, video, or other images or sounds to our work. We may want to put our stories into a digital format, allowing the reader freedom of navigation or providing forms that would be hard to bring into an essay—puzzles, video games, moving images, and more. You may want to tie your words to something physical, like the quilt we'll discuss later in this chapter. We have enormous freedom now, with the possibilities of online publication and with the accessibility of paintings, music, and other nonliterary arts. Nonfiction requires your presence as an author, your own slant. Within that, however, so much is possible.

It can be a little daunting to think of taking your nonfiction beyond the bounds of a traditional essay. Perfecting that form can be hard enough! But what our students have found, over and over, is that the opportunity to expand the means of creative expression becomes exhilarating. Even if it's on a screen, your text can become a broader sensory experience than words alone. You may, with mixed media, add a physical piece to your writing. Mixing in other genres might give you a chance to do more lyrical or speculative writing than the traditional essay. All of us love more than one kind of book, more than one artistic medium. The modes we discuss here give you a chance to combine your passions.

Combining Text and Other Media

In his book *A Postcard Memoir*, Lawrence Sutin juxtaposes images from his extensive postcard collection with the brief, vivid reminiscences and ruminations these images inspire in him. Sutin uses fragmentation and interplay between image and text to powerful effect. For example, in his piece "Man and Boy," Sutin uses an old black-and-white portrait of an anonymous father and son to ruminate on the nature of his relationship to his own father. He sees in this photograph not just the figures of a man and a boy, but the emotional underpinnings and connection implied by the placement of a hand on a leg, the identical smiles, the way man and boy imperceptibly lean toward one another.

Sutin does not spend time describing the photograph; in fact, the prose itself hardly refers to it. Rather, his own story arises from the image, and the details he chooses enable us to look at this photograph through his eyes. In this way, the reader becomes a participant in the creative process. As Sutin remarked in an interview with the *Bellingham Review*, "The reader can float along with the image in their own way, too, because it's clear that these aren't real photographs of my life, so there's a *shared* quality to them."

By using the form of postcards to tell his own story, Sutin automatically gives himself parameters that both contain and liberate his personal history. The images lead him into memories he may not have expected. "In some cases," Sutin says, "the response to the postcard allowed me to see more clearly what my life meant, more than I knew in advance." The form of the postcard also necessitated brief vignettes, rather than drawn-out narratives, he explains:

> Obviously many, if not all, of my pieces are longer than you could fit on the back of a postcard, even if you had very spidery, tiny handwriting. But the idea of the postcard being a brief recollection, and in my mind, an intense recollection was something that I used. . . . I suppose the typical postcard message is, "Hi, we're having a great time, wish you were here," and I was going totally beyond that. Something about the brevity of the message, and the fixed, chosen quality of the image to represent the time or place, those things were important to me.

The postcard medium also carries within itself, intrinsically, the intent of communication—an intimate yet public communication between writer and reader. After all, a postcard is meant only for the recipient, but in the course of its journey can be read by many eyes. By working in the genre of the postcard, Sutin automatically brings these philosophical issues to bear on his writing, and so he is able to craft a voice that is intimate and public at the same time.

This mix of image and text is a relatively simple example of how writers can use other media in their work. But such projects can be as simple or complex as the material demands and in accord with the artistic skills of the writer. For example, book artist Susan King created a piece titled *Treading the Maze: An Artist's Book of Daze.* King was diagnosed with breast cancer after returning from a trip through Europe. The book that came out of these experiences, using artwork from Chartres cathedral, charts her travels through these two different types of terrain, physical and medical.

Our students, though generally not trained as artists, have found mixed media both a challenge and a delight. They've created a plethora of artifacts incorporating written texts, visual arts, photographs, and whatever other medium the student finds appropriate. We've had students incorporate their own music into their presentations or create a website for their final projects. One student printed her essay on strips of paper baked into fortune cookies, and another brought to class a planter full of specimens from an arboretum, each with its own fragment of a nature essay attached. In this last case, the student, Anna, asked her classmates to choose the pieces at random and read the fragments aloud. We all got our fingers covered in dirt, and in so doing collaborated with Anna in creating the shape of the final essay. Another student enlisted the help of her family to sew a quilt that had fragments of her essay (all about family) embedded within.

The possibilities are endless, and one of the side effects of such work is that it so wholly depends on the viewer's participation for the project to come to fulfillment. In this way, perhaps, mixed-media works are the perfect vessel for creative nonfiction because you connect with your reader in such a concrete way. The use of different media in your creative nonfiction work also allows you to discover new sources of creativity within yourself. Too often, we get bogged down in habitual ways of writing; the requirement to use other media forces us to approach writing from a fresh perspective, and it adds a wonderfully tactile quality to our personal expressions.

Cross-Genre Writing

Cross-genre writing refers to literature that blends more than one literary genre in a single piece, moving across genres or subgenres within the realm of text. A graphic memoir, or illustrated text, would not typically fall under the heading of cross-genre.

This intra-literary movement can happen in many ways: nonfiction that brings in fiction or poetry, for instance, or books that include elements of science fiction or suspense in a text otherwise outside this mode. Unlike hybrid forms, cross-genre writing tends to embrace each literary medium for what it is. In fact, cross-genre writing often underscores the differences between what these forms can do. Truman Capote's *In Cold Blood*, a book he termed a "nonfiction novel," melded the novel's immediacy of action with a continually acknowledged presence of journalistic fact.

In Joy Harjo's memoir, *Crazy Brave*, the author, a Native American of Creek and Cherokee heritage, blends memoir with forms that reflect both her ancestry and her personal awakenings. Harjo introduces each section of the book with a collective view of the direction it's named for, such as "East is the direction of beginnings. It is sunrise. When beloved Sun rises, it is an entrance, a door to fresh knowledge." These invocations present the author's life as belonging to what preceded her, to the power of her history.

As Harjo's own life grows out of what she calls "an ancient dance," she begins to make more memoiristic realizations, such as how necessary poetry becomes to her in making sense of her world. As the power of poetry dawns on Harjo, poetry breaks into the prose. Here is an example, from the first chapter.

I had no way to translate the journey and what I would find there until I found poetry.

THIS IS MY HEART
This is my heart. It is a good heart.
Weaves a membrane of mist and fire.
When we speak love in the flower world
My heart is close enough to sing to you
In a language too clumsy
For human words.

Telling the reader how she fell in love with poetry would not provide the power Harjo creates when a poem breaks into her narrative. In this moment, we sense how the author depends on poetry to navigate her life.

The Hybrid Form

The idea of blending literary forms with other literary forms, or other artistic modes, has always existed as a writer's strategy, cropping up in works as diverse as William Blake's illustrated poems, or Chaucer's *Canterbury Tales,* which unite prose and verse, religious tract and flatulence joke.

As an identified genre, the hybrid work has been growing in literary importance. Hybrid pieces share qualities with mixed-media and cross-genre works. But hybrids unite more than one element—more than one "meaning-making mode," in the words of critic Catherine Beavis. Unlike mixed media pieces and cross-genre works, hybrids qualify as hybrids only when those modes influence and change each other, forming something new.

Author Judith Kitchen calls the hybrid form "a mix, a twining, something that makes it neither one nor another." The introduction to the Rose Metal Press hybrid anthology, *Family Resemblance: An Anthology and Exploration of Eight Hybrid Literary Genres,* describes the result of two (or more) modes in one hybrid work as necessarily a "fertile tension." Neither mode can simply support or be swallowed up in the other. Photos with text, for example, don't offer hybridity, if the effect is only to illustrate what the writer has described.

Nick Flynn's memoir of his relationship with his father, *Another Bullshit Night in Suck City,* uses hybridity as a tool. Flynn's father was homeless, and his disruptive life serves as the crux of the book. Flynn writes at the opening of his chapter "Santa Lear," "Each night, like another night in a long-running play, I wander the empty streets, check on every sprawled man until I find him. . . . I am forced to play the son." The chapter moves from that opening into an actual play, set at the Dunkin' Donuts where Flynn's father spent many nights. The characters in this short play are five men in Santa costumes and three daughters. The script draws heavily from Samuel Beckett as well as Shakespeare's *King Lear.*

SANTA FOUR exits cell, again to applause, picks up the bullhorn, coughs into it, rubs sleep from his eyes.
DAUGHTER TWO: Froze to death, couldn't pry the bell from his hand.
SANTA ONE: I was a goner from the first moment, the first check. Doyle set me up. He knew about you kids.

Flynn's chapter illustrates the "fertile tension" of hybridity. We readers cannot escape from the theatricality of this passage—there is a presumed audience, stage directions, and, as in absurdist theater, some dialogue has no obvious meaning. Flynn's father has no daughters, nor does he dress as Santa. We cannot dismiss the script material as pure theater either. Flynn introduces the play by saying he himself plays a part, and Santa One's dialogue in this excerpt is taken directly from Flynn's father. The scene becomes more than theater and more than memoir.

Digital Literature

Digital literature, also called electronic literature, hypertext, hypermedia, and by other terms, is defined here as literature that takes advantage of organizations, such as linking, available when writing in digital programs. In the early days of digital writing, the organization of a story or an essay was likely done through link-node organization—the familiar way we experience most web texts, with selectable links that move the viewer from one screen to another.

Digital literature is becoming more and more innovative and varied. Literary texts may exist in the form of video with voiceovers, moving paper cutouts, streaming images, with or without link-node movement. Video games, Rubik's cubes, and games of chance have been used as ways of creating a digital work. A piece by Eric LeMay published in the fall 2016 *Bellingham Review,* "Nonsense," offers a mashup of randomly generated text and a Charlie Chaplin film.

A digital work is often spatial in every direction, truly nonsequential—nothing follows by necessity anything else. You can read screen by screen, if the work is organized that way, or read only the first few words of the first screen, then move elsewhere, and so on. You may come to a screen that describes a car accident and only later reach the text that tells you how it happened. The text may be set up to move you without user choice.

Scholars of digital literature use the term *decentered*—it can (though doesn't necessarily) become impossible to say where the core of such a digital work lies. French critics Gilles Deleuze and Félix Guattari compare this writing strategy more poetically to the branching systems of rhizomatic plants such as mints and strawberries, plants spreading via a loose root system that establishes nodes for new plants but has no base: "any point on a rhizome can be connected with any other, and must be. This is very different from a tree or root, which fixes a point and thus an order." Vannevar Bush, a midcentury thinker who anticipated the development of the internet, pointed out that such a writing system comes much closer to the way we think and learn: nonsequentially, interactively, working off association.

The branching and associational quality of digital writing forms a natural fit with much nonfiction, particularly the type of nonfiction we describe in "What Is the Lyric Essay?" (see Chapter 9, "Innovative Forms: The Wide Variety of Creative Nonfiction"). If you tend to braid your work or imagine a varying organizational structure, this kind of text may be for you. Mixed-media digital literature offers a natural way to use visual images and other media as well: music, chanting, sounds of a tempest at sea. There are few limits on what elements you can weave into your digital nonfiction.

If you have the tech skills, try putting your writing into a format in which you can play around—add music, video, photos, to get a feel for balancing visual elements. Offer linking organization, allowing the viewer to shape the textual experience. Strive for combinations that work together in ways that surprise. As with hybrid work, the most interesting mixing of multiple forms results in something more than either form would be on its own. If you do not have adequate computer skills, don't give up. Ask around among your friends and even post ads for someone who does have such skills to help you. It is not unusual for digital artists using complex forms to have technical help. Many with computer abilities do not often get offered such interesting, creative challenges.

Blogs and Social Media

As we experience daily, online writing takes many forms. There are the complex forms of much digital literature, and then there are the common genres of blogs, Facebook posts, and those of other social networking sites.

When blogs first began, they were generally web diaries with an author-centered, generalized focus; the term *blog* was coined in the late nineties as a shortened version of *weblog*. There are blogs specific to nearly every sector of human society. Even fictional characters on television shows have their own blogs, with legions of avid followers.

Blog as Writing Practice

At its most basic, a simple blog can be a way to focus and structure your own writing practice, giving you deadlines and some measure of accountability. You can use a blog to work out your ideas and begin to draft, and you can interact with other writers through your blog. The blog form lends itself to writing practice because the posts can be short, "occasional" (i.e., tied to a particular occasion or trigger for the thought), and are usually fairly informal while retaining a sense of craft. They could be a way to discipline yourself to work through a particular topic you've had on your mind, with more structure than a paper journal entry, but with the same sense of spontaneity and intimacy. Your blog can become the foundation for a subject you want to explore in more depth.

One writer we know set herself a goal of writing fifty blog entries, under the title "Fifty Ways to Be a Brilliant Mom Without Having a Baby." She chose this topic because, as she puts it, "It could be that I'm a poet with a secret desire to be an advice columnist. So when I couldn't find any good sites about becoming a stepmom, or having an eccentric elderly mom for a friend, I started this blog." At first it was to be a private blog, but she wanted the accountability that came with having it available to the public. And by choosing a finite number, fifty, she had a concrete goal and was able to narrow down an overwhelming task to a workable routine. As a result, she wrote her fifty entries, attracted a small but solid group of followers, and now has the beginning of a book around this topic.

TRY IT

1. Create a mixed-media piece that uses other kinds of documents and images along with your own prose. Make several photocopies of these documents so you can cut them up and experiment. Create collages, paying attention to the kinds of textures you create with these elements.

2. Collaborate with a photographer, a musician, a painter, a sculptor, or a graphic artist to create a mixed-media work for presentation to an audience.

3. What literary genres do you love, besides the genre you work in most of the time? Make a list for yourself of literary forms you feel attracted to, using each form as a heading—your list might start with terms like *memoir*, *thrillers*, *poetry*, *theater*. List qualities of each. What does each genre or subgenre accomplish that the others don't? The answers might be compression, lyric beauty, excitement, a sense of real time. Pull out an essay of yours that hasn't quite worked yet, or perhaps a new idea for an essay. What qualities would you like this piece to have that belong to other modes on your list? How could you incorporate both into one cross-genre piece?

4. Do the preceding activity, but with an eye toward greater blending of your "meaning-making" modes. Add other arts: photography, watercolors, video. The difference between writing cross-genre and hybrid work is often a matter of how you manage reader expectations. Think of Nick Flynn and write a genre mashup in which expectations of each of the modes you work in are never fully realized. Imagine that these modes intertwine, forming something new.

5. The *haibun* (the term was probably coined by the great Japanese poet Basho) combines highly lyrical prose segments with haiku. The brief poems end each section of prose, adding a still, focused moment to pieces that may be full of narrative and movement. Read some masterful haibun, then try this form. Note that the five-seven-five syllable structure of haiku is more restrictive in English than it is in Japanese. You may want to experiment with other line lengths, keeping the three-lined, reflective quality of these poems.

6. Edward Falco, in response to a question about how authors start a piece in hypertextual digital form (with all its many components), said, "There are probably as many different ways of writing hypertext as there are hypertext writers." Some authors start with a print piece and gradually accrete other nodes of material; some write directly to a hypertext program. One method we've found useful is to have everyone assemble index cards and actually map out the architecture of a site—including visual elements like photos and art, if you plan to use them. Lay the potential screens out in front of you, see where links would occur, and practice different navigational options. Seeing your work spatially can ignite ways of using the form. Many website creation programs have prompts that can make linking organizations, the addition of other media, and similar moves easy.

Variation for a group: Create a group site to house your group's online "anthology" of digital literature.

7. Start a simple piece writing directly into a digital program. Challenge yourself to use just three text links (text linked to other screens of text), and only use simple visual images, if you use them at all. Starting out in hypertext by trying to include complicated animation or the like may give you the false impression that this form is too difficult to master. It isn't; it's a series of small steps. Start with a few steps, and you will most likely be excited by the possibilities you see before you.

8. Spend some time reading blogs on a topic that's close to your heart. Take note of the voices that attract you, those that repel you, and those that leave you neutral. Write up a list of those attributes, and then see how you might learn from them for your own writing—on a blog or otherwise.

9. Start a blog with the idea of a finite number of entries: "Fifty Ways" or "Twenty-Five Views of" or "Thirty Considerations," and so on. Commit to posting at least once a week, no matter what.

For Further Reading

Resources Available Online
- Electronic Literature Organization
- *Treading the Maze: An Artist's Book of Daze* by Susan King
- "Nonsense" by Eric LeMay in the *Bellingham Review*
- *The New River: A Journal of Digital Writing and Art*

Print Resources
- *In Cold Blood* by Truman Capote
- *Another Bullshit Night in Suck City: A Memoir* by Nick Flynn
- *Crazy Brave: A Memoir* by Joy Harjo
- *Family Resemblance: An Anthology and Exploration of Eight Hybrid Literary Genres,* edited by Jacqueline Kolosov and Marcela Sulak
- *A Postcard Memoir* by Lawrence Sutin

PART III

Honing Your Craft

Let men and women make good sentences. Let them learn to spell the sound of the waterfall and the noise of the bathwater. Let us get down the colors of the baseball gloves, the difference in shade between the centerfielder's deep pocket and the discreet indentation of the catcher's mitt. . . . Let us enlist the Vocabulary, the Syntax, the high grammar of the mysterious world.

—Stanley Elkin

11

The Particular Challenges of Creative Nonfiction

But how, exactly, is the truth in nonfiction determined? How much of what is being told should be true? And who is the final arbiter of truth . . . ? The line between fiction and nonfiction is often debated, but is there a single dividing point or an all-encompassing truth a writer is supposed to tell?

—Lee Gutkind

I'm writing an essay about my grandmother. I'm not sure why I'm writing this; there are just certain scenes and images that haunt me and I have to get them down on paper: my grandmother immobilized in a hospital bed, the ties of her hospital gown undone around her collarbone; my mother crying quietly in a restaurant as she tells me she can't bring herself to care for her mother in her home. As I write, I have to make several questionable choices: Do I really remember massaging my grandmother's back that day in the hospital? Now that I've written it, the scene's taken on the stamp of truth, seems to have replaced any "real" memories I might have of that day. And do I relate the scene of my mother's shame; is it really my story to tell? Can I imagine a scene between my mother and my grandmother, the difficulty of touch between them?

In the end, several months later, I decide to leave in the massage scene—it has an emotional truth to it, a resonance that indicates to me the memory is valid, not only for the essay but for myself. But I delete the scene with my mother in the restaurant; though the facts of this moment are more readily verifiable, I've decided that it oversteps some boundary I've set up for myself. That part is not my story to tell—I don't have the authority or the permission—and it feels too risky. I also, therefore, need to cut the scene where I imagine my mother and grandmother together in our family home. This is a difficult cut—I love the writing in that section—but it needs to go because the scene no longer fits in with the trajectory of the essay.

Yet I know that none of this writing has been wasted. Through writing the scenes I eventually eliminated, I came to understand what was important for this particular essay: to focus my attention on the metaphors of touch, the difficulties of such simple gestures within the family. I also learned how I draw the theoretical lines for myself, how I choose to go about negotiating the ethical land mines of creative nonfiction.

—Brenda

A Few Caveats About Writing from Life

Creative nonfiction is a tricky business. On the one hand, you have the challenge—and the thrill—of turning real life into art. But on the other hand, you have to deal with all the issues that come attached with that "real life." A fiction writer is able to create the set amount of characters necessary for the story's action; can you do the same thing with the characters you encounter in your own life and research? When fiction writers need dialogue, they write dialogue. As a nonfiction writer, can you make up dialogue you don't remember verbatim? When you're writing essays based on research, how much of your imagination can you use? Does "nonfiction" mean "no fiction"?

Also, how do you create a piece inhabited by the self without becoming self-centered? And how do you negotiate all the ethical and technical obstacles that come with writing from real life?

The Pact with the Reader

In creative nonfiction—more so, perhaps, than in any other genre—readers assume a real person behind the artifice, an author who *speaks* directly to the reader. Just as in spoken conversations, it's a symbiotic relationship. The reader completes this act of communication through attention to the author's story, and the author must establish right away a reason for the reader to be attentive at all.

Simply presenting your work as an "essay" rather than a piece of fiction sets up certain assumptions. The reader will be engaged in a "true story," one rooted in the world as we know it. Because of this assumption, readers need to know they are in good hands, in the presence of, in Vivian Gornick's words, a "truth-speaking" guide who will lead them somewhere worthwhile. Philippe Lejeune, in *On Autobiography*, calls this the "pact with the reader." The essayist pledges, in some way, both to be as honest as possible with the reader *and* to make this conversation worthwhile.

Or your authorial presence may be more slippery, even unreliable. Writers like John D'Agata, in his book *The Lifespan of a Fact,* play with truth to create narratives that aim to accomplish something different from a story built on pure reporting. Defending himself for changing details and dates of a tragedy in Las Vegas, D'Agata writes flatly, "It's called art." D'Agata is clear that, for him, facts pale in the face of larger aesthetic demands. Other authors' unreliability can be a self-revelation that also transcends the facts of their experience. Robin Hemley, in the preface to his book *Nola: A Memoir of Faith, Art, and Madness*, writes, "As for me, I have a larcenous heart." Sometimes, truth is not the truth of facts, but something deeper.

So *how* does a writer establish this pact with the reader? In the introduction to *The Art of the Personal Essay*, essayist Phillip Lopate writes that "part of our trust in good personal essayists issues, paradoxically, from their exposure of their own betrayals, uncertainties, and self-mistrust." When we reveal our own foibles, readers can relax and know they engage in conversation with someone as human as they are.

Good writers can also establish this pact through their skillful manipulation of the techniques that make for vivid writing (see Chapter 12, "The Basics of Good Writing in Any Form"). We assume that the writer has shaped the material for its best literary effect, while at the same time remaining as true as possible to the acts of the world and history.

Let's take a look at some skilled essayists and see how they establish a pact with the reader early on in their work, combining craft with content:

- **Joan Didion ("Goodbye to All That")**: "That first night I opened my window on the bus into town and watched for the skyline, but all I could see were the wastes of Queens and the big signs that said MID-TOWN TUNNEL THIS LANE and then a flood of summer rain (even that seemed remarkable and exotic, for I had come out of the West where there was no summer rain), and for the next three days I sat wrapped in blankets in a hotel room air-conditioned to 35° and tried to get over a bad cold and a high fever. It did not occur to me to call a doctor, because I knew none, and although it did occur to me to call the desk and ask that the air conditioner be turned off, I never called, because I did not know how much to tip whoever might come—was anyone ever so young? I am here to tell you that someone was."
- **Bernard Cooper ("The Fine Art of Sighing")**: "You feel a gradual welling up of pleasure, or boredom, or melancholy. Whatever the emotion, it's more abundant than you ever dreamed. You can no more contain it than your hands can cup a lake. And so you surrender and suck the air. Your esophagus opens, diaphragm expands. Poised at the crest of an exhalation, your body is about to be unburdened, second by second, cell by cell. A kettle hisses. A balloon deflates. Your shoulders fall like two ripe pears, muscles slack at last."
- **Jenny Boully ("Choom")**: "Her skin was the color of the old catfish that my father dredged from the bottom of the lake. Her skin was like its skin: mottled and blotchy, a yellow bruise. The yellow-browns and the brown-yellows leaked like watercolor. She said she had been playing so hard at the pool; she said she had just been flirting so much at the pool and had just splashed around and jumped around in the water too hard and that's why she had such a blossoming of splotches."
- **Eula Biss ("Time and Distance Overcome")**: "'Of what use is such an invention?' the *New York World* asked shortly after Alexander Graham Bell first demonstrated his telephone in 1876. The world was not waiting for the telephone.

  Bell's financial backers asked him not to work on his new invention because it seemed too dubious an investment. The idea on which the telephone depended—the idea that every home in the country could be connected by a vast network of wires suspended from poles set an average of one hundred feet apart—seemed far more unlikely than the idea that the human voice could be transmitted through a wire.

Even now it is an impossible idea, that we are all connected, all of us."

What do you find in common with these four very different essayists? They write about divergent subjects, and their presences within the essay also differ. Didion opens with a memoiristic first person, while Boully starts "Choom" with a poetic, yet disturbing description of another woman. Biss's tone is initially factual and distant, but moves to a larger idea. Cooper uses second person, slipping the reader into his shoes as he contemplates the human sigh. What these writers have in common is that they've constructed a voice that speaks directly to the reader, and immediately engages us.

In her long, breathless sentences, Joan Didion reveals her embarrassment and timidity at being in a city where she knows no one and is unsure of the social conventions. Not only does she reel us in because of the details (we get to be on that bus with her), but she also laughs at herself and invites the reader to laugh with her. "Was anyone ever so young? I am here to tell you that someone was." These two sentences establish that Didion has perspective on her experience. We know the material will be shaped and presented by someone who is able to distance herself from the "I" who is a character in her story.

Bernard Cooper reaches out a hand and tugs us into his essay by starting off with the second-person point of view: "You feel a gradual welling up of pleasure." He makes us a participant in his essay by recreating a sigh on the page. Read the passage aloud and see if you can keep from letting out a long, hearty sigh. And the "you" makes an assertion that's difficult to deny. The experience he creates on the page does indeed become a universal sigh, exhaled in common with thousands of others.

Boully is not telling a primarily personal story. In this brief essay, she describes a woman named BaNoi, an ill woman who makes sausage with Boully's mother while the young author plays nearby. Though this piece is not memoiristic in the way Didion's essay is, the lush descriptions capture the world of the author: the catfish her father catches, the "blossom" reference, the importance of the pool. Immediately, we're engaged as we wonder about this mysterious woman's story, such as the reasons she needs to lie about the splotches on her skin.

Biss is the most personally removed as a presence in this lineup of essayists. Her opening is factual, but not in a way that feels boring. We're immediately captured, in this era of perpetual contact, by the fact that at one time Americans couldn't imagine wanting phones. Nor is Biss absent as an author. The voice she uses in the third paragraph is the first-person plural, the collective "we." She speaks for the group, a position she's earned. The story of Bell's invention underscores how impossible human connection can feel in the abstract. And Biss's first-person plural voice still contains a sense of the author. She is not just amused or intrigued by this quirky anecdote of the invention of the telephone. She wants to understand what it means in a larger sense, what hints it gives us toward the human condition.

All these writers, along with the multitude of creative nonfiction writers we admire, must immediately make a case for taking up a reader's time and attention. In doing so, they also take care of the "so what?" question that plagues writers of creative nonfiction and of memoir in particular. Why should anyone care about your personal story or your perspective on the world? What use will the essay have for anyone outside of yourself? By engaging you in their essays through vivid details and an authentic voice—through imaginative uses of form and structure—these essayists show that the personal can indeed become universal. We care about their stories because they have become *our* stories.

The Permutations of "Truth": Fact Versus Fiction

The simple acts of writing and reconstructing experience on the page are essentially creative acts that impose a form where none before existed. Beyond that, what kinds of fictions are allowable and what are not in creative nonfiction? Just how much emphasis do we put on "creative" and how much on "nonfiction"?

Some writers believe that nothing at all should ever be knowingly made up in creative nonfiction. If you can't remember what color dress you wore at your sixth-grade graduation, then you better leave that detail out or do some studied research to find the answer. If you had five best friends in high school who helped you through a jam, then you better not compress those five into one or two composite characters for the sake of efficient narrative.

On the other hand, some writers believe that small details can be fabricated to create the scenes of memory, and they knowingly create composite characters because the narrative structures demand it. Some writers willingly admit imagination into factual narratives; others abhor it and see it as a trespass into fiction.

It's interesting to note that when a writer publishes a piece of fiction that contains highly autobiographical elements, no one flinches; in fact, such blurring of the boundaries is often presumed. But to admit fictional techniques into autobiographical work creates controversy and furious discussion. The nature of an "autobiographical pact" with the reader—creating a sense of trust—demands this kind of scrutiny into the choices we make as nonfiction writers.

We believe that writers must negotiate the boundary between fact and fiction for themselves. What constitutes fabrication for one writer will seem like natural technique to another. But what we can do here is show how some writers employ fictional techniques and the effects these choices have on your credibility as an essayist.

Memory and Imagination

If your work is rooted in memory, you will find yourself immediately confronted with the imagination. Memory, in a sense, *is* imagination: an "imagining" of the past, recreating the sights, sounds, smells, tastes, and touches (see Chapter 1, "The Body of Memory"). In her essay "Memory and Imagination," Patricia Hampl writes, "I am forced to admit that memoir is not a matter of transcription, that memory itself is not a warehouse of finished stories, not a static gallery of framed pictures. I must admit that I invented. But why?"

We invent because our lives and the world contain more than simple facts; imagination and the way we imagine are as much a part of ourselves as any factual résumé. In creative nonfiction, the creative aspect involves not only writing techniques, but also a creative interpretation of the facts of our lives, plumping the skeletal facts with the flesh of imagination. Hampl continues, "We find, in our details and broken and obscured images, the language of symbol. Here memory impulsively reaches out its arms and embraces imagination. That is the resort to invention. It isn't a lie, but an act of necessity, as the innate urge to locate personal truth always is."

Look back to the tonsil story at the beginning of Chapter 1. There's no real way to verify either the fact or fiction of the tonsils floating in a jar on the bedside table. What I, Brenda, can do with this image is admit the bizarre and unlikely nature of this mental picture that imagination has called forth in conjunction with memory. I can say, "Why do I remember this jar of tonsils at my hospital bedside?" In so doing, I readily admit the imagination into memory and can then proceed to construct an essay that both interprets the image for metaphorical significance and allows it to become a jumping-off point for a longer meditation on the topics this metaphor suggests. I do not discount or omit this image because its factual veracity is in question. Rather, I relish the opportunity to explore that rich boundary zone between memory and imagination. And I do so in full view of my audience, disclosing my intent, and so maintaining my pact with the reader.

Emotional Truth Versus Factual Truth

Mimi Schwartz in "Memoir? Fiction? Where's the Line?" writes,

> Go for the emotional truth, that's what matters. Yes, gather the facts by all means. Look at old photos, return to old places, ask family members what they remember, look up time-line books for the correct songs and fashion styles, read old newspapers, encyclopedias, whatever—and then use the imagination to fill in the remembered experience.

If we allow imagination into memory, then we are naturally aligning ourselves with a stance toward an emotional or literary truth. This doesn't mean that we discount factual truth altogether, but that it may be important, for *literary* purposes, to fill in what you can of the facts to get at a truth that resonates with a different kind of veracity on the page. Facts only take us so far.

Schwartz continues, "It may be 'murky terrain,' you may cross the line into fiction and have to step back reluctantly into what really happened—the struggle creates the tensions that make memoir either powerfully true or hopelessly phony." We may reconstruct certain details, imagine ourselves into the stories *behind* the facts, but certain facts cannot be invented. Or as novelist and memoirist Bret Lott puts it in his essay "Against Technique": "In fiction you get to make up what happens; in creative nonfiction you don't get to mess with what happen*ed*."

Take a look at the case of a highly publicized memoir, *Fragments: Memories of a Wartime Childhood*. In this lyrical narrative told from a child's point of view, Binjamin Wilkomirski recreates scenes from his experience as a child survivor of the Holocaust. He recounts his father's execution in graphic detail, scenes of rats scurrying over piles of corpses. The prose is beautifully rendered, and some scenes move the reader to tears. But shortly after publication of this memoir, critics began to question Wilkomirski's veracity. One journalist did some investigation and found evidence that showed the writer had never been in a concentration camp at all. Birth certificates and adoption records showed him born in Switzerland in 1941 and adopted into a family shortly thereafter. However, Wilkomirski stood by his memories, which were recovered, he said, in therapy. To him, these memories were as real—they carried just as much emotional truth—as the factual history.

Though we've presented arguments that claim emotional truths can be just as veracious as facts, it is not acceptable to appropriate or wholly invent a history that has little or no relation to your own. You still need to use your own history as a scaffolding for the emotional truths you will uncover. There are facts and then there are *facts*. Which ones are hard and fast?

One of the most publicized controversies in creative nonfiction came with the promotion of James Frey's memoir, *A Million Little Pieces*. Chosen for the coveted Oprah's Book Club, this memoir told in riveting detail Frey's story of drug and alcohol abuse, criminal activity, and many other unsavory events. Oprah Winfrey, on her show, told viewers it was "like nothing you've ever read before. Everybody at Harpo is reading it. When we were staying up late at night reading it, we'd come in the next morning saying, 'What page are you on?' "

But something didn't sit right with several critics and watchdog groups. *The Smoking Gun* conducted an in-depth investigation, which revealed that most of what Frey had written was highly exaggerated, if not completely fictionalized. Frey defended his actions, saying that he had "embellished" the truth for "obvious dramatic reasons." Oprah had Frey back on the show to chastise him for this deception, and the publisher, Nan A. Talese, even went so far as to offer refunds to offended readers.

It could be that the response to Frey's artifice was so strong because those who "stayed up late at night reading it" felt their own emotions had been trifled with. At the same time, when we read memoir, should we do so with a grain of salt? Five years after her admonishment, Oprah had Frey back on her show to apologize for her reaction; in this interview, Frey said he wasn't ashamed of his actions, because he believes all memoir writers "do what I did." Would you be comfortable inserting such fictions in your own nonfiction writing?

"The Whole Truth?"

Sometimes you'll be troubled not by "facts" that are made up, but by those that are omitted. In essay writing, it's nearly impossible to tell the "whole" truth. Of necessity, you'll find yourself needing to pare away certain details, events, and characters to create an essay that makes narrative sense. For example, if you're writing about something that happened in school when you were ten years old, you'll have to decide just how many members of your fifth-grade class will make it onto the stage. Who is important and who is not, for this particular essay?

This is an easy one: you'll naturally choose to flesh out the one or two characters closest to you at the time. More difficult will be knowing when and how to omit the characters that felt important in real life but just get in the way once you land them on the page. For example, Bernard Cooper included his brothers in his early book *Maps to Anywhere*, but when he wrote the essays collected in *Truth Serum*, he made a conscious decision to leave his brothers out. This left him open to criticism from reviewers who said he deceived his audience by implying he was an only child. Here is his reply to them, from his essay "Marketing Memory":

> I had three brothers, all of whom died of various ailments, a sibling history that strains even my credulity. . . . Very early in the writing of *Truth Serum* I knew that a book concerned with homosexual awakening would sooner or later deal with AIDS and the population of friends I've lost to the disease. . . . To be blunt, I decided to limit the body count in this book in order to prevent it from collapsing under the threat of death. . . . There is only so much loss I can stand to place at the center of the daily rumination that writing requires. . . . Only when the infinite has edges am I capable of making art.

"Only when the infinite has edges am I capable of making art." Perhaps that should be a credo we creative nonfiction writers etch on the walls above our desks. For that is what we're up to all the time: creating those edges, constructing artful containers that will hold some facts and not others.

These "edges" might also be formed by choosing to create "composite characters" or to compress events in time. A composite character is a fictional construction; the author blends the traits of several characters into one or two, thereby streamlining both the cast of characters and the narratives needed to take care of them. Compression of time means that you might conflate anecdotes from several trips home into one composite visit. As a writer and a member of a writing community, you'll want to think about these devices—and talk about them—to see how they conform to your own writing ethics.

The Dodge

Nonfiction can be deeply personal. It may mean reviving periods in your life that were painful, even traumatic. Many of us get caught between our desire to share our stories, painful or not, and our desire to protect ourselves. We all try, at times, to avoid what is painful, and this problem appears in essay drafts in a variety of ways. Two we see often are what we call "the metaphor dodge" and "the blanket-statement dodge." If you are writing tough material, it's worth your while to learn to look for these dodges.

The "metaphor dodge" involves using metaphor—sometime long series or "flights" of metaphor—to take the place of telling the reader what is or was happening. Metaphor gives us a way of comparing an actual thing or event to something else that describes it. In Robert Burns's line, "O my love is like a red, red rose,"the loved one is the subject of the metaphor—the rose is used for comparison, bringing that concept of a fragrant, lovely (and perhaps, thorny) rose to the reality of the lover. If you find yourself relying on metaphor in sensitive places, check to make sure it is clear what you are actually describing.

The "blanket-statement dodge" is just what it sounds like—using a broadbrush declaration like "childhood was the worst time of my life," without further scene, detail, or even explanation. Check for these kinds of statements in your drafts, and make sure you are answering not just the "what" question of your reactions, but the "why." You may be giving the broad-brush version as part of doing "the dodge."

Of course, it is important to honor your feelings and calculate the personal cost of probing certain subjects. You may need to put off writing certain pieces until you feel ready. Give yourself permission to take your time, moving in small steps, looking for the small details and effective structures that will contain your story (see also Chapter 2, "Writing the Family," for a discussion of "permission to speak," and Chapter 12, "The Basics of Good Writing in Any Form").

Some Solutions

As with any obstacle, there's always a way to rise to the challenge and become a better writer for it. Here we offer you a few tried-and-true methods for working your way through the difficulties of writing from personal experience.

Cueing the Reader

As you continue to develop your skills in creative nonfiction, you'll find that you'll create your own tools for negotiating some of these tricky areas. Some simple ones to keep in mind, however, are *taglines* that let the reader in on what exactly you're up to. Phrases such as "I imagine," "I would like to believe," "I don't remember exactly, but," "I would like to remember," or even a simple "Perhaps," alert the reader to your artistic agenda.

In her essay " 'Perhapsing': The Use of Speculation in Creative Nonfiction," Lisa Knopp coins the term *perhapsing* as a way to describe the ways we can cue the reader that we are entering the realm of the imagination, filling in the details. She writes: "Perhapsing can be particularly useful when writing about childhood memories, which are often incomplete because of a child's limited understanding at the time of the event, and the loss of details and clarity due to the passage of time."

Cueing the reader can be accomplished even more subtly. If you have trouble writing a scene for a family event because it happened ten years ago, try beginning it with a line like, "This is how my father sounded," or, "This is what Sundays were like at my house." Then watch the pieces fall into place.

These statements are unobtrusive, but they make it clear that you're not claiming to provide a verbatim transcript of an event.

Breaking the Fourth Wall

Writers can also directly tell the reader what they're up to. In a daring move, Lauren Slater titled a book *Lying: A Metaphorical Memoir*. Though this book is full of details that prove to be untrue, Slater stands by her work with an obvious defense: the title tells us, quite bluntly, that she's fabricating metaphorical experiences. Though you may or may not buy this as a reader, you can't claim that she didn't warn you.

If you are dealing with emotional material and find yourself doing "the dodge," one solution might be to tell the reader why you need to stop telling the story. Try statements that describe to the reader honestly why you are dodging, if that seems appropriate: "This is not my story, but my sister's, to tell." With these kinds of statements, you're doing what we call "breaking the fourth wall."

In film, theater, and television, "breaking the fourth wall" means breaking out of the piece and in some way acknowledging awareness of—generally, establishing dialogue with—the audience. Often it involves the direct address of a character or characters to the audience. Think of the film *Deadpool*. The hero, or antihero, of the movie complains to the camera about the hokey conventions of the superhero movie he is trapped in.

By its very nature, creative nonfiction has a permeable fourth wall. Speaking directly to the reader, telling us something about the writing process itself, establishes intimacy, enhances your control of the story, can foreground how you think and/or remember, and can also readjust the contract with the reader. It can, as in this example from Mary Karr, give *more* rather than less information.

Karr, in *The Liar's Club*, tells of a time when her dysfunctional parents farmed her out as a child to live with another family. She writes:

> I will leave that part of the story missing for a while. It went long unformed for me, and I want to keep it that way here. I don't mean to be coy. When the truth would be unbearable, the mind just blanks it out. But some ghost of an event may stay in your head. . . . The ghost can call undue attention to itself by its very vagueness.

This fourth wall technique teaches the reader about the effects of Karr's trauma, her intentions as an author, and the quality of her memory itself. Of course, you can't rely on breaking the fourth wall every time you don't remember, or would rather not address, a piece of your story. Karr's words, however, give us a path to navigate around lost or untouchable material.

Sometimes an author can bring in another voice or character to break that fourth wall. This character can help the narrator speak more clearly or directly. For example, in her memoir *Safekeeping: Some True Stories from a Life,* Abigail Thomas allows her sister to articulate what might be on the reader's mind. After the first few short chapters, the sister appears:

> There are already a lot of husbands floating around, my sister says.
>
>   Well yes, I say, I married three times.
>
>   That's what I'm saying, a lot of husbands. Somebody's going to get confused. Maybe even annoyed.
>
>   Well then, I'll spell it out. . . .

The sister's voice recurs throughout the book, in conversation with Thomas, usually at a moment when the narrator appears to be struggling with how to convey the totality of her experience or the complexity of her emotions. In an essay Thomas wrote for *The Iowa Review* about the process of writing this memoir, she describes the crucial part her sister played—both in real life and on the page:

> My sister and I drank a lot of coffee and I would show her what I was writing and when she thought there was more going on than I'd gotten at, she insisted I look harder. She was pitiless. She knew me, she knew about my life. . . . She could put me in context, seeing me as part of the times we'd lived through, a perspective I didn't have. I used our conversations verbatim.

Pitfalls to Avoid: Revenge Prose and the Therapist's Couch

Ironically, while creative nonfiction can be a tool of self-discovery, you must also have some distance from the self to write effectively. You must know when you are ready to write about certain subjects and when you are not—when you are still sorting them out for yourself. Perhaps you will be able to write about a *small* aspect of a large experience, focusing your attention on a particular detail that leads to a larger metaphorical significance. See any of the essays in the Anthology for examples of how writers use small details to lead to larger ideas.

This is not to say that creative nonfiction is devoid of emotion; on the contrary, the most powerful nonfiction is propelled by a sense of urgency, the need to speak about events that touch us deeply, both in our personal history and those that occur in the world around us. The key to successfully writing about these events is *perspective*.

As readers, we rarely want to read an essay that smacks either of the discourse appropriate to the "therapist's couch" or "revenge prose." In both cases, the writer has not yet gained enough perspective for wisdom or literature to emerge from experience. The writer may still be weighed down by confusing emotions, or feelings of self-pity, and want only to share those emotions with the reader. In revenge prose, the writer's intent seems to be to get back at someone else. The offender does not emerge as a fully developed character, but only as a flat, one-dimensional incarnation of awful deeds. In both cases, it is the writer who comes out looking bad.

The best writers also show a marked generosity toward the characters in their nonfiction, even those who appear unsympathetic or unredeemable. For example, Terry Tempest Williams, in "The Clan of One-Breasted Women," writes an essay that is clearly fueled by anger, but it does not come across as personally vengeful or mean-spirited. Most of the women in her family died of cancer, an illness that could have been caused by the government's testing of nuclear weapons in her home state. By channeling her energy into research, she shows herself as someone with important information to impart, aside from her own personal history. She creates a metaphor—the clan of one-breasted women—that elevates her own story into a communal one. By directing her attention to the literary design of her material, she is able to transcend the emotional minefield of that material. "Anger," she has said, "must be channeled so that it becomes nourishing rather than toxic."

The Warning Signs

In your own work, always be on the lookout for sections that seem too weighed down by the emotions from which they spring. Here are some warning signs. Read the piece aloud and see if the prose has momentum. Where does it lag? Those are the sections that probably haven't found the right details and scenes. And seek out any sections that too directly explore your feelings about an event rather than the event itself. Where do you say words such as "I hated," "I felt so depressed," "I couldn't stand"? The "I" here will become intrusive, a monologue of old grievances.

If you find yourself telling the reader how to feel, then you're probably headed the wrong way. Channel your creative energy, instead, into constructing the scenes, images, and metaphors that will allow readers to have their own reactions. On the page, your life is not just your life anymore. You must put your allegiance now into creating an artifact that will have meaning outside the self.

Try It

1. Have an individual or group session in which you plumb your own sense of non-fiction ethics. What would you do and what wouldn't you do? Would you recreate a scene or invent dialogue for someone without a clear cue to the reader? Would you invent a fact? It's useful to proceed in your writing with a defined sense of your own boundaries.

2. Practice writing cueing lines. This can be fun to do in a group, while passing one another's essays around or just writing inventive cueing lines to pass ("If I dreamed this scene, this is how I would dream it."). Sharing ideas will get you in the habit of using cueing lines creatively.

3. Try writing out a memory in scene from the perspective of at least two people who were present (members of your family, perhaps). Get their memory down as accurately as you can by questioning them, and write it as carefully and lovingly as you write your own. Think of this as an exercise in the quirks of individual perspective. If you like the results of this exercise, try juxtaposing pieces of each narrative, alternating the voices, to create a braided essay.

4. Try compressing time by creating one scene out of several similar events. For instance, take moments from several Christmas dinners and create one specific scene that encapsulates all of them. What do you gain and/or lose by doing this to your material?

5. Are you doing "the dodge"? Go through your drafts and identify those moments most difficult for you to write. Ask yourself simply: How clear is what is happening here? A series of "it was like" or similar type sentences built on metaphor always needs to be scrutinized, asking the question of whether or not the reader knows what exactly was like that. Likewise, search for broad-brush statements giving "that relationship was a nightmare" kinds of declarations.

   If you are dodging, write a clear paragraph describing that moment or event purely factually. At this point, decide what of this material you actually need to incorporate into your piece. Or consider other strategies like "breaking the fourth wall." Let your readers tell you if that move works.

6. If it is odd that you have no memory of a crucial event from a time period when your memories are otherwise clear and accessible, you may want to state this fact and probe why that might be the case. Your meditation on this trick of memory might, like Karr's, tell us more about that time than the facts of the memory would.

7. As Abigail Thomas does in *Safekeeping*, bring in another character's voice to speak more directly. How can this character act as a foil to your own memory or experience? How can this voice help you bring in more information?

8. Read again the opening to Paisley Rekdal's "The Night My Mother Met Bruce Lee" (see Anthology). How does she let you know that she is creating an experience using her imagination? How does she convince you, if she does, that it's okay to recreate her mother's memory? Would you be comfortable doing so?

9. Comb through an essay you're writing to ferret out any hint of therapist's couch or revenge prose. See if you can replace these moments with concrete details or images instead.

FOR FURTHER READING

In Our Anthology

- "The Fine Art of Sighing" by Bernard Cooper
- "The Night My Mother Met Bruce Lee" by Paisley Rekdal

Resources Available Online

- "Time and Distance Overcome" by Eula Biss
- "Choom" by Jenny Boully
- "Goodbye to All That" by Joan Didion
- "The Creative Nonfiction Police?" by Lee Gutkind
- "'Perhapsing': The Use of Speculation in Creative Nonfiction" by Lisa Knopp
- "Against Technique" by Bret Lott
- "Memoir? Fiction? Where's the Line?" by Mimi Schwartz
- "The Clan of One-Breasted Women" by Terry Tempest Williams

Print Resources

- "Marketing Memory" by Bernard Cooper in *The Business of Memory: The Art of Remembering in an Age of Forgetting*
- *The Lifespan of a Fact* by John D'Agata
- "Memory and Imagination" by Patricia Hampl in *I Could Tell You Stories: Sojourns in the Land of Memory*
- *Nola: A Memoir of Faith, Art, and Madness* by Robin Hemley
- *The Liar's Club: A Memoir* by Mary Karr
- "For You, For Me" by Abigail Thomas in *The Iowa Review,* Volume 36, Number 1
- *Safekeeping: Some True Stories from a Life* by Abigail Thomas
- *Inventing the Truth: The Art and Craft of Memoir* by William Zinsser

12

The Basics of Good Writing
in Any Form

I was delighted to find that nonfiction prose can also carry meaning
in its structures and, like poetry, can tolerate all sorts of figurative language, as well as alliteration and even rhyme. The range of rhythms in
prose is larger and grander than it is in poetry, and it can handle dis-
cursive ideas and plain information as well as character and story. It
can do everything. I felt as though I had switched from a single reed
instrument to a full orchestra.

—ANNIE DILLARD

I am working with a group of novice nonfiction writers, and we're about two-
thirds of the way through our time together. My students have plumbed their
lives in ways they never thought possible: as environmental records, as living
history, as a movement through various forms—scientific, spiritual, cultural,
aesthetic—of inquiry. They sort themselves through the door of my classroom with varying degrees of eagerness and pull out their notebooks, pens
cocked and waiting. They're used to coming in and interrogating themselves
in different ways: Who are they really? How have they lived?

Today, however, I know I'm going to make them groan. Instead of prompts
like writing about the latest election or a probing of an early memory, I have
them pull out a piece of their own prose and count the number of words in
each sentence for three paragraphs. I also have them jot down comments on
the kinds of sentences they use: simple declarative (basic subject-verb), complex, fragmented, and so forth. They do the assignment, because it would be

even more boring to sit and do nothing, I suppose. Suddenly a little exclamation breaks out from a corner of the room.

"Ohmigod!" says one young woman. "All of my sentences are eleven words long!"

This woman has been concerned about what feels to her like a flatness or lifelessness to her prose. Here, in one rather mechanical but not painful exercise, she's put her finger on the reason, or one of the reasons. On further analysis she discovers that she has a penchant for writing one simple declarative sentence after another: "I drive to the forest in April. My car is almost ready for a new clutch. The forests are quiet at that time of year." The metronomic beat of same sentence structure, same sentence length, has robbed her otherwise sparkling essays of their life.

For the sake of comparison, listen to the difference created in those three sample sentences by a little more rhetorical inventiveness: "In April, a quiet time of year, I drive to the forest. My car almost ready for a new clutch."

—SUZANNE

Scene and Exposition

Generally speaking, scene is the building block of creative nonfiction. There are exceptions to this statement—more academic or technically oriented writing, the essay of ideas perhaps—but overall, the widespread notion that nonfiction is the writer's thoughts presented in an expository or summarizing way has done little but produce quantities of unreadable nonfiction. Scene is based on action unreeling before us, as it would in a film, and it will draw on the same techniques as fiction—dialogue, description, point of view, specificity, concrete detail. Scene also encompasses the lyricism and imagery of great poetry.

Let's begin by defining our terms. *Expository* writing, as the term implies, exposes the author's thoughts or experiences for the reader; it summarizes, generally with little or no sensory detail. Expository writing compresses time: *For five years I lived in Alaska.* It presents a compact summation of an experience with no effort to recreate the experience for the person reading.

On the other hand, *scene*, as in fiction, uses detail and sensory information to recreate experience, generally with location, action, a sense of movement through time, and possible dialogue. Scene is cinematic. Here is a possible reworking of the preceding sentence, using scene: *For the five years I lived in Alaska I awoke each morning to the freezing seat of the outhouse, the sting of hot strong coffee drunk without precious sugar or milk, the ringing "G'day!" of my Australian neighbor.*

The latter version of this sentence clearly presents the reader with a more experiential version of that time in Alaska, with details that provide a snapshot of the place: the slowness of time passing is stressed by the harsh routine of the coffee and outhouse; we get a sense of scarcity of supply; the neighbor even has a bit of swift characterization. Of course, for an essay in which Alaska is totally unimportant the expository summation might be the better move. But if you find yourself writing nonfiction with very little scene, you are likely to produce flat writing readers have to struggle to enter.

In his essay "The Knife," author and surgeon Richard Selzer moves fluidly between scene and exposition; Selzer forces us to *live* the awesome power and responsibility of the surgeon before allowing himself the luxury of meditating about it.

> There is a hush in the room. Speech stops. The hands of the others, assistants and nurses, are still. Only the voice of the patient's respiration remains. It is the rhythm of a quiet sea, the sound of waiting. Then you speak, slowly, the terse entries of a Himalayan climber reporting back. "The stomach is okay. Greater curvature clean. No sign of ulcer. Pylorus, duodenum fine. Now comes the gall-bladder. No stones. Right kidney, left, all right. Liver . . . uh-oh."

Selzer goes on to tell us he finds three large tumors in the liver. "Three big hard ones in the left lobe, one on the right. Metastatic deposits. Bad, bad." Like fine fiction, this passage contains a clear setting—the hospital room, characterized appropriately enough by sound rather than appearance: the silence of life and death. There is action mimicking real time, containing the element of surprise. We learn along with the surgeon about the patient's metastasized cancer. There's dialogue, as the surgeon narrates to himself, to his surgical assistants, seemingly to the fates, his discovery of the patient's mortality. And like fine poetry, this piece of writing also organizes itself through imagery: the "quiet sea" of the passive patient's breathing versus the labored voice—like a "Himalayan climber's"—of the surgeon emphasizes the former's loss of control.

Selzer's passage would be easy to change to an expository sentence: *Often in surgery I found unexpected cancer.* But the author's final purpose—an extended meditation on the relationship of human and tool, soul and body—would fall flat. The reader, lacking any feel for the grandeur and potential tragedy of exploring the body, would dismiss expository statements such as, "The surgeon struggles not to feel. It is suffocating to press the feeling out," as merely odd or grandiose.

Representative and Specific Scenes

There are several other moves worth noting in Selzer's passage. Like the sample Alaska sentence given previously, Selzer's surgical description is a *representative scene*. In other words, he doesn't pretend this operation occurs at one specific time and place, but it represents a typical surgical procedure, one among many.

In contrast, here's an example of a *specific*, not representative, scene, from Jo Ann Beard's essay "The Fourth State of Matter." The scenes comprising the essay all occur at specific moments in time. Here is Beard at work, with her physicist colleagues having a professional discussion around the chalkboard:

> "If it's plasma, make it in red," I suggest helpfully. We're all smoking illegally, in the journal office with the door closed and the window open. We're having a plasma party.
>
> "We aren't discussing *plas*ma," Bob says condescendingly. He's smoking a horrendously smelly pipe. The longer he stays in here the more it feels like I'm breathing small daggers in through my nose. He and I don't get along; each of us thinks the other needs to be taken down a peg. Once we had a hissing match in the hallway which ended with him suggesting that I could be fired, which drove me to tell him he was *already* fired, and both of us stomped into our offices and slammed our doors.
>
> "I had to fire Bob," I tell Chris later.
>
> "I heard," he says noncommittally. Bob is his best friend.

This is a pinpointed event, not representative but presumably unlike any other moment in Beard's life. Notice how much suggestive detail Beard packs into a short space. These characters break rules, argue, and exist in complex relationship to one another. Her relationship with Bob is established in this scene—a relationship that seems suffused with a genuine but relatively harmless tension, given their ability to issue dire threats to each other without consequence. The dialogue sounds real and secures the characters, capturing the nuanced pretense of Bob's stressing the "plas" part of the "plasma." Chris, the man in the middle, seems to have heard all this bickering before.

We all tend to use too little scene in creative nonfiction. We especially forget the possibilities of representative scene. Even when we're reporting a typical rather than a specific event, use of scenic elements, as in Selzer's surgery, conveys a sense of character and situation far more effectively than does summary.

Remember those "shocks of memory" from Chapter 1? Go back and see how the examples in that chapter use both specific and representative scenes to stay focused on a particular moment in time. They rarely summarize or skim over these moments; they have the patience to keep looking. Or study a particular essay in the Anthology, identifying representative scenes, specific scenes, and exposition. This will be good practice for your own writing.

Specificity and Detail

Scene forces us to use specificity and detail, elements that get lost in the quick wash of exposition. Even in discussing the largest ideas, our brains engage with the small workings of the senses first. And the specificity of a piece of nonfiction is generally where the sensory details lie: the aroma of honeysuckle, the weak film of moonlight. While it is possible to go overboard with detail, generally in drafting it's best to keep going back and sharpening as much as possible. You leaned not just against a tree but against a weeping silver birch; the voice at the other end of the phone sounded like the Tin Man's in *The Wizard of Oz*. When you write scene, your job is to mimic the event, create an experiential representation of it for the reader.

Look at the examples given earlier, and think about how much the details add to those scenes: the hushed silence of the hospital room and three hard tumors on the left lobe of the liver in Selzer's essay. In Beard's, we see the bickering but ultimate acceptance of this close group of coworkers. We sense the author's ambivalent position in the group—shut out of their "talking physics," as she tells us earlier—but also her authority within the group. We sense, in the hyperbolic description of Bob's pipe smoke ("like daggers"), a bit of foreshadowing of a coming tragic event.

In *The Elements of Style*, William Strunk, Jr., explains that the one point of accord among good writers is the need for detail that is "specific, definite, and concrete." (We also address this point in Chapter 1.) Concrete detail appeals to the senses; other writers call such details "proofs." If Selzer told readers that sometimes in surgery he found cancer, we might abstractly believe him, but it's hard to associate that fact with real life and death. In this passage, we're convinced by the specifics: three hard tumors on the liver, the surgeon's voice mumbling, "Bad, bad."

Abstract language—the opposite of relying on concrete detail—refers to the larger concepts we use that exist on a purely mental level, with no appeal to the senses: *liberty, justice, contentment*, and so on. These terms may contain the implication of sensory detail (you may flash on "warmth" when you hear "contentment," but that's a personal reaction that wouldn't make sense to, say, a penguin), but they are in themselves broad categories only. Beard could have summarized her relationships with her coworkers; Selzer could have presented a few expository sentences about soul and body, surgeon as God. We want experiences, not lectures. We want to enter into events and uncover their meanings for ourselves.

Paying attention to concrete detail and the input of our own senses also helps save us from the literary pitfall of cliché, an expression or concept that's been overused. Frequently, clichés are dead metaphors, and we don't pay attention anymore to the comparisons they contain. If Beard had described Bob's pipe tobacco as smelling like "dirty socks," or "killing" her nose, she would have been indulging in cliché. Instead, she used the information of her senses to create a fresh image.

Next time you work on a piece of creative nonfiction, hear yourself talking through the story to friends in a crowded coffee shop or club. There's plenty to divert their attention: music, people-watching, smoke, and noise. Which details do you use to hold their attention? Do you imitate the look of someone's face, the sound of a voice? Do you screech to demonstrate the sound of car tires on asphalt? Your reading audience will be equally distractible. Think about how to render these attention-grabbing devices in your prose. You may want to consult Chapter 1, "The Body of Memory," to remind yourself how to use sensory detail.

Developing Character

Character development, like learning to write effective dialogue, is part of writing scene. It's another particularly easy-to-miss demand of good creative nonfiction. After all, *we* know what our parents, children, or lovers look like. Unconsciously, we tend to assume that everyone else does as well.

Suzanne has, by marriage, a very funny grandmother. She wasn't intentionally funny, but nonetheless the mere mention of her name tends to bring down the room when the family's together. The family bears in mind, as courteous people, that we need to break through our uncontrollable giggling and clue other listeners in to the source of our amusement: "Well, she came from a tiny town in south Georgia and talked about nothing all day long but her ar-ther-itis and her gallbladder that was *leakin'* plus she lied compulsively and pursed her mouth in this funny way when she did. . . ." After a few minutes of this our listeners understand why we find her so endlessly amusing. This kind of filling in, also natural in conversation, is the essence of character development.

Nothing demonstrates the power of fine characterization like studying writers who, in a few strokes, can help us apprehend someone sensually (through sight, sound, or feel) as well as give us a sense of their essence. The following are examples of quick, effective character development from essays we love:

- **Albert Goldbarth in "After Yitzl":** "My best friend there shoed horses. He had ribs like barrel staves, his sweat was miniature glass pears."
- **Lawrence Sutin in "Man and Boy":** "In the case of my father and myself, I had the fullness of his face and his desire to write, which had been abandoned when he came to America with a family to raise. . . . He was a middle-aged man who was sobbing and sweaty and his body was heavy and so soft I imagined his ribs giving way like a snowman's on the first warm winter day."
- **Judith Kitchen in "Things of This Life":** "Mayme would step onto the platform wearing a dark purple coat, her black braids wound tightly around her head. Her skin was too soft and wrinkly. When you kissed her cheek, it wobbled, and you wished you didn't have to do that."

Details that show the essence of individuals—in both their typical (commonness with their type; grandmothers typically have soft and wrinkly skin) and specific glory ("sweat like miniature pears")—are blazingly effective when you come upon them. Think, when you write about someone close to you, how you would characterize that person in a stroke or two for someone else.

Dialogue

It can be difficult to allow ourselves to use direct dialogue in creative nonfiction. After all, memory's faulty; we can't recall conversations word for word, so why try? The answer is that we need to try, because insofar as nonfiction attempts to be an honest record of the observant mind, dialogue matters. We recall voices, not summaries; we observe scenes in our head, not expository paragraphs.

Dialogue generally moves action forward. Selzer quotes himself finding the metastasized cancer, and Beard gives a sense of the dynamics of her office. Dialogue must characterize and capture the voice of the speaker, however, not simply give information. The latter is called in fiction writing "information dumping," and it occurs when you have people say things like, "Well, Carmen, I remember you told me you were taking the cross-town bus that day only because your white 1999 Volvo had developed a gasket problem." Information dumping is less of a problem in nonfiction because this genre is reality based (and people really *do not* talk that way). But, if you cue your readers that you are recreating a conversation, it may be tempting to lard the dialogue with information you can't figure out how to get in any other way. Don't do it.

Everyone has a natural cadence and a dialect to his or her speech. We nearly always speak in simple sentences, not complex-compound ones. We might say, "When the rain comes, the grass grows," which has one short dependent clause beginning with the word *when*; we aren't likely to say, "Whenever it happens the rain comes, provided the proper fertilizer's been applied, the grass grows"—a simple sentence or *main clause* ("the grass grows") festooned with wordy subordinate clauses. We frequently speak in sentence fragments or ungrammatical snippets—for example, the how-are-you question "Getting along?" instead of the grammatically correct "Are you getting along?"

One exception to these rules of natural speech might be a person who *is* pompous and wordy. Perhaps you're writing dialogue to capture the voice of a stuffy English professor you know. In that case, go to town. Just bear in mind that what bores you will bore others fairly quickly. In the case of people who are boorish, dull, or otherwise hard to listen to, give readers a sample of the voice and they will fill in the rest. A little goes a long way.

One final caveat: beware of elaborate taglines, which identify the speaker, such as "he said," "she argued," and so forth. In dialogue between two people taglines are often dispensable after the first two. Even when you must use them, stick as much as possible to "said" and "asked," two fairly invisible words in the context of dialogue. It's an easy mistake to make—and a difficult one to overlook as a reader—to have all of your characters "retort," "storm," or "muse." And make sure the words themselves contain tone as much as possible. (Tone can also be conveyed in a character's gesture, as in Beard's colleagues casually breaking the rules by smoking in their office.) Don't follow each speech tag with an adverb such as "angrily," "sadly," and so on. If you feel the need to use those words, ask yourself why the dialogue itself doesn't seem to contain those feelings.

Point of View

Every story is told by a storyteller (even in a piece with multiple speakers, one speaker dominates at a time), and every storyteller must be situated somehow within the frame of the work. This situating is called *point of view* (POV), and we express it through choice of pronouns: *I* (first person); *you* (second person); *he, she, they* (third person). Though it may seem at first blush as though all nonfiction must be told in first person, skillful writers do use the techniques of second- and third-person POV to wonderful effect in nonfiction. Some writers also use the first-person plural (*we*) POV, to create "communal" or "community" memoir.

Here's a sentence from "The Fourth State of Matter" again, a classic first-person approach: "It's November 1, 1991, the last day of the first part of my life." Compare that with a short passage from Richard Selzer, who uses second person liberally throughout his essay. Watch the careful way he slips from first- to second-person POV, as if inviting the reader to experience the fearfulness of a surgeon's power:

I must confess that the priestliness of my profession has ever been impressed on me. In the beginning there are vows. . . . And if the surgeon is like a poet, then the scars you have made on countless bodies are like verses into the fashioning of which you have poured your soul.

In contrast, Judith Kitchen's essay "Things of This Life" uses third person throughout the piece to create a sense of freshness and excitement in a childhood memoir:

Consider the child idly browsing in the curio shop. She's been on vacation in the Adirondacks, and her family has (over the past week) canoed the width of the lake and up a small, meandering river. . . . So why, as she sifts through boxes of fake arrowheads made into key chains, passes down the long rows of rubber tomahawks, dyed rabbits' feet, salt shakers with the words "Indian Lake" painted in gold, beaded moccasins made of what could only in the imagination be called leather, is she happier than any time during the past week?

Kitchen, further along in the essay, tells us, "Now consider the woman who was that child." It seems at first an odd choice, to write about the self as if it were someone completely apart, a stranger. But as Kitchen unfolds her sense of her life as "alien," a space she's inhabiting that raises questions she still can't answer ("How can she go on, wanting like this, for the rest of her life?"), the strategy becomes a coherent part of the architecture of the essay.

Imagine the paragraphs it would take to explain such an alienation from the self—a sense of distance from one's own desires—and the relative powerlessness such an explanation would have. Annie Dillard writes in our introductory quote that she "delighted" to learn that nonfiction, like poetry, can carry meaning in its structures. Kitchen here has wisely chosen a structure to convey her feeling—a feeling open only to the clumsiest articulation.

In "People Are Starving" (see also Chapter 5, "The Body of Identity,"), Suzanne Rivecca chooses to make her personal story of eating disorders a communal one by using the *we* pronoun throughout. Sometimes the "we" narrator conveys what all the members of this "we" would have in common, but sometimes the "we" also shows a multiplicity of experiences, such as in the following list-like passage:

We had milk money. We had lunch money. We had a Bee Gees lunchbox. We had a plaid Thermos full of soup that smelled like sweat. We had a brown paper sack. Our mom put notes in our lunch: on stationery with kittens on it; on folded-up loose-leaf; on pastel Post-its; on scraps from yellow legal pads. The notes said, *Have a great day.* They said, *I love you.* They said, *God loves you.* They said, *Be good today.* They meant, *Remember who you are.* They meant, *Come back safe.* They packed us notes every day and we wished they wouldn't. They never packed us notes and we wished they would. Our moms packed us damp baby carrots. One pale piece of string cheese. A sandwich composed of geometric slabs of meat and cheese—perfect circles, perfect squares. A rectangular brownie, a perennially uneaten orange, a zip-lock bag of humid saltines, a Fruit Roll-Up, a slippery hard-boiled egg, browning slices of apple, a bent granola bar. A handful of cornflakes in a plastic bag, a wedge of lasagna wrapped in foil, a bunch of lettuce in Tupperware. A single pancake in the shape of our first initial. A wilted five-dollar bill. Five one-dollar bills, so crisp they looked fake. A handful of candy corn. Nothing at all.

This list—so vivid in its concrete details!—immerses the reader in the world of school lunch and may even trigger memories of our own school lunches. The experiences are all so different and sometimes contradict each other, yet within these differences a commonality emerges: the messages we're given around food, and how food defines our home, class, and cultural environments.

Image and Metaphor

Janet Burroway, in her text *Writing Fiction*, describes metaphor as the foundation stone "from which literature derives." Image (any literary element that creates a sense impression in the mind) and metaphor (the use of comparison) form the heart of any literary work. Notice how, trying to impress this importance upon you, we strain to make strong metaphor: metaphors are the foundation stones of a building; they're the pumping hearts of literary writing.

For example, in "First" (see Anthology), Ryan Van Meter allows many of his concrete details to have metaphoric overtones. In the first paragraph, he describes in detail where he and his friend Ben are situated in the station wagon—separate from and turned away from the parents—and then characterizes it as feeling "like a secret, as though they are not even in the car with us." This image of facing in different directions recurs throughout the essay and emphasizes the essential themes of the piece: this memory highlights a sense of secrecy, as well as a rupturing in perspective between children and parents.

While essays can be organized many ways—through topic, chronology, or passage of time—organization through image and metaphor has become much more common. Clustering thoughts through images and loose associations (and metaphors are, at the most basic level, associations) seems fundamental to the way the human mind works.

You can often find clues to your own imagistic or metaphoric organizations when you recall the sensory association a thought or experience calls to mind. If the summer your best friend was killed in a diving accident always comes back to you with a whiff of honeysuckle, stay with that image and explore it in writing for a while. Does it lead to concepts of sweetness, youth, temptation, the quick blooming? If you let yourself write about the image alone for a while—not rushing to get to the subject your mind may insist is "the real story"—a more complex series of themes in your story will probably emerge.

A Note on Cliché

Most clichés, as we mention previously, are concepts or images that are emptied of meaning. Often, they are metaphors or similes that have lost their imagistic connections. When we hear the phrase "good as gold," we don't picture a transaction backed by the value of gold, rather than by payment that is devalued or counterfeit—the origins of the term. We probably don't think of "gold" in a tangible way at all.

Our student, writer Lindsay Petrie, came up with a method of breathing new life into a cliché, for those times when such a phrase seems somehow appropriate, or those times when you want the little surprise of making your reader really experience those words again. She called this move the *clicheze,* as it is like spraying a freshener like Febreze on your cliché, refreshing it and bringing it to life. A clichézed "good as gold" might be ironic, like "as good as gold if the gold were a ring and you can't get it off your finger." Or serious: "as good as gold if you're a prospector and you haven't eaten in three days." You can see how the clicheze treatment makes the words and the image come to life again.

The Rhythm of Your Sentences

It's a well-known fact that sentences must contain some variation. You must have become acquainted with this fact already. It's clear if you read a certain kind of prose. A work must use different kinds of sentence structures. Different kinds of sentence structures help alleviate that numbing feeling. It's a feeling you don't want your readers to have.

The previous paragraph contains six sentences, each composed of about ten words, and each is a simple sentence, beginning with a subject and its verb. Unlike this sentence you're currently reading, none begins with a clause. None is short. None, unlike the twenty-five-word sentence introducing this second paragraph, engages us for very long. Read both of these paragraphs together. Do you sense a difference? Do you, as we do, begin to go blank by the middle of the first paragraph and finally feel some relief at the second one?

Notice that the second paragraph in this section of the book, while clarifying many of the ideas that the first paragraph contains, varies sentence structure and length. It also varies voice. One sentence uses the *command* voice ("Read both paragraphs together"), two are cast in the *interrogative* voice—they ask questions. Clauses like "Unlike this sentence" and "as we do" appear at the beginnings, middles, and ends of sentences to break up that repetitive simple structure.

The Poetry of Prose

Virginia Woolf, who many writers would list as a "favorite poet," began work not with an idea but with a "rhythm," writing to a friend, "Style is a very simple matter; it is all rhythm. Once you have that, you can't use the wrong words." Though it's become popular, and helpful at times, to divide up nonfiction into lyric essays and non-lyric essays, doing so can obscure the fact that all language is controlled by rhythm—especially a highly stressed, partly Germanic language like our own. If you learn to see how language operates through rhythm and sound, as well as how sentence structure affects meaning, you will be delighted at the new power of your prose.

Let's examine a paragraph of Woolf's prose, one that appears at the start of her novel *Mrs. Dalloway*:

> What a lark! What a plunge! For so it had always seemed to her, when, with a little squeak of the hinges, which she could hear now, she had burst open the French windows and plunged at Bourton into the open air. How fresh, how calm, stiller than this of course, the air was in the early morning; like the flap of a wave; the kiss of a wave; chill and sharp and yet (for a girl of eighteen as she then was) solemn, feeling as she did, standing there at the open window, that something awful was about to happen; looking at the flowers, at the trees with the smoke winding off them and the rooks rising, falling; standing and looking until Peter Walsh said, "Musing among the vegetables?"—was that it?—"I prefer men to cauliflowers"—was that it?

Woolf begins with two short, emphatic sentences that illustrate the joyous, "plunging" movements of her heroine, Clarissa Dalloway, going out on a trip to purchase flowers. She follows that with two long sentences, the first ending with the prepositional phrase "into the open air," the sentence structure itself mirroring the protagonist's entry into the larger world beyond her doors. Those emphatic semicolons that first set off the arrival of waves in her mind cue us that the "kiss of a wave" may not be an entirely pleasant thing, and prepare us for the "foreboding." The final use of dashes to set off the question "was that it?" enables that phrase to "float" syntactically, not clearly connected to anything else in the sentence—is she wondering what Peter Walsh said, what she was thinking then, or something else? Author Virginia Tufte uses the term *syntactic symbolism* to describe syntax that creates emotional effects.

Here is an excerpt from writer Dorothy Parker, a description of a breakup:

> But I knew. I knew. I knew because he had been far away from me long before he went. He's gone away and he won't come back. He's gone away and he won't come back, he's gone away and he'll never come back.

Here the repetition of "knew" captures the author's sense that she cannot drive this devastating knowledge out of her mind. Even the tense shifting—past "knew" to present "He's gone"—reflects her inability to cease feeling the painful emotion.

The choices you make as a writer either charge your prose with energy and support your narrative, or represent a missed opportunity. Sometimes, as with the unvaried sentence lengths we mentioned, your choices work against you. Sentence length and sentence structure, syntax, paragraphing, clause placement, and similar elements deeply influence the meaning of your prose.

In Brian Doyle's "Leap" (see Anthology), variations in sentence length and patterns of repetition underscore the terrible story of the September 11 attack on the World Trade Center. Doyle stresses the detail of victims choosing to jump from the towers rather than die in the building, and of reaching for one another's hands as they did so. Here is the essay's opening:

> A couple leaped from the south tower, hand in hand. They reached for each other and their hands met and they jumped.
>
> Jennifer Brickhouse saw them falling, hand in hand.
>
> Many people jumped. Perhaps hundreds. Who knows.

Doyle begins this essay with a terse, abbreviated style. He uses short, factual sentences, and naming the witnesses of this event—Jennifer Brickhouse, in this excerpt—increases the reportorial nature of the prose. The one poetic element of this opening is the repetition of "hand in hand" at the end of two sentences that follow each other in quick succession (this type of repetition is known in rhetoric as an *epistrophe*). The words *hand* and *hold* repeat frequently in this essay, reinforcing Doyle's focus on this small act of connection within the midst of such tragedy.

As "Leap" progresses, Doyle breaks the pattern with several sentences that are much longer. These break out of that tone of terse recital:

> I try to whisper prayers for the sudden dead and the harrowed families of the dead and the screaming sounds of the murderers but I keep coming back to his hand and her hand nestled in each other with such extraordinary ordinary succinct ancient naked stunning perfect simple ferocious love.

This sentence is not only long, it is also underpunctuated: Doyle leaves out the commas we expect to find between clauses and between adjectives. The pause-less, rushing feel of this sentence performs the chaos of the event as well as the writer's breathless horror and awe. The voice of the essay, contemplating what happened that day, becomes overwhelmed. A pileup of nine adjectives in a row would generally feel overdone, but the contrast it creates with the held-back quality of Doyle's earlier writing makes this move feel justified and powerful. And the adjectives are so surprising, and in some cases contradictory, or almost contradictory—"extraordinary ordinary," "simple ferocious"—that we move with Doyle through the impossibility of fully capturing the victims' response.

Nonfiction Structures and Containers

As we described in Chapter 8, "The Tradition of the Personal Essay," essays often have two lines of movement: the horizontal (plot, story, linear development) and the vertical (insight, reflection, delving below the surface). You can envision your work in these terms. Is it more horizontal or vertical? Does the balance between the two feel adequate, or is it unbalanced in some way? Is there a beginning, middle, and end?

Even in experimental or lyric work—works that aren't dependent on plot—we need to figure out what is creating forward movement in the piece. John Gardner, a fiction writer, has translated the archaic term *profluence* (which literally means "onward") onto literary craft, using the term to describe the way a story lets us know that it is getting somewhere. In creative nonfiction, we can think about profluence too: Are we "getting somewhere"? What kind of container or structure will help this movement along?

Sometimes, the story itself will lend itself to profluence: for example, a travel narrative often has natural starting and ending points. Other times, we need to find a small thread that will act as this propellant, perhaps even something quite mundane. For example, in his essay "Burl's," Bernard Cooper "bookends" his essay with a simple task: at the beginning of the essay, Cooper's father sends the boy outside a diner to get a newspaper from the vending machine. While doing this task, the child narrator notices two flashily dressed women teetering on high heels down the sidewalk, and as they draw closer he sees they also carry the gender markers of men: stubbles of beard, Adam's apples, broad shoulders. When one of the women trips and her wig shifts, the narrator sees "a rift in her composure, a window through which I could glimpse the shades of maleness that her dress and wig and make-up obscured." This observation leads him into a rumination on how things are not always as they seem:

> Any woman might be a man; the fact of it clanged through the chambers of my brain. In broad day, in the midst of traffic, with my parents drinking coffee a few feet away, I felt as if everything I understood, everything I had taken for granted up to that moment . . . had been squeezed out of me.

He breaks from this scene to the heart of the essay, where Cooper meditates for several pages on the concrete memories that gave him his first inklings of his own blurred sexual boundaries. We then return to the newspaper at the end of the essay: "I handed my father the *Herald*. He opened the paper and disappeared behind it. My mother stirred her coffee and sighed."

Though we had almost forgotten about the small task at this point, it returns to provide a satisfying, small "plot" for the piece. He has suspended a small moment in time, and in the few moments while he performed this task, the narrator has gained new insights into his experience.

In your own essay, think about the structure of your piece and whether there might be some small "plot," a container that will hold your deeper musings in place. Read several essays in our Anthology with this idea in mind: How do these writers begin and end their essays? What creates profluence? How do we move across space and time?

The Looping Essay

If you map nonfiction structures, you'll find many shapes: the woven pattern of the braided essay, the rising and falling pattern of conflict-crisis-resolution, and so on. One classic structure that particularly lends itself to the movements of creative nonfiction is the *looping essay*. Creative nonfiction often involves holding a subject, idea, or image, up to the light: establishing it on the page, examining its shifting facets, studying its evolution. In the looping essay, you loop back again as you close to the place you started. You do not repeat what you've already done—that moment where you began comes back, yes, but with a new insight.

In Brent Staples's "The Coroner's Photographs" (see Anthology), the essay opens in the midst of a searing scene: the author views images of the body of his murdered brother, seen lying in a morgue. The essay winds back to recall the brother's childhood, and his life as a drug dealer. Staples takes us through his deep emotional connection with his brother's body. "I know his contours well," he writes. "I bathed and diapered him when he was a baby and studied his features as he grew." The coroner's report on this death serves as a stark and clinical contrast to the author's memories—the weight of Blake Staples's heart and lungs, the minutiae of his gunshot wounds. The end brings us back to the scene where we began, but only after we've lived Staples's difficult journey to choose to see the coroner's files.

Virginia Woolf's essay "Street Haunting" is a classic "looping" essay. This meditative essay begins with a mundane purpose:

> No one perhaps has ever felt passionately towards a lead pencil. But there are circumstances in which it can become supremely desirable to possess one; moments when we are set upon having an object, an excuse for walking half across London between tea and dinner.

With these lines, Woolf creates a reason for the essay that follows: a physical reason that sets us (both writer and reader) moving. She then embarks on the walk with a purpose, and what follows is an extended meditation on the permeable nature of the self, triggered by the sights and people she encounters on this walk. After being distracted again and again on our way across London—privy to the intimate lives taking place behind lit windows—we finally return triumphant with pencil in hand:

> Here again is the usual door; here the chair turned as we left it and the china bowl and the brown ring on the carpet. And here—let us examine it tenderly, let us touch it with reverence—is the only spoil we have retrieved from all the treasures of the city, a lead pencil.

If, as Joan Didion says, we write "to learn what [we] are thinking," it makes sense that the thought that compels an essay may be the one to which it wants to return, refreshed and refracted. This is particularly true of the meditative essay, but the structure is common even in more narrative pieces. Sometimes, when you cannot find your ending, you will discover that the germ of it is already planted, ready for your loop back.

Humor

Of all the audience responses writers may want to elicit, none is harder to gauge than humor. It's hard to argue about the sentimental value of people falling in love or the tragedy of war, but we all tend to have a comedy vocabulary peculiarly our own. Emily Dickinson, who lends our book its title, had a peculiar habit of roaring with laughter over the obituaries every day. The juxtaposition of odd or unexpected things makes up a lot of what we find comic. So do word choice, sentence structure, and the stance authors take toward the world and toward themselves.

In his essay "The Drama Bug," well-known humorist David Sedaris falls in love with theater and affects a Shakespearean speech that becomes hilarious in juxtaposition with the ordinary events occupying his teenage years. Over a chicken dinner with family, he proclaims, "Methinks, kind sir, most gentle lady, fellow siblings all, that this barnyard fowl be most tasty and succulent." Humor writers like Sedaris are constantly mining their lives for incongruities to use in their work.

Exaggeration, or hyperbole, is also a classic technique of humor. Sedaris clearly exaggerates in the long-winded pseudo-Elizabethan speeches he delivers in "Drama Bug"; no one could remember their own monologues that precisely. (And surely his family would have swatted him with the barnyard fowl before listening to all of that!) Writer Anne Lamott is another comic exaggerator. It's a device she uses again and again to great effect, as when she describes a reading in which "I had jet lag, the self-esteem of a prawn, and to top it off, I had stopped breathing. I sounded just like the English patient."

One characteristic that Sedaris and Lamott have in common is the self-puncturing qualities of the authors. They laugh at themselves so freely we feel encouraged to laugh with them—and, if we're honest with ourselves, we all have a gold mine of material in self-deprecation.

TRY IT

1. Go through a piece of your writing and find a passage of summary that could or should be in scene. Don't fret right now about whether scene is absolutely necessary here: the point is to develop the skill of automatically asking yourself whether that option will help you.

Sometimes we stymie ourselves by imagining we must remember *everything* or we can't describe *anything*. So work with what you do remember. You may forget the look of a room but remember the sound or smell of it (think of Selzer's defining silence in that hospital room). Or create a bridge, such as writing a few sentences about how this is what a dialogue sounds like in your memory as you try to recreate it, giving yourself permission to fill in what you don't remember word for word. Remember that almost any device for reconstruction is fine, as long as you let readers in on what you're doing.

2. To get a feel for writing scene, recreate an event that took place in the last week— one with characters you can delineate and dialogue you can remember. It doesn't have to be important—it probably will help if it isn't. The point is simply to write two to three pages in which a location is established through description, people are characterized and talk, and something happens.

3. Finally, when you feel confident of your basic skills, remember a scene out of your own life that does contain the utmost importance. Write the scene with as much fidelity as possible. Don't question right now why what matters *matters*. Trust your intuition, and tap into all of the passion you have invested in this scene.

   Now question yourself. Why was a certain gesture or inflection so important? The chances are that your emotional story is locked into the details you remember of your life. When you begin to question the scene in this way, scrutinizing every detail, you'll probably discover an essay waiting to be written about this crucial moment.

4. Think of someone close to you and try to convey their essence, through clothing, sound, dialogue, gestures, and so forth, in two or three paragraphs. Don't aim to write scene; this portrait doesn't need to contain action, merely characterization.

   When you're reasonably finished, trade your piece with a writing partner. Read each other's sketches and then elaborate on the person described, giving an overall, abstract sense of that individual's personality. How close did you come? Discuss with your partner ways this sketch could be refined: important details that may have been omitted, or others that could be misleading. Is this character sketch on its way to becoming an essay? Articulate to yourself why this character matters, why she is different, or why he is intriguingly typical.

5. Write a page or two of dialogue. Practice for this by using your notebook to record snippets of speech verbatim: exchanges with classmates, friends, spouses,

parents. Pay attention to the syntax of speech. How much is grammatically correct or incorrect? How much slang or dialect appears in different speakers' voices? When you feel ready, write a page or two of typical dialogue—you can record it and write it down, or try to recreate it—with someone fairly close to you. Do the same partner swap with this dialogue you did with characterization, and see how much of the person you're describing comes through in his or her voice.

6. The only way to fully understand point of view is to experiment with it. Pull out an earlier essay of yours, or write a simple paragraph about some subject you've thought about as a likely one. Then recast the point of view, from first to second or third or first-person plural. Force yourself to keep going through at least one paragraph.

7. Try writing a piece entirely from the first-person plural (we) point of view. See how this move might help you make connections between your personal experience and a communal one.

8. Do a quick diagnostic of two to three paragraphs of your own prose (less might not be representative enough). How long do your sentences tend to be? How do you structure them? Do you vary voices or speech acts, such as questioning, stating, and commanding, or do you simply use the declarative or simple statement voice? Challenge yourself to approach a piece of prose in a way you haven't in the past—more short sentences or sentence fragments, perhaps, or more shifts in voice. See how this change alters your work and opens up the possibilities of the essay.

9. Considering Brian Doyle's powerful changes in sentence length, take a page of your own prose that doesn't feel quite right to you yet, and deliberately vary your sentence length. Go from short and terse to long and rich, snappy to overwhelmed and overwhelming. Vary your punctuation, both over- and under-using it. You will certainly not want to keep all of the changes you make in this exercise, but underline or circle those sentences that do seem to work, articulating to yourself why and how they do.

10. Try to identify a simple "container scene" in your piece that you could use to hold the essay in place. Begin the piece with this scene, and return to it periodically, or just at the end of the essay. Use this scene as anchoring thread and see if the essay feels more shaped or polished.

11. Create a visual diagram that describes the "profluence" of your essay. Does it move in a straight line? Does it spiral? Does it look like a spiderweb? or a series of peaks and valleys? There are any number of ways to envision the forward movement of your essay. See if this kind of representation might open up some new ideas about the structure of the piece that might enhance its effect.

12. When you are struggling to find an ending to an essay, consider the looping structure. Go back and reread only your first paragraph. List for yourself what is there: the characters, events, images, suggestions, ideas. Imagine the metaphoric possibilities of each, the capacity of the images you are already using to recur and be extended. Write a closing paragraph after carefully considering only the first— or first and second—paragraph. If the looping structure feels right, continue to revise and refine it.

13. Practice writing deliberate incongruities, twists, exaggerations, and understatements. What is the strangest sight you've seen over the last year? Was it a man in a tuxedo kicking his shoes off and jumping into the surf? A Santa Claus withdrawing money from an ATM? What experience in your own life led to the most unexpected sight?

14. What irritates you? Write a few paragraphs on the most constant irritants in your life, whether it's telemarketers, the fact that you have almost the same phone number as the local pizzeria, whatever. Write dialogue and scene; strive to be funny. At the same time, think, as previously, of larger subjects this irritant suggests.

15. Study any essay in the Anthology (or in your outside reading) and see if there is one technique you can "borrow" to strengthen your own piece. Notice variety in the sentence structures, the way the author uses image and metaphor. Study the larger structure: how does the essay move from beginning to end? Study the transitions from one paragraph or section to another. Observe closely, like an apprentice, and see how you can practice incorporating the writer's techniques into your own work.

FOR FURTHER READING

In Our Anthology

Note: All the sample essays in our anthology, of course, showcase elements of strong writing. Cited in this chapter:

- "Leap" by Brian Doyle
- "The Coroner's Photographs" by Brent Staples
- "First" by Ryan Van Meter

Resources Available Online

- "The Fourth State of Matter" by Jo Ann Beard
- "People Are Starving" by Suzanne Rivecca
- "The Knife" by Richard Selzer
- "Street Haunting" by Virginia Woolf

Print Resources

- *Truth Serum: A Memoir* by Bernard Cooper
- "After Yitzl" by Albert Goldbarth in *A Sympathy of Souls*
- "Things of This Life" by Judith Kitchen in *Only the Dance: Essays on Time and Memory*
- *The Elements of Style* by William Strunk, Jr., and E. B. White
- *A Postcard Memoir* by Lawrence Sutin

13

The Writing Process and Revision

I have rewritten—often several times—every word I have ever published. My pencils outlast their erasers.

—Vladimir Nabokov

In graduate school, I once submitted a workshop story that nobody liked, not one person. I remember one woman: she dangled my work in front of her and said, her lips curling in distaste, "I don't understand why this story even exists!" As I walked home that night—dejected and furious—I could still tell that her comment, though poorly worded, had something in it I needed to hear. It has stayed with me throughout the years, and now, when I'm at the final stage of revision, it's her question I hear in my head: *Why does this essay exist?* I go back to work.

At this stage in the writing process, the draft becomes nothing more than a fruitful scavenging ground. Right now, as I write, I'm in the middle of Wyoming, and down the road a huge junkyard lies at the intersection of two minor highways. Against the rolling fields of wheat grass, this junkyard rises as ten acres of glinting metal, bent chrome, colors of every hue. One of my fellow colonists, a sculptor, began buying scraps to incorporate in her work: gorgeous landscapes with ribbons of rusted metal juxtaposed across blue skies.

Now I've come to see the junkyard as a place of infinite possibility. What useful parts still hum in the innards of these machines? How will they be unearthed? What kind of work would it take to make them shine?

—Brenda

The Drafting Process

> Writing is easy; all you do is sit staring at a blank sheet of paper until the drops of blood form on your forehead.
>
> —GENE FOWLER

When you first sit down to work, you may have no idea what the writing will bring. Maybe it even scares you a little, the thought of venturing into that unknown territory. Perhaps you circle your desk a while, distracting yourself with chores or email, wary of the task at hand. Or maybe you are the type of writer who can sit down and start writing without hesitation, training yourself to write at least one full paragraph before stopping. You know you'll go back and trim and revise, so you just keep the words coming.

Either way, the important thing to know, for yourself, is your own style. In the first case, to the untrained eye, you may appear engaged in nothing but mere procrastination. But if you know yourself well, you understand that puttering is essential to your writing process. Or, in the second case, you act more like an athlete in training, knowing that routine and discipline are essential for your creative process. You write quickly because that's the only way for you to outrun your inner critic. Neither way is "correct." The only correct way to write is the way that works for you.

The writing process is just that: a *process*. You must have the patience to watch the piece evolve, and you need an awareness of your own stages of creativity. You must know when you can go pell-mell with the heat of creation, and when you must settle down, take a wider view, and make some choices that will determine the essay's final shape.

Discovery Drafts

> I don't write easily or rapidly. My first draft usually has only a few elements worth keeping. I have to find what those are and build from them and throw out what doesn't work, or what simply is not alive.
>
> —SUSAN SONTAG

First drafts can be seen as "discovery drafts"; much of the writing you did from the prompts in Part 1 will fall into this category. You are writing to discover what you know or to recover memories and images that may have been lost to you. You are going for the details, the unexpected images, or the storyline that reveals itself only as you go along. The best writing you do will have this sense of exploration about it; you allow yourself to go into the unknown, to excavate what lies beneath the surface.

It's important to allow yourself permission to write *anything* in a first draft; otherwise you might censor yourself into silence. The first draft is the place where you just might light upon the right voice for telling this particular story; once you're onto that voice, you can write for hours. If you train yourself to write without overthinking the material, it will also become easier to let some of that writing go when it comes time to revise. (For ideas on how to use writing groups, contracts, and challenges to spur new writing, see Chapter 14, "The Power of Writing Communities.")

The Revision Process

No matter how good your discovery draft material seems at first glance, most often it will need some shaping and revision before it is ready for public eyes. Revision, perhaps, is an acquired taste, but you may find that revision actually becomes the most "creative" part of creative nonfiction. It is in revision that the real work begins.

Global Revision

Revision can often be mistaken for line editing. There is a time, naturally, for going back to your prose to fine-tune the grammar, change a few words, and fix typos. But first you need to look at the essay as a whole and decide what will make this essay matter. What is the *real* subject of the piece? What image takes on more significance than you realized? What now seems superfluous? We call this "global revision."

Elizabeth Jarrett Andrew, in her book *Living Revision: A Writer's Craft as Spiritual Practice,* describes global revision this way:

> I recently learned a new way to understand the word "respect." The roots are the same as "revise"—to see again. The surprising similarity between these

words shines a fresh light on revision: When we see something anew, we come to respect it. Each new perspective, each layer of understanding, deepens our regard. Seen in this light, revision is the most respectful approach to our writing.

It's beneficial to take some time between drafts at this stage of the process. After that first heady flush of creation settles down, you'll better be able to pinpoint the areas that sing and those that fall flat. You'll be able to notice an unexpected theme that emerges organically through the imagery you chose. You'll hear how the ending may actually be the beginning of your piece. Or the beginning may make for a better end. Andrew describes this process as listening for the "heartbeat" of your piece. Where is it most alive? What new material does the writing demand to flourish? (See Try It #1 at the end of this chapter for ideas on how to go about this global revision process.)

At this point you need to see the work as fluid, with infinite possibilities still to come. What you may have intended to write may not be the most interesting part of the essay now. Be open to what has developed in the writing process itself, and don't be afraid to cut out those areas that no longer work.

Ask yourself this question: What is the essence of the topic *for this particular essay*? Many times it's easy to think that we have to put in everything we know or feel about a topic in one essay. You have to figure out what is necessary for this essay *and this essay alone*. You will write other essays about the topic, don't worry. As writer Natalie Goldberg put it, "Your main obsessions have power; they are what you will come back to in your writing over and over again. And you'll create new stories around them."

You may keep only a small portion of the original work, perhaps even just one line. But by doing this kind of pruning, you enable new, more beautiful and sturdy growth to emerge. Take comfort in knowing the old work may find its way into new essays yet to come. If it's hard for you to let go of a section completely, put it in a "fragments" file and know that you will call it back sometime in the future. Time and again, we have found new homes for those bits and pieces of prose that just didn't work in their original homes.

The Role of the Audience

When you're writing a first draft, it's often necessary to ignore any concept of audience just so you can get the material out. An attentive audience, hanging on your every word, can be inhibiting at that stage of the writing process. But when you're revising, some concept of audience will help you gain the necessary distance to do the hard work that needs to get done.

This audience can be a single person, an ideal reader you have in mind. Or the audience can be much larger. Many times, having a reading venue or publication in mind can focus your attention in a way that nothing else can. Many towns have readings in cafés or bookstores where beginning and experienced writers are invited to read their work to an audience. If you are brave enough to commit yourself to reading one night, you will find yourself in a fever of revision, reading the piece aloud many times and getting every word just right.

Or you might decide that you're ready to start sending your work out for publication. Find one journal and read as many copies as you can, then revise your piece with this publication in mind. You'll surprise yourself with the focus you can generate once the piece leaves the personal arena and goes public. (See Chapter 15, "Publishing Your Creative Nonfiction," for more details on the publication process.)

Three Quick Fixes for Stronger Prose

After you've done the hard labor on your essay, you'll want to do the finish work, the small things that make the prose really shine. This is often called "local revision." (We don't mean to suggest these two processes are mutually exclusive; naturally you will find yourself adjusting the prose as you go along.) We have three quick fixes that make any piece stronger: "search and destroy," "the adjective/adverb purge," and "the punch."

Search and Destroy

The most overused verbs in the English language are variations of *to be*—these include *is, are, were, was*, and so forth. While these verbs are necessary (note how we just used them!), often you can sharpen your prose by going over the piece carefully and eliminating as many of these weak verbs as you can. To do this you will need to look closely at the words surrounding the *to be* verbs; often you can find a stronger verb to take its place or a juicier noun. Even if you eliminate just an *is* here or a *was* there, the resultant prose will seem much cleaner and lighter. It's the kind of work the reader won't notice directly (except for word nuts like us), but it will immediately professionalize your prose.

Take a draft of an essay that is nearly finished. Go through it and, with a red pen, circle all the *to be* verbs. Go back and see if you can rework any of those sentences to replace them with verbs that feel more "muscled," have more impact to them. Sometimes you'll find you don't need the sentence at all, and you'll have eliminated some deadweight. If you're working in a group, exchange essays with one another and do the same thing. Suggest new lines that eliminate the *to be* verbs.

The Adjective/Adverb Purge

Often, adjectives can be your enemy rather than your friend. Adjectives or adverbs can act as crutches, holding up weak nouns or verbs, and they actually water down your prose rather than intensify it. As with the search-and-destroy exercise, the point here is not to eliminate adjectives and adverbs altogether, but to scrutinize every one and see if it's necessary for the point you want to get across.

Take an essay you think is nearly finished and circle every adjective and adverb. Go back and see if you can rework the sentences to eliminate these words and replace them with stronger verbs, nouns, or both. Or you can take stronger measures. For at least one writing session, ban adjectives and adverbs from your vocabulary. See how this exercise forces you to find more vivid nouns and verbs for your prose.

The Punch

Professional writers develop a fine ear for language. Writers are really musicians, aural artists attuned to every rhythm and nuance of their prose. And when you study the writers you admire, you'll invariably find that they tend to end most of their sentences, all of their paragraphs, and certainly the closing line of the essay, with potent words that pack a punch. They do not allow their sentences to trail off but close them firmly and strongly, with words that leave the reader satisfied. When you work toward strong closing words in your sentences, the prose also takes on a new sense of momentum and trajectory, the sentences rearranging themselves in fresh ways to wield that satisfying "crack."

Read your essay aloud, paying attention to the sounds of the words at the ends of sentences and paragraphs. Do they ring clearly, firmly ending your thought? Or do they trail off in abstraction? Circle any words that seem weak to you; then go back and rework these sentences for better closing effects. Pay particular attention to the word you use to end the entire essay. How do you leave your readers? What will they remember?

An Example of the Writing Process

We asked the writer Bernard Cooper for his thoughts on the writing process. Here is what he had to say:

> I edit relentlessly—have already revised this very statement. My prose itself tends to come in short bursts, while the bulk of my time is involved in trying different words and sentence structures and punctuation so those word-bursts say exactly what I want them to. Revision seems to me the writer's most crucial task; you are given the chance to make your work as powerful as possible. "Words are all we have," said novelist Evan Connell, "and they'd better be the right ones." Anyone who has written for long knows the pleasure in finding the word that makes a description suddenly more vivid, or finding the structure that makes a sentence more taut, surprising, rhythmic, or funny.

When you write well, revision becomes not a chore, but the essence of the writing act itself. What came before cleared the way for what is to come; no writing is ever wasted, no time spent at the desk useless. Writing creates its own rhythm and momentum, and you must be willing to go with it, to become absorbed in the task, to let go of the writing you once thought precious.

At one time or another, many writers experience what they call "gifts"— essays or poems or stories that seem to come effortlessly, full-blown onto the page with little revision or effort. But as the poet Richard Hugo put it, "Lucky accidents seldom happen to writers who don't work. . . . The hard work you do on one poem is put in on all poems. The hard work on the first poem is responsible for the sudden ease of the second. If you just sit around waiting for the easy ones, nothing will come. Get to work."

TRY IT

1. Practice global revision. Take out a piece you wrote at least a month ago. Read it aloud, either to yourself or to a kind audience. Here are some specific questions to ask yourself as you go about the global revision process:

   - What is the piece *really* about? Write this theme or idea or emotion down in a word or short phrase and use it as a guiding force for revision.
   - Is there one image that can be used as a cohesive thread throughout the piece? How can you amplify this image and transform it from beginning to end?
   - Have you chosen the most effective point of view for telling the story? What happens when you experiment with third person? Second person?
   - Look closely at the beginning paragraph of your essay. Do you begin in a way that draws the reader in? Often, the first few paragraphs of a rough draft act as "clearing the throat." Is the true beginning really a few pages in?
   - Look closely at the end of the essay. Do you end in a way that leaves the reader with a compelling image? Often it's tempting to "sum up" the essay in a way that can be wholly unsatisfying to the reader. Can you end on an image rather than an idea?
   - How do the beginning and ending paragraphs mirror or echo one another? The first and last paragraphs act as a frame for the piece as a whole. They are, in a way, the most important places in the essay, because they determine everything that happens in between. If you make an effort to connect them in some way—repeating a key image from the beginning, bringing back on stage the major players for a final bow—you will find a stunning finish to the piece.

2. In Elizabeth Jarrett Andrew's book *Living Revision,* she suggests creating a visual diagram of your essay. Draw a circle that represents the core or the "hub" of your essay. Write inside it one or two words that distill the essence of your essay so

far: the theme you identified in Try It #1. Then draw a larger circle around it, and within this circle write down notes about what you've already written in the essay. Then draw a third larger circle, within which you'll jot notes about the scenes, memories, and/or experiences that are *not* in the essay yet and possibly should be. Contemplate this diagram to see if it gives you a road map on how to proceed in global revision. What needs to stay? What needs to go? What new sections still need to be written?

3. Practice local revision, using the "Three Quick Fixes for Stronger Prose" section in this chapter. Go through an essay that you feel is nearly done, circling first the verbs, then the adjectives and adverbs, then the end words of each sentence. What do you notice when you highlight these important areas of your sentences? How can you rework even a few of these sentences for stronger effects? Share this process with others to get their eyes on this material as well.

4. Refer to Chapter 1, "The Body of Memory," and Chapter 12, "The Basics of Good Writing in Any Form." Use the categories in those chapters to revise your work. Look for places that could use more sensory detail or scene. Is there a moment where you could slow down and expand the imagery? Consider your characters: Are they fully formed? What about your structure? How about your tenses? Are you tied to past tense or present tense? Where can you make some changes to strengthen the overall effect of your piece?

FOR FURTHER READING

Resources Available Online:
- *Grammar Girl* sends out a weekly newsletter with handy tips for common grammar and stylistic challenges.

Print Resources
- *Living Revision: A Writer's Craft as Spiritual Practice* by Elizabeth Jarrett Andrew
- *The Elements of Style* by William Strunk, Jr., and E. B. White

14

The Power of Writing Communities

The fiction that artistic labor happens in isolation, and that artistic accomplishment is exclusively the provenance of individual talents, is politically charged and, in my case at least, repudiated by the facts. While the primary labor on *Angels* [*in America*] has been mine, more than two dozen people have contributed words, ideas and structures to these plays.

—Tony Kushner

In graduate school, I had the dream writing group: friends who made me laugh and who were also careful and attentive readers. We met in a quirky little room at a local tavern, a room decorated with Moët and Chandon champagne posters. Before settling into our work, we shared what we'd all been doing that week, in the areas of writing, submitting, and acceptance or rejection. Nothing seemed so terrible once we laughed about it, sometimes passing around our form rejection slips (these were the days of paper submissions!).

One evening during our critique session, my friend Dan pointed out to me something I had not noticed in my work and that I needed to know: I tended to end every poem I wrote with an apostrophe, a direct address to the reader. Once I heard that, I looked my poems over and realized Dan was absolutely right. I hated writing endings, and I had developed this literary tic of speaking out of the page to make them easier. Read five poems of mine in a row, and the reader might feel shouted at! I needed to get out of this habit.

A strong writing group provides much more than feedback on your individual pieces (though that is a gift). Group members become one another's cheerleaders, informal literary agents, even cocreators. They stay alert for the journals and presses suited to each other's work. And they notice strengths, and also those weaknesses—those tics, those unconscious repetitions—that build up in everyone's work over time. A good group also helps us internalize the ability to read our own work with a critical eye. Decades later, I still scan my work for the kinds of strengths and problems my groupmates pointed out to me under the champagne signs.

—Suzanne

The Need for Feedback

Tony Kushner, in the quote introducing this chapter, states the case strongly but not, we think, too strongly. Writers need feedback. The myth of writers as loners who follow their vision and remain true to their inner muse, bucking rather than embracing outside help, is very much a myth. It was created largely by the writers of the British Romantic period, whose artistic mythologies we still cling to, though those writers themselves used one another unceasingly as idea sources and sounding boards. Virtually all writers do.

The modern writing workshop or writing group is not an innovation but a form of learning that can be traced back as long as literature and the arts have flourished. You can use this chapter to find ways to create your own workshop group—one with members you trust, who can grow with you and your work—or to get the most productive working relationship you can out of a classroom workshop or an established writing group.

Setting Guidelines for Discussion: A Practice Approach

In the following section on learning to give useful responses, we will provide very specific suggestions for shaping workshop discussion. You may use or adapt these as your group sees fit. For now, it is a good idea to have a preliminary talk with your peers about what does or does not work for you as a group in receiving feedback. You can and should discuss the entire practice of workshopping, come up with a procedure, and devise your own workshop etiquette—a collective sense of what is OK and not OK in talking about your writing. Logistical questions to discuss include how far in advance you will share your work, whether you will read pieces aloud at any point, and whether you want to include written comments or limit yourself to oral critique. If you are doing this as a workshop leader or teacher, consider having the group create a specific "contract" that you will all try to follow.

It is essential to find a method of discussion with which the group feels safe and comfortable; don't flounder around trying to shape your valuable writing without first defining what helps you. To guide this process, find an essay, perhaps from a literary magazine, for practice. Read the piece and offer comments as you would in a workshop setting, and together monitor the discussion for responses that seem diminishing, unconstructive, or unhelpful.

Safety to speak and inclusion should be your priorities, so listen carefully and be sure everyone in your group articulates their needs and their experience of what is said, and how it is said. The writer Beth Nguyen writes of her writing workshop experience, including the rule of author silence during discussion, as creating a "forceful imbalance of power." Talk openly about what makes us feel comfortable or uncomfortable as writers and workshop citizens, particularly for writers of marginalized identities.

Helpful Language

You may want to ask the group to rule out feedback based on "I like, I don't like" formulas. These are by their very nature subjective comments and hard to use in the revision process. One way to train ourselves out of the "I like, I don't like" reflex is to begin the discussion by using the phrase "I notice" instead. For example, "I notice the image of the maple tree recurs three times in the essay," or "I notice the strong connection between the dog and the woman," or "I notice the momentum of your sentences." By noticing, instead of judging right away, the reader allows the writer to hear what stands out in the piece, and to hear it in a way that does not automatically flatter or degrade the writer. It takes away some of the emotional energy—both positive and negative—that can get in the way of a writer really absorbing what the reader sees in his or her piece. Once several readers have "noticed" what is happening in your piece, you will get an in-depth sense of what stands out and what has not yet emerged. Your respondents can then go on to explicate the meaning or theme they see developing in the things they noticed, and how these images or scenes or sentences can lead to fruitful revisions.

All of you together can watch out for unhelpful critical language—"stinks," "lame," "one cliché after another." Of course, we don't advocate only praise; those words probably do hold suggestions for revisions that need to be made. What's important is that you work together as a group to find more constructive approaches. "This doesn't come up to the level of the rest of the essay," "I'm not seeing this scene yet," or "The language here could be more original" might be suitable comments to replace the offending ones.

Even when you hear responses that feel appropriate, use this practice session to sharpen them. If someone says he or she can't quite get a feel for a character, question why that is and try to formulate the most specific response possible. "I can't quite see David because he's never described and never speaks until you find him crying in the kitchen." Try reformulating your feedback comments two and three times to make them as specific as possible. Practice together until you feel good about one another's feedback style and the comments feel supportive, encouraging, and full of ideas to take back to your writing desk.

The Agenting Approach

One workshop strategy we have had great success with is the agenting approach. It is a role-play method. All the members of the writing group agree to function as one another's literary agents for the duration of the group.

Literary agents take on their author-clients because they believe in them. Agents feel certain they can sell their clients' essays and books. They derive their income from sales of their authors' work, so their faith in their authors is concrete and tangible. At the same time, agents become valuable critics and editors. They must bring their clients' work to the publishing market in its finest possible form.

As an agent your comments are always couched in terms like, "I think this will really work once the dialogue feels more authentic/Jack has a fuller character/we know where Luke ended up." Like an agent, you will always begin your responses by citing what *does* work, and, where appropriate, providing ideas for transferring that success to less polished parts of the essay.

When beginning this approach, it can help to write out comments in the form of letters—the type of communication you'd likely get from a literary agent. These letters will begin with an affirmation of your faith in your client; a summary of what works well in the piece; and a careful, detailed listing of what needs to be addressed before the piece is finally ready. These letters can be used to fuel discussion and passed to the author at the end of a workshop session. A wonderful side benefit of the agenting approach can be, when you reach a phase in your group relationship where lots of revision has taken place, you can decide to devote an hour or two to browsing at the periodical section of a bookstore or a library or looking online to find suitable publication venues for one another's work. (See Chapter 15, "Publishing Your Creative Nonfiction.")

Here are a few more guidelines to consider.

- **Don't be subjective or start talking about your own experience** unless there's a specific reason to, such as an expert knowledge you can add to the work at hand. ("I've worked at an emergency room and I don't think it would be painted bright pink," not "I've worked at an emergency room; isn't it weird?")
- **When you give praise,** see if you can add even more to your comment by suggesting another place where the same writing tactics can help the essay. Do provide revision suggestions freely, along with support and encouragement. The other side of the workshop coin from the pick-it-all-apart session is the lovefest, which ultimately disrespects your peers' ability to bring their work to a higher level, and does them no good.

Remember always that as you give to others in your group, you will get back. You have a deep commitment to their growth as writers and to the productive workings of the group as a whole, so always act accordingly. Also, we often learn the most about our own writing while listening carefully to critiques about someone else's work. What is true for that person struggling with a satisfying ending is probably true for you as well. Don't assume that the only time you learn anything is when your own piece is up for discussion.

Some Useful Workshop Guidelines

Here are a few tips for making the group work.

- **Agree to distribute copies of writing to be workshopped no less than forty-eight hours in advance of your meeting.** Agree beforehand whether emailed copies are acceptable, or whether your group would prefer printed copies, or an online group document program such as Dropbox. Agree on whether or not you will write comments directly into the document, or save all comments for discussion. Make sure your essay is carefully proofread. Some readers will also appreciate being able to make typed comments directly on the manuscript.
- **Set an amount of time you will spend on each essay, with a five- or ten-minute degree of flexibility.** Twenty minutes to half an hour usually works.
- **Have one of you agree to facilitate the discussion.** Facilitating means making sure the conversation stays within or lasts until the assigned period. Facilitators can also throw out topics or questions as necessary (each piece under discussion can have a different facilitator). We remember one poorly run graduate workshop in which the instructor simply allowed the group to go on as little or as long as it liked, leading to discussions that ranged anywhere from five minutes to an hour. That's a frustrating, insulting experience for an author, so agree in advance to monitor your time and keep comments on track. If you are the facilitator of the group, you can decide whether to guide each discussion or to assign others to lead for one another.

One method we've found useful for some mature groups is to have the teacher or leader hold off on making comments on the manuscript itself or during the workshop, but instead take on the role of "scribe," writing down as much as possible during the discussion, being the impartial observer on behalf of the writer. Then, after the workshop, leaders can write up a summary of what they heard, as well as revision suggestions based on the group's comments and their own opinion. For example, they can couch responses with phrases such as, "I heard many voices saying _____, while others disagreed and felt the most important part of the essay was _____. You have a few choices here in how to revise." In this way, the writer—who is often too nervous or overwhelmed to clearly hear what is being said—can relax, knowing another is listening carefully. This technique also models how to begin sifting through comments and dealing with contrary opinions, understanding that there is always more than one way to approach revision. Writers must learn how to both trust their own intuitions and take guidance from others.

This method also gives teachers or leaders a chance to think about their own responses in light of the group's feedback, and by doing so validates the democratic nature of group discussion. The leader is often a privileged responder, which can make the group members lax in their own feedback; by sitting back and taking on the role of invested listener, facilitators empower the group process itself and may also hear responses that shift their own perception of the piece.

Small-Group Versus Large-Group Workshops

The workshop approach we have described works well in a group of eight to fourteen people; often, at the college level—or in a larger community group—your class sizes are likely to be larger. You can still choose to do a whole-class workshop, but one way to help modulate the responses is to have every other person in the circle respond directly to the writer (it is helpful to structure the discussion loosely on the "Workshop Checklist" later in this chapter), varying the order for different questions.

Another way to approach discussion is to break the group down into smaller workshop circles. The advantage to this method is that all participants will be heard and will feel freer to speak; the writers all gain a certain amount of trust and understanding with one another over time. The disadvantage, of course, is that the leader cannot oversee each discussion group. Leaders can offset this by handing out workshop guidelines ahead of time and by assigning each person in the group to be the "advocate" for one other person in the group. This advocate is responsible for ensuring that the discussion stays on track, that the group answers the writer's questions, and that a positive, helpful atmosphere takes precedence. Leaders might consider varying small-group with large-group workshops to provide a variety of responses.

A Workshop Checklist

In addition to the general suggestions outlined earlier, here is one intuitive way to read an essay to be discussed. We suggest you use the following questions when you read, picking and choosing as seems appropriate, rather than marching through them one by one in the group. Facilitators can also keep this checklist handy as a way of sparking conversation when it begins to lag.

1. **Jot down the scenes, descriptions, and images that stick with you:** the "Velcro words and phrases," as writer and teacher Sheila Bender puts it. Put the essay down and make note of the first thing you remember about it. Generally these passages are the ones that not only are the best written, but the most key to what the essay is doing at a deep level.

2. **Identify the emotional tones of the essay and its prose.** You may sense the pleasure of a friend's visit, of a hike, the anxiety of sentences that all begin with "I think" or "I believe." Do you get the sense of over-formality in a phrase like "I am perturbed"? Do you wonder why the author calls her mother by the definite article, "the mother"? Does it feel somewhat chilly? In all cases, are these feelings ones the author intended to convey, or do they seem unintentional and perhaps working against the movement of the essay?

3. **Identify your curiosity.** Make note of where specifically you want to know more. "I want to know more about that distant definite-article mother," "about that feeling of perturbation in the pit of the stomach," "about the author's uncertainty," "about the rest of the family," and so forth. Which locations and characters would benefit from more description? Which characters' voices do you want to hear? Where do you want to know more about the author's responses and feelings? These curiosities help locate places for expansion.

If you need help going deeper with your comments, here are some **content questions** to consider:

- **What is the organizing force of the essay,** and does it sustain the piece? If this essay has a clear narrative (a story to tell), is the story clear? If it is a lyric essay organized around images, do the images keep it going?

- **Are characters effectively presented** and fully developed?
- **Is dialogue believable,** important to the overall essay, and used where it needs to be? Does it help shape character?
- **Are there places where exposition should be replaced by scene** for greater reader involvement or scene replaced by exposition for greater compression?
- **Is the point of view working well?** Would it help to try another point of view, for example, substitute first person for second?
- **If this is a meditation or essay of ideas, is there an ideology behind it?** Is it presented clearly? Is it presented in a way that respects the reader, rather than becoming preachy or heavy-handed?
- **Are the images fresh and interesting?** Do they work together in a way that supports the essay?
- **Is the language strong throughout,** avoiding sentimentality and cliché?

Here are some **form questions** to keep in mind:

- **Does the form of the essay add to or enhance its content?**
- **Is the organization effective?** Look closely at elements such as collaging, the use of white space "jumps" between material, and whether the piece's organization is purely chronological, following the order in which events happened, or something else.
- **Does the piece begin and end in a way that feels satisfying?** Note that "satisfying" does not necessarily mean providing closure or full answers to any questions it might raise. Does the essay open in a way that makes you want to keep reading, and end in a way that provides some sort of aesthetic stopping point?

These samples will help you with **diction questions**:

- **Does the language seem appropriate to the subject?** Is it at times overly fussy or formal or overly slangy and flip?
- **Does the essay contain any archaic or outmoded language**—a trap we all fall into in literary writing—that doesn't belong?
- **Are the sentence structures and rhythms appealing and effective?**

You might also look back to Chapter 13, "The Writing Process and Revision," and think about feedback in terms of "global" versus "local" responses. Train yourself to begin with "big picture" responses: What is the piece *really* about for you? What theme or idea seems interesting, ripe for future development? What connections are being made in an original way? What one image really stood out for you? Why? Then shift your group's feedback to more "local" concerns, looking at what can be cut, what can be modified, what can be added, and what can be moved around.

Creating Your Own Writing Group

The veteran publisher Stanley Colbert wrote, "Your journey to the bestseller list begins with a single reader." All of the people you come in contact with who share your interest in writing and literature are resources for forming a writing group. Even if you are writing in a creative writing classroom, an out-of-class group with compatible peers will help you generate much more work, and receive feedback on it.

Who are your friends or acquaintances who love to write? If you've never talked with them about forming a response group, try it. Most writers spend their lonely writing time dreaming of an audience of enthusiastic readers—chances are, you will be proposing something they'll regard as a dream come true. If you're shy about your writing and find it hard to think about sharing it with your cat, let alone a group, try this: Look at the first few questions in the workshop checklist, given previously in this chapter. Now think of a piece of your writing and imagine answers to those questions. Chances are the thought of hearing a list of your Velcro scenes and images, the places you've made a reader curious, will actually seem pretty pleasant.

The fact is, when we worry about sharing our work, we imagine ourselves handing an essay to someone and saying, "What do you think?" and standing, knees trembling, for the final judgment. Well, first of all, no one has the all-knowing literary judgment to do that (J. K. Rowling got dozens of rejections, some quite "rude," in her words, for the first *Harry Potter* novel). Second of all, delivery of verdicts is not what writing groups are for, and you should never let yours drift into that destructive habit. Remember, you can and should exert control about the feedback process, and talk about it as a group until you get it right.

Kate Trueblood, an author and teacher of writing, formed a group with three other writers she knew who seemed compatible. Though the group was friendly and supportive, the workshop did spend a few meetings having to fine-tune their discussion style. "At first it was a little jumbled and unfocused, and feelings were hurt," Kate remembers. The group communally generated a list of rules that's kept them going successfully for many years now. "We talk about what's successful first, then acknowledge amongst ourselves when we're moving to critique. We work from global issues to smaller issues. And each time we pass out a manuscript we designate what kind of feedback we want, and what stage the work is in."

If you don't know anyone interested enough or compatible enough to form a workshop group with you, you still have another excellent resource—your local bookstore. Many bookstores have active writing groups that meet regularly and often welcome new members.

If you find your bookstore(s) does not have a workshop group, start one. Ask to speak to the store manager of a bookstore you like, or in a larger store, the community relations coordinator. These folks will generally help you, by posting signs and advertising in store newsletters and calendars, to find other folks in your community interested in sharing their writing. From the interviews we've done with bookstore personnel, the response will almost certainly be strong: there are a lot of writers seeking readers out there. From the bookstore's point of view, it's a way to lure literature lovers into their store on a regular basis. From your point of view, it's heaven: a group of peer reviewers, and a comfy place to meet.

For many writers, an online writing group works very well, too, as it can bring in people who don't live in your area, as well as be adapted to everyone's schedule. This could be a generative writing group, where you give each other writing prompts (perhaps from this very book!) and deadlines, or it could be focused on providing feedback on work written on your own. If it is a generative writing group, you might want to stay focused simply on "Velcro" phrases and images, speaking back to the writer the areas that seem rich with meaning and beauty. You might want to rotate the duties of facilitator so that there can be some order and cohesion in how you function together.

The Writing Group as Writing Practice

Throughout history, writers have depended on their artist friends to help generate new and fresh ideas. During the Romantic period, four writers—Percy Shelley, Mary Shelley, Lord Byron, and Dr. John William Polidori—challenged one another to write a ghost story. Polidori wrote *The Vampyre*, the start of reams of vampire literature. Mary Shelley wrote *Frankenstein*, one of history's most renowned novels. Sylvia Plath and her husband Ted Hughes created constant writing assignments for themselves, many based on what they could see from their home—a full moon in a yew tree's branches, an ancient elm.

Writing groups can commit to generating new writing together in addition to providing critique, or they can simply exist as generative groups. When we write with others, we feed off one another's energy and focus. We're accountable to stay on task for the allotted time, and we have a reason to be writing. This type of generative writing group doesn't have to be large (even one other person can be plenty!), and it's probably best to keep it fairly small to nurture the focus and camaraderie necessary to this endeavor—fewer than ten members (though some of us thrive in larger groups). Like critique groups, generative groups can work beautifully together online. Large or small generative groups are also a powerful addition to a creative writing classroom.

Writing Contracts and Challenges

Sometimes it helps to have a formal "contract" to get your writing done. In such a document, you would set forth your goals for a time period: say, a week, a month, or a summer. These goals can be anything: writing for a certain amount of time per day; writing a certain number of words per day; writing a certain number of pages a week; completing a certain number of short pieces or a long essay; submitting work to journals; and so on. You can create a contract with just one other person, or with a group of friends.

This next part is key: you must have either *rewards* or *consequences* for fulfilling or not fulfilling your end of the bargain. One writer we know allows herself a piece of high-quality chocolate when she finishes her daily goal. Another writer agrees to clean her friend's oven if she doesn't fulfill the contractual obligation (that's a powerful motivator). You get the idea. By making yourself accountable in a concrete way, you may have more motivation to make your writing life a priority.

Like a contract, a writing challenge can take place over a specified time period, and usually involves much more intensive, daily work, with a wider literary community. In recent years, we've seen the rise of programs such as National Novel Writing Month (NaNoWriMo) in November, and National Poetry Writing Month (NaPoWriMo) in April. Recently, November also became National Memoir Writing Month (NaMeWriMo). If you join in one of these national challenges online, you'll often receive a daily prompt for your writing and a way to share that writing with others. You can adapt the format of one of these challenges for your own writing group.

TRY IT

1. It is so simple, and yet so wildly creative, to create writing challenges for a group. Bring this book to your group meetings, with everyone choosing a favorite Try It. Then riff on these: you can select a formal structure, like a hermit crab, for all of you. If you meet in person, pick an element of your surroundings to write about, as Plath does in her poem "Elm" (you may want to bring this poem to read). Borrow from Michel de Montaigne and choose an innocuous body part to write about, as he does in "Of Thumbs," or a sense to explore, as he does in "Of Smells" (see Anthology). It can be helpful to share your pieces as you go, possibly by reading aloud, but without critique.

2. Each group will have its own character and working style, of course, but we can offer you some suggestions for how to use the time effectively. Groups that can't or would rather not meet in person can follow the same procedures, using a video calling/conferencing program, or whatever system works for your group.

   • Begin with a timed writing (about five to ten minutes). You can choose a word at random to start the writing, or a phrase from a book you have handy.
   • Decide whether you want to share this writing. If sharing, do not give feedback. Simply listen.
   • Each person can be responsible for bringing a writing prompt for the meeting. This prompt can be from a text such as this one or a prompt the

writer devises. You can each write to this prompt for a specified period, between fifteen minutes to an hour, or whatever works for your group.

- Or: You can work on individual projects for a specified time, such as forty-five minutes to an hour.
- Share what you did at the end of the time. Again, no feedback, to keep this space purely generative and judgment-free.

For Further Reading

Resources Available Online

- "Unsilencing the Workshop" by Beth Nguyen
- "Towards a Better Nonfiction Workshop" by Will Slattery

15

Publishing Your Creative Nonfiction

Essays end up in books, but they start their lives in magazines.
(It's hard to imagine a book of recent but previously unpublished
essays.) . . . The influential essayist is someone with an acute sense
of what has not been (properly) talked about, what should be talked
about (but differently). But what makes essays last is less their
argument than the display of a complex mind and a distinctive
prose voice.

—Susan Sontag

It's 1993, and I've just received my copy of the *Georgia Review*, where my
essay "A Thousand Buddhas" sits among the pages. It's my first acceptance
by a national literary journal, and I can hardly believe it. It took a long time
to write that essay and even longer to figure out where to send it, to wait
through the evaluation process, and then to work with the legendary editor,
Stan Lindberg, over the phone. It's both thrilling and terrifying to finally see
it in print.

It's 2018. I've submitted a piece to a journal using the online submission
manager Submittable. The program creates an account for me so that I can
see where my submission is at every stage of the process. Within a week, I
have my answer from the editor, and a couple of weeks after that, the essay
actually appears in the online edition. The process seems a little dizzying in
its swiftness. And I'm still both thrilled and terrified to see the piece in print.

The publishing world has changed a lot in the last twenty-five years, but
some things never change: the need to write the best creative nonfiction I

can, and then to do the necessary work of finding it a good home—whether that home be in a traditional print journal or in a quality online publication. The writing process, for me, does not feel complete until I've sent the work out into the world to stand on its own.

—Brenda

Getting published involves more than just writing your best work; it means knowing where that work will get a good reception and how to revise so that the essay makes it past the eyes of the first readers. It means understanding the type of publication that might be receptive to your work: A print literary journal? An online journal? A venue that can offer multimedia capabilities? Or perhaps what you have written belongs in a magazine like *Harper's*, a women-oriented magazine like *O* or *Elle*, or a specialty magazine like the environmental magazine *Orion*. All of these venues are possibilities, but it is vital to learn how to gauge and approach your potential audience.

Once you start aiming toward publication, your writing will take on a new level of professionalism. You may find focus where before there was just a blur, or you'll finally figure out the dead prose that's slowing down your first paragraph. Think like an editor, with hundreds of essays crossing your desk or your computer every month: What will make your essay stand out from the crowd?

Publication Venues

Literary Journals

These journals are literary publications, often but not always housed at colleges and universities, run by people who are in the business of publishing mostly because they love literature. They offer prestige, a small (around the low thousands, typically) but devoted readership, and exist on the low end of the payment scale. Acceptance rates are low, too, frequently 1 to 2 percent, and even lower for prestigious journals like the *Kenyon Review*. Literary journals often have particular editorial directions, such as *Image*, a journal of spirituality and the arts, or *Seneca Review*, which leans strongly toward the lyric essay. Some literary journals print artwork and other media. It's important to read carefully as you select potential homes for your work.

The good news? You can develop warm, even mentoring relationships with editors of literary journals, who are passionate about great writing. Literary agents also read literary journals to get ideas about potential new clients whose writing they find exciting.

Online Journals

Online literary journals are as important a venue for literary writers as print journals. Print journals tend to have readerships in the low thousands; online journals may average ten thousand or more views per issue. The difference is largely due to accessibility and reading habits on the web—most web users surf and sample many different websites. Finally, the cost of creating an online publication is minimal—you have to learn the programming, which isn't hard, and find a server that can accommodate your files. Most universities have servers students can request space on. The low cost of start-up, however, means online journals frequently pay little to nothing.

There's a distinction between online publications that publish traditional print literature—posting it as it would appear on the page—and those that publish a mix of traditional print literature and literature that is by its nature web-based. There are also online journals that publish only hypertext- and hypermedia-type digital literature. In the first category would be a quality online journal like *Brevity*, which publishes short—750 words or less—creative nonfiction. In the second category would be journals like *TriQuarterly Online*—whose formats encourage interactive reading—and in the third category would be *The New River*, a gold-standard site publishing some of the best hypertext- and hypermedia-type digital literature around.

Browse online journals using a site such as *LitLine* and the list hosted by *Every Writer's Resource* (see the list of websites at the end of this chapter). Enjoy the spirit and experimentation of this medium: streaming audio, streaming videos, art, even virtual communities are common. Let both your mind and your eye become engaged, and new possibilities will open for your own nonfiction.

Target Your Work

To target your work to the markets most likely to publish your particular brand of nonfiction writing, do your research. Browse in the library, bookstores, and newsstands as well as on your computer. Send away for sample issues of magazines. This will save you time and money. Editors hate getting work that comes from writers who obviously have never even cracked the covers of one of their issues.

Visit the websites of your target publications and read the submission guidelines posted. These guidelines will let you know the submission format the publication prefers, and they give further details on how to submit, such as the publication's reading period—most do not read unsolicited material year-round—payment, and length limits. Also go online to the Association of Writers and Writing Programs (AWP) for a list of quality literary journals; other lists can be found at *New Pages*, *LitLine*, and other sites on the web.

Most publications these days use an online submission service. Many use a service called Submittable, which allows you to upload your work onto a host site for editors to consider. Online submission enables you to check in on your submission, and you can even click a box to withdraw your work if it should be accepted elsewhere. Just because you are using online submission services, do not skip the cover letter! It should be as polished and complete as with a print submission.

Aim high, but not unrealistically so. It's important to start establishing a publishing history, so don't hesitate to send off to smaller, lesser-known journals. Getting your name out there in the publishing world will lead to greater and greater opportunities. Finally, look for contest and anthology submission opportunities. Good resources for these are *The Writer's Chronicle* (published bimonthly by AWP and *Poets & Writers* (published bimonthly, available in bookstores).

Breadcrumbing

Read widely, fall in love with other writers, research literary journals and publishers. Check out agents, if that's appropriate for you. Even when you do all of these things, though, it can feel overwhelming to figure out just what people and places are right for you. Who are the literary professionals most likely to be smitten with your work?

A process we and the writers we work with use is one we call "breadcrumbing," and it is enormously helpful. Create a list of writers you admire and whose work feels similar to yours, in form, aesthetics, subject matter, or other qualities. Perhaps your writing uses a similar compressed lyric style, incorporates history or food, explores body image. List writers whose work shares this kind of DNA with your own. Then find these authors' books. Note for yourself what literary publications publish these authors. Read these writers' Acknowledgements pages (or other forms of thank-yous) very carefully. Add to your list the names of literary agents and editors they thank. If these writers thank friends who have helped by reading their manuscripts, you may want to check these folks out too—many active writers also edit.

This breadcrumbing will give you a running start on submitting your work—a list of venues, editors, and publishing houses tailored specifically to your particular interests and talents.

Elements of Your Submission

1. **Your essay, polished to perfection,** with extra care taken on the first and last paragraphs. There should be no typos, grammatical errors, punctuation errors, messy print, or anything else that will undermine the professionalism of your work. Put your name, address, phone number, and email address on the upper left-hand corner of the first page. Number the subsequent pages on the upper right-hand corner, using your last name as part of the header. Example: "Miller—2."

2. **Your cover letter.** Use standard business format. Keep it short and simple. Avoid the impulse to be jokey or overly familiar. If you can, offer sincere praise of the publication that shows you are a reader as well as a would-be author. Do *not* tell the editor what your essay is about! The essay should stand on its own.

3. **For print submissions, include a business-size self-addressed stamped envelope (SASE)** for the magazine's response. If you want your manuscript returned, use a large enough envelope and sufficient postage.

Generally, your submission process will happen online; the journal may charge a small fee that covers their costs.

Keep a record of your submissions, noting the date, the place sent, the title of the essay, and the result of the submission. You can also use an inexpensive submission manager, like Duotrope, to track your submissions.

Literary Agents

The function of literary agents tends to be something of a mystery for many writers, even for those well along in their careers. The fact is, many writers write and publish successfully without a literary agent. You should aim to work with a literary agent only if you feel you have a book project well underway, or have amassed excellent publication credentials, *and* you do not see yourself placing your work at a smaller, independent publisher or a university press. Agents exist to get your work placed at the larger publishing houses that pay substantial advances and publish books that they anticipate receiving substantial royalties. These are the publishing houses that exist, whatever individual editors may feel about literature, to earn money and maintain a healthy bottom line.

Agents earn their living by taking about 15 percent of their authors' earnings. In return for that, they talk up your work to editors they know and have a strong working relationship with, submit your work for you, and make sure your interests are represented when an offer comes along. Bear in mind that no reputable agent ever charges a "reading fee" or any fee other than what can be deducted from your advances and royalties, along with compensation (once the book is placed) for copying and other costs attached to the actual submission process.

Publishing a Book

Collecting Your Essays

As you become more adept at writing short pieces of creative nonfiction, you may find yourself looking at these pieces with an eye toward developing a book. This is where a different kind of fun begins! You'll begin to ask yourself these kinds of questions: What themes seem to naturally arise in your work? How are your essays connected? What happens when you put them together to mingle?

Rebecca McClanahan, in her essay "Forest in the Trees: The Challenges of Shaping a Book (Not a Collection) of Essays," makes a distinction between a "collection," which might simply gather together the best of your work in one place, and a "book," which she describes this way: "A well-shaped *book* of essays is another genre altogether; though each essay can and should stand alone, each also relates to the other essays in significant ways." She elaborates:

> I never set out to write a *book* of essays, nor do most of the essayists I know. Rather, we find ourselves writing one essay, then another, then another. (I like how that sentence came out—*we find ourselves writing*—as if writing helps us find ourselves, which of course it does.) After a while, the essays accumulate. "How many do you have now?" a writer-friend asks. "Enough for a new book?" Well, that depends. Maybe enough for a collection, but a book? I'd have to think about that. Do all the essays talk to each other in interesting ways? Is there a center point, a hub, into which all the spokes fit? If I had to write the cover copy for this book, what central elements would I highlight?

If you think you might be ready to consider putting together a book of individual essays, have patience. Give yourself the time and space necessary for such an endeavor. One way to do this is to print out the essays. Find a big table, or use the floor, to spread them out, seeing them in new ways. Shuffle them around like puzzle pieces. What kind of invitation do you give the reader with the first essay? On what kind of tone or note does the book conclude? What is the role of the midpoint essay? How do the essays transition from one to the next?

Try several different orders, keeping an open mind. As with an individual essay, look for a guiding theme. What will this book be about? There will be some hard decisions: some essays you love just might not fit in this design, or they might be too similar to other essays in the book. Or the voice might be too jarring for the tone of the book as a whole. You might see gaps, opportunities for new essays that have not yet been written.

Study books of essays you love. How do they keep you engaged? How do they set the tone and theme from the very beginning? You might find that some books invite the reader in with a very short prologue essay that telegraphs what is to come. For example, in her book *Just Breathe Normally,* which collects short fragments detailing her recovery from traumatic brain injury, Peggy Shumaker opens with a prose poem titled "Just This Once." It begins:

> Once, in a wild place, I felt myself quiet down. I listened, drew silent breaths. It was dangerous not to warn the bears I was there, no question. But I wanted to live one moment in a wild place without disturbing the other creatures there. This delicate moment laced with fear—a life wish.

Though this scene has nothing to do, directly, with her injury and recovery, Shumaker (who is also a poet) decides to use lyric language and imagery to highlight deeper themes that will be an undercurrent for the book as a whole: how we deal with fear; how fear is an inherent part of being fully connected with life.

The Book Proposal

If you think your writing might lead you to a book-length project, it's useful to know that many nonfiction books now—particularly the ones placed at the larger publishing houses—are sold on proposal (following we give an outline of a typical proposal structure). Writing a good book proposal has become an art in itself—proposals can range anywhere from twenty to forty pages long or longer and may take months to complete. Philip Gerard spent four months researching and writing the book proposal for *Secret Soldiers: The Story of World War II's Heroic Army of Deception*, a time commitment that's not unusual. As with publications of individual essays, book publications cover a variety of venues. There are the large, mostly New York–based houses that would include W. W. Norton, Knopf, Doubleday, Penguin, Random House, HarperCollins, and other imprints. These are the publishers that pay top dollar in advances and have access to the best publicity machines in the business, the kind that can get valuable TV and radio spots and take out prestigious and visible advertisements.

These large houses are, of course, the hardest publishers to get interested in your project, and the hardest to keep interested in you as an author: they publish books for the purpose of making money, and the fact is, in this competitive arena, the majority of books do not earn out their advance money. With the exception of W. W. Norton, these publishers are owned by large conglomerates, so you may find that many book imprints—Viking, Penguin, Putnam, Tarcher—are all housed in the same company. When you try your manuscript with one editor in the conglomerate, the rejection is typically final; much of the time you cannot go back and try other editors in the firm. Agents are particularly qualified to know what editor in the maze of imprints owned by one publishing conglomerate would be best for your project.

Nonfiction books can go out to smaller presses and to book contests in complete form, but generally, larger publishers make offers based on book proposals. At times, agents want to see a book proposal before taking on a new client. There are many books and websites with valuable information on writing a successful book proposal. Literary agents, too, will have a great deal of input about what kind of proposal will make your project shine. What follows is a typical proposal format. And note that even if you do not want to present a complete book proposal to a publisher, the information on marketing, comparable books, audience, and author bio and platform are useful to keep in mind for *any* book submission.

How to Write a Book Proposal

The Overview

This should be a short—three-to-five page—overview of what the book is about and why it matters. Editors will want to know what happens in your book, but they also want to know the significance of it to the reader. Why is this book important? What is it doing that is new?

Chapter-by-Chapter Outline

This will do just what it sounds like it will do—provide two to three paragraphs about each chapter. Consider what events happen in each chapter, but also what characters and concepts are introduced, and how the elements of the chapter work toward the whole. Make sure this stays congruent with your overview.

Author Bio

Most of us have brief bios we use that outline our educations, achievements, publications, and so forth. While that information is useful here, what editors will be looking for is "platform"—what have you done professionally that will enable you to connect with readers? Perhaps you have a blog with thousands of followers, or you have lived in a particular place and had an experience few others have had. Use every scrap of information that makes you seem like the right person to write this book and to find a wide audience.

Comparable Books

Sometimes this category goes under the name of "Competition" or "Competitive Titles," which indicates the kind of dance authors have to do with this section. You want to indicate that there are books out there that are similar to yours and that they have found an audience. It's tempting to write in screaming capitals in this section that THERE IS NOTHING OUT THERE LIKE MY BOOK! NOTHING! (See? We just did it.) But if it's the case that no book like yours exists—and it rarely is—you are asking publishers to take a heck of a risk on you. You do want to make it clear that your book is going to add something to the literary world that is new and necessary. Provide a few sentences, at most a paragraph, on each title you regard as comparable or competitive, and how you build on them.

Target Audience

Clarify as definitively as possible who will buy your book. What people will be invested enough to purchase it? Be specific and do your homework. And don't broad-brush it: publishers don't want to know how many readers there are for researched nonfiction, or for memoir, or family history. State as clearly as you can how many potential readers there are for this topic. Explain how you know this potential group of readers exists.

Marketing

In this section, you will list what you can do to market this book, making your plans as practical as possible. Describe what you have already done in the way of gaining publicity—working with readings, newspapers, interviewers, radio, and so on—and how you will use this previous experience to market this book. Can you arrange a "blog tour," in which you will contact established bloggers offering to write a guest post? Would journals that have published your writing be willing to help publicize it? If you know of influential writers who will offer to give you a blurb, give their names. Be creative. Publishers want to know what you will do to promote your own work.

Sample Chapters

This section is just what it sounds like. Include one to two chapters of your book (more if they are short) that show both your writing, and your book's intentions, in the best possible light.

Small Presses

You are not stuck if you cannot get a press like Knopf interested in your book. Small, independent presses and university presses publish books that win major awards and reach important audiences. These presses may not offer the same advance money as the larger houses, but they are less likely to over-edit your work and more likely to commit to you as an author over the long term. Their marketing can be hit-and-miss. You should always check out how well any smaller publisher is able to distribute its books—actually get them into bookstores—as well as get them reviewed and advertised.

Self-Directed Publishing

More and more presses out there will help you publish your book as well as provide a variety of support services, for a cash investment from you, the author. These presses often go by the terms *independent* or *indie* publishers (though, confusingly, small presses might use the term *indie* as well). Their price for a publishing "package" can run into many thousands of dollars. And services like copyediting can be extra, adding to the bill. The support services they offer may include publicists and cover designers, as well as in-house editors. They should have a sound distribution process in place. Unless you know the press well, ask a lot of questions, including what kind of support they will give, and how other books of theirs have done. Finally, your royalties with presses like this will be quite high—above 50 percent of sales, or higher.

Presses that have a curating process—in other words, they don't simply accept every manuscript that comes in—call themselves *hybrids*. As with other indie presses, hybrids will charge for publication and other services. These presses will have the advantages of other indie publishers, along with some degree of consistent quality in their list. Indies and hybrids can grow to a size that gives them advantages in the complex publishing market. She-Writes Press, for instance, is a hybrid publisher that uses Ingram, one of the most important book distributors in the business, for its books.

Yet another avenue of self-directed publishing is the *cooperative* press. These are presses run by the authors themselves, though they may have publicists and designers, as well as other professionals, on call for their authors. Book View Café is a well-known cooperative press, founded by Ursula K. Le Guin. Book View publishes mostly ebooks, and membership is open to any author who has received in the past a traditional advance-and-royalties book contract. Members pitch in to do the work of providing feedback and editing to their peers' books, as well as publicity after publication. Some writers' cooperatives are founded just to publish the work of the founding authors. Many, though, are open to new members.

There are many online forums offering advice and how-tos for self-publishing. *Self-Publishing Review*'s website offers a lot of valuable information for authors considering this route. The Independent Book Publishers Association also has a wealth of information on their website.

A Final Note

It is wonderful—and a privilege—to think ahead to a lifetime of being a writer. Self-expression constitutes one of the great joys of life. And one of life's most common—and keenest—regrets remains, "I should have written it down." People lament not having written down their stories for a book-buying audience, for children and grandchildren, for others who have shared similar experiences, and ultimately for themselves.

You, our readers, have this to look forward to: the fact that your own indelible imprint on the world can be captured in the nearly indelible medium of language, be it ink or pixel. You need to ask yourself the question of what you want your written legacy to accomplish, and set your publishing goals accordingly. All the while, keep in mind that most important of all, you are building the tools of self-expression you need to satisfy the one you most need to satisfy in life—you.

TRY IT

1. Give yourself a period of time—perhaps one or two weeks—to focus on bread-crumbing. List ten authors you love whose writing you find resonates with your own. You can't always see these connections, so you might ask writer friends for ideas. Create a comprehensive list of editors, journals, publishers, and agents (if you are seeking agents), based on your breadcrumb trail. We always advocate buying books if you possibly can. But if buying all these books is financially pro-hibitive, browse a literary bookstore. Do your background research, and then plan submissions based on your breadcrumbing.

2. Write a sample cover letter:

   March 6, 2019

   Wendy Woe, Editor
   A Great Little Journal
   Anywhere, Any State, U.S.

   Dear Wendy Woe:

   I've enclosed the personal essay "The Road Home" for your consideration. It covers a time period I spent working at a New Age ashram in Sedona, Arizona. I think, given your interest in personal essays that involve larger social commentary, it would be a good fit for your journal.

   My work has appeared or is forthcoming in _____ (and/or) I am currently studying nonfiction writing with _____ .

   Thank you for your time and consideration.

   Sincerely,

   Signature

   Print your name, street address, phone number, email address, and website address, if you have one, at the bottom of the page.

Variation for a group: Pass around your cover letters, and write cover letters for one another. You may think of ways to present each other's work that you would not come to on your own.

FURTHER READING

Resources Available Online
- American Association of University Presses offers a listing of university presses.
- Association of Writers and Writing Programs has links to numerous journals, magazines, and presses, as well as other useful information.
- *Electronic Literature* offers a portal site for a great deal of nonfiction published on the web.
- *Every Writer's Resource* offers an excellent list of literary publications and a wealth of other information.
- *LitLine* contains many literary publishing listings.
- *New Pages* offers a listing of independent presses.
- *Poets & Writers.*
- *Self-Publishing Review.*
- *WritersNet* offers a variety of useful resources and advice on everything from agents to freelance writing for writers looking to publish their work.

Print Resources
- *How to Write a Book Proposal* by Michael Larsen
- *Literary Market Place*
- *Write the Perfect Book Proposal: Ten That Sold and Why* by Deborah Levine Herman and Jeff Herman (presents ten actual book proposals that resulted in book deals, with analysis)
- *Writer's Digest*

16

Putting on Our Editors' Hats

I submitted work seventeen times to *The Georgia Review* before any was accepted. This makes me think that often we stop too soon, just when an editor is finally getting used to the voice or the style, just before an editor is sure that you have staying power. . . . I've only met one person who has never received a rejection slip.

—Judith Kitchen

Every week, I spend many hours reading submissions for the *Bellingham Review.* I get as comfy as possible: a soft chair, a good view of our local, snow- and cloud-tipped volcano. I do this because reading submissions takes a lot of time. Like most editors-in-chief, I have several layers of pre-readers. Initial readers forward material that seems strong to my genre editors, who read in the areas of nonfiction, fiction, poetry, and hybrid works. All my editors are keen and savvy and the work they forward to me contains much that is praiseworthy. And yet the great majority of what I read, I know I will have to decline. Like all literary magazines, the *Review* accepts only a small fraction of what we get—in our case, about 2 percent.

As I read through my forwarded submissions, two essays stop me. I return to them and reread them several times. Both have much to recommend them—striking characters, a unique story. Yet both also pose problems. One essay weaves together many narrative threads, yet rushes through them to an oversimplified ending. The other lacks characterization and detail. It is tempting in both cases to go back to the author with a provisional acceptance, contingent on revision. How do I make this call?

Well, Author One wrote a precise, yet detailed, cover letter making it clear that author knew our journal well and respected our editorial mission. This person used editors' names and had read and thought about recent issues. Author Two sent a generic note addressed to "Dear Editor," with no letter, only a canned bio.

With little hesitation, I write a detailed, provisional acceptance to Author One, and send a note of rejection to Author Two. Perhaps I'm wrong in my assumptions, but I have little to go on besides how these writers address me and my journal. The sense I get from their letters is that Author One admires us and would be pleased to work with us. Author Two appears to be doing scattershot submissions with little sense of each publication. If I am going to put my time into a complex letter with revision ideas, I want to feel I am investing my time wisely and directing it toward an interested writer. And in this way many editorial decisions are made (and unmade!).

—Suzanne

I've been asked to be a judge for a national literary contest. The initial screeners for the contest have forwarded to me ten finalist pieces, all anonymous; these are the essays that have risen above the rest (most contests receive hundreds, if not thousands, of entries). Now it's up to me to evaluate the essays side-by-side to determine the winner.

I begin by reading the first paragraph of each essay, no more. The first paragraph is so important in this situation (and really any publishing situation): it's where you will establish the content, the theme, the form, and the writer's unique voice. The first paragraph must be perfect. In this case, most of them are; they must be, to make it this far.

But even in this elite group, a few stumble: they use the first paragraph to summarize, rather than engage us directly with the story; or there's a phrase that's either clichéd or what I call "packaged language," something we've heard so often that anyone could have written it. Some writers are too flippant in the first paragraph or too melodramatic. With some, the real essay starts later in the piece.

And then I turn to the end and read the last paragraph of each piece. That's odd, you might think, to read the ending before seeing the entire piece. But just as with beginnings, the ending can often signal whether a writer has polished this essay to its brightest shine. If a writer summarizes with a "moral of the story," the essay will fall flat. But if the essay just "stops," without any sense of closure, it will leave the reader feeling a bit empty. The writer must walk a fine line here, providing closure while still keeping the essay open for interpretation. Ending on a strong image, rather than an idea, is usually what I'm looking for.

About half the finalist essays pass these tests. So I read those first, allowing myself to fully engage with them on their own terms. Before ranking them, I read the others, noting how these essays might succeed with a few revisions, and to make sure my initial impressions play out. Then begins the hard work of picking the winner, a big responsibility, knowing this decision might be huge in this anonymous person's writing career.

—Brenda

Between us—Brenda and Suzanne—we have twenty years of editorial experience. Both of us have served as editor-in-chief of the *Bellingham Review*, housed at Western Washington University. Suzanne has also guest-edited two online journals, and we've served as judges for national and university contests. Our editing has covered four genres and print as well as online platforms. Both of us know the exhaustion and exhilaration of editing—receiving far more submissions, even top-notch submissions, than we can use. And discovering new writers whose work we are thrilled to find and to present. Here are our best tips, as we don our editors' hats.

- **The cover letter.** A great cover letter, as we discussed in Chapter 15, "Publishing Your Creative Nonfiction," should be one page at most, not jokey or overly familiar, and knowledgeable about the journal addressed. Tell us about yourself, but also show that you are familiar with our publication. Better no cover letter at all than the generic "Dear Editor" followed by a canned bio.
- **Polish your first paragraph to perfection.** Make sure it will draw the reader in. Eliminate *any* clichéd language. As you do your final revisions, be open to changing your first paragraph, or moving a paragraph from later in the essay to the beginning.
- **Understand the successes that precede publication.** Few writers go from zero to acceptance. To put our opening Judith Kitchen quote—citing the one rejection-free writer—into context, Kitchen knew

thousands of writers. Editors look out for writers they find exceptional in some way, and even if they can't make an offer of publication, write notes of encouragement. Do not underestimate the importance of these kinds of positive responses. In our experience as editors-in-chief, about 10 percent of submissions make it through the preliminary reading process to us. Out of that fraction, perhaps another 10 percent warrants a personal letter. If you receive a note of praise, mark it down somewhere and try that journal again when you have work that is top-notch.

- **Proofread.** Nothing gets you out of the editorial queue faster than errors. This is true no matter how your work resonates on other levels. Cleaning up misspellings, grammatical errors, and typos is more work than editors are prepared to do. And a sloppy submission feels disrespectful. If you are not a proofreader, cultivate someone who is. Swap favors, bake that good proofreader some cookies. And practice. Proofreading is a cultivated skill, like any other.

- **Understand that truly, it is almost always not you.** All journals share the need to mix up their content. Once at the *Review* we realized we had published several essays in a row featuring animals. Editors keep an eye out for repetitions, whether of form or of content, and they happen to us all the time. We also experience sudden increases in one genre, or geographical clustering. A surprising percentage of editorial decisions are based on these kinds of factors.

- **Submit widely and submit a lot.** The greatest error committed by new submitters is not sending out enough. In this era of multiple submissions, each essay you feel is ready should go out to four or five venues. Having ten or more submissions out at a time, if you have multiple pieces, is reasonable. Don't choose one "perfect" journal for each piece and submit only to that one. Take the "it is almost always not you" bullet point to heart. There are far too many reasons beyond quality that your perfect publication cannot take your work.

  Look at it this way: a 2 percent acceptance rate is typical for a literary journal, and some are more selective than that. You have to be rejected ninety-eight times just to be normal!

- **Choose a submission tracking method that works for you.** Sending more work to a journal that already has your work under consideration, or sending back the same thing, feels to us editors as a sloppy manuscript does—you're not doing your homework. There are inexpensive submission tracking services. Excel spreadsheets work for other writers. For yet others, their tracker is a stack of note cards. Whatever you do, make sure you keep on top of your submissions.

TRY IT

1. Most communities house presses and literary journals. Volunteer to read submissions for a publishing venue in your area (if you have a connection to a journal or press elsewhere, you may be able to read long distance through their submission service). This sort of reading can provide a quick and powerful education in the dos and don'ts of submitting.

2. If you're in a class, ask the instructor to have an editor visit to provide you and your peers with an overview of the publishing world as that editor sees it. Schedule a question-and-answer session to get a picture of how professionals make those selections of literary work to publish. Or ask an editor to visit your writing group.

3. Do a feedback session where you look only at the first and last paragraphs of a piece. Be ruthless. How does the writing draw you in (or not)? Does the essay end on a vivid, original note? If you were reading hundreds of anonymous submissions, how would this piece stand out (in a good way)?

PART IV

ANTHOLOGY

Read, read, read. Read everything—trash, classics, good, and bad, and see how they do it. Just like a carpenter who works as an apprentice and studies the master. Read! You'll absorb it. Then write. If it is good, you'll find out. If it's not, throw it out the window.

—WILLIAM FAULKNER

Reading as a Writer

There's no getting around it. Reading and writing go hand in hand. You cannot be a good writer without also being a good reader. You read to hear other writers' voices, but you also read to tune up your *own* voice, to remember what gets you excited about writing in the first place. Through reading, you continually learn the craft all over again.

Throughout *Tell It Slant*, we refer to many fine essays to illustrate key points in writing creative nonfiction, and at the end of each chapter we provide a list to guide you in further reading (these lists are by no means a comprehensive accounting of great creative nonfiction!). Many of these readings are available online as well as in print. For your convenience, we've also compiled the following anthology with essays that illustrate a wide variety of the concepts we've introduced in this book.

Reading For Craft

The following questions can help focus your reading on craft, skills, style, and techniques. We suggest you read the essays once for content, then again with a few of these questions in mind. You can reflect on each of the essays in writing or in discussion with fellow learners.

You might also develop your own writing prompts from each reading. What skills would you like to practice? What content does the writing inspire in you?

Questions for Reading as a Writer

1. What are the major themes (ideas, moods, lessons) in this piece? Are there any minor themes as well? Do you see a motif (a recurring pattern or theme) in this piece?

2. What specific, small details stay in your mind? Why? What senses are involved in creating these details? How do these small details lead to larger ideas (or themes)?

3. Does the author use details or images to create metaphor or simile? Is the metaphor an effective way to communicate meaning?

4. What kind of rhythm (or voice) does the writer create? Is there variety in the sentence structure or line length? Read the piece aloud to get a sense of the writer's voice.

5. Try to identify scenes (that include concrete writing) in contrast to reflection or expository writing (which tends to be more abstract). What is the balance between the two?

6. How does the writer suspend key moments in time? In other words, how do we linger in a scene that might take only a few moments in real life? Why do you think the writer suspended this particular moment?

7. What tenses does the writer use (present, past, future, speculative)? What are the effects of these tenses? How does the writer combine tenses to create layers of time?

8. What point of view does the writer use? Is it always from the first-person (I) point of view? Does the point of view remain the same throughout the piece? Does the narrator speak from a child's perspective or an adult perspective? or both?

9. How does the writer structure the piece and to what effect? (Why does it begin where it does? Why does it end with the image or scene the writer chooses?)

10. Look at the transitions between paragraphs or between stanzas. How does the author make these transitions? What effect do they have on the forward momentum of the piece?

Questions for Creative Nonfiction in Particular

1. What is "creative" about "creative nonfiction"?
2. When does the "creative" part become "fiction"?
3. What ethical considerations must writers take into account?
4. How does a writer gain access to memory? How can this memory be represented both accurately and aesthetically?

5. How do writers incorporate research in creative nonfiction?
6. How do we overcome inhibition while writing in this genre?
7. How can personal stories become interesting to others? What makes them "universal?" Do they need to be? Are some stories relevant only for a particular audience?

1

The Fine Art of Sighing

Bernard Cooper

You feel a gradual welling up of pleasure, or boredom, or melancholy. Whatever the emotion, it's more abundant than you ever dreamed. You can no more contain it than your hands can cup a lake. And so you surrender and suck the air. Your esophagus opens, diaphragm expands. Poised at the crest of an exhalation, your body is about to be unburdened, second by second, cell by cell. A kettle hisses. A balloon deflates. Your shoulders fall like two ripe pears, muscles slack at last.

My mother stared out the kitchen window, ashes from her cigarette dribbling into the sink. She'd turned her back on the rest of the house, guarding her own solitude. I'd tiptoe across the linoleum and make my lunch without making a sound. Sometimes I saw her back expand, then heard her let loose one plummeting note, a sigh so long and weary it might have been her last. Beyond our backyard, above telephone poles and apartment buildings, rose the brown horizon of the city; across it glided an occasional bird, or the blimp that advertised Goodyear tires. She might have been drifting into the distance, or lamenting her separation from it. She might have been wishing she were somewhere else, or wishing she could be happy where she was, a middle-aged housewife dreaming at her sink.

My father's sighs were more melodic. What began as a somber sigh could abruptly change pitch, turn gusty and loose, and suggest by its very transformation that what begins in sorrow might end in relief. He could prolong the rounded vowel of *oy*, or let it ricochet like an echo, as if he were shouting in a tunnel or a cave. Where my mother sighed from ineffable sadness, my father sighed at simple things: the coldness of a drink, the softness of a pillow, or an itch that my mother, following the frantic map of his words, finally found on his back and scratched.

A friend of mine once mentioned that I was given to long and ponderous sighs. Once I became aware of this habit, I heard my father's sighs in my own and knew for a moment his small satisfactions. At other times, I felt my mother's restlessness and wished I could leave my body with my breath, or be happy in the body my breath left behind.

It's a reflex and a legacy, this soulful species of breathing. Listen closely: My ancestors' lungs are pumping like bellows, men towing boats along the banks of the Volga, women lugging baskets of rye bread and pike. At the end of each day, they lift their weary arms in a toast; as thanks for the heat and sting of vodka, their aahs condense in the cold Russian air.

At any given moment, there must be thousands of people sighing. A man in Milwaukee heaves and shivers and blesses the head of his second wife who's not too shy to lick his toes. A judge in Munich groans with pleasure after tasting again the silky bratwurst she ate as a child. Every day, meaningful sighs are expelled from schoolchildren, driving instructors, forensic experts, certified public accountants, and dental hygienists, just to name a few. The sighs of widows and widowers alone must account for a significant portion of the carbon dioxide released into the atmosphere. Every time a girdle is removed, a foot is submerged in a tub of warm water, or a restroom is reached on a desolate road . . . you'd think the sheer velocity of it would create mistrals, siroccos, hurricanes; arrows should be swarming over satellite maps, weathermen talking a mile a minute, ties flapping from their necks like flags.

Before I learned that Venetian prisoners were led across it to their execution, I imagined that the Bridge of Sighs was a feat of invisible engineering, a structure vaulting above the earth, the girders and trusses, the stay ropes and cables, the counterweights and safety rails, connecting one human breath to the next.

2

Leap

Brian Doyle

A couple leaped from the south tower, hand in hand. They reached for each other and their hands met and they jumped.

Jennifer Brickhouse saw them falling, hand in hand.

Many people jumped. Perhaps hundreds. No one knows. They struck the pavement with such force that there was a pink mist in the air.

The mayor reported the mist.

A kindergarten boy who saw people falling in flames told his teacher that the birds were on fire. She ran with him on her shoulders out of the ashes.

Tiffany Keeling saw fireballs falling that she later realized were people. Jennifer Griffin saw people falling and wept as she told the story. Niko Winstral saw people free-falling backwards with their hands out, like they were parachuting. Joe Duncan on his roof on Duane Street looked up and saw people jumping. Henry Weintraub saw people "leaping as they flew out." John Carson saw six people fall, "falling over themselves, falling, they were somersaulting." Steve Miller saw people jumping from a thousand feet in the air. Kirk Kjeldsen saw people flailing on the way down, people lining up and jumping, "too many people falling." Jane Tedder saw people leaping and the sight haunts her at night. Steve Tamas counted fourteen people jumping and then he stopped counting. Stuart DeHann saw one woman's dress billowing as she fell, and he saw a shirtless man falling end over end, and he too saw the couple leaping hand in hand.

Several pedestrians were killed by people falling from the sky. A fireman was killed by a body falling from the sky.

But he reached for her hand and she reached for his hand and they leaped out the window holding hands.

The day of the Lord will come as a thief in the night, in which the heavens shall pass away with a great noise, wrote Peter, *and the elements shall melt with a fervent heat, the earth also and the works that are therein shall be burned up.*

I try to whisper prayers for the sudden dead and the harrowed families of the dead and the screaming souls of the murderers but I keep coming back to his hand and her hand nestled in each other with such extraordinary ordinary succinct ancient naked stunning perfect simple ferocious love.

There is no fear in love, wrote John, *but perfect love casteth out fear, because fear hath torment.*

Their hands reaching and joining is the most powerful prayer I can imagine, the most eloquent, the most graceful. It is everything that we are capable of against horror and loss and death. It is what makes me believe that we are not craven fools and charlatans to believe in God, to believe that human beings have greatness and holiness within them like seeds that open only under great fires, to believe that some unimaginable essence of who we are persists past the dissolution of what we were, to believe against evil hourly evidence that love is why we are here.

Their passing away was thought an affliction, and their going forth from us utter destruction, says the Book of Wisdom, *but they are in peace. They shall shine, and shall dart about as sparks through stubble.*

No one knows who they were: husband and wife, lovers, dear friends, colleagues, strangers thrown together at the window there at the lip of hell. Maybe they didn't even reach for each other consciously, maybe it was instinctive, a reflex, as they both decided at the same time to take two running steps and jump out the shattered window, but they *did* reach for each other, and they held on tight, and leaped, and fell endlessly into the smoking canyon, at two hundred miles an hour, falling so far and so fast that they would have blacked out before they hit the pavement near Liberty Street so hard that there was a pink mist in the air.

I trust I shall shortly see thee, John wrote, *and we shall speak face to face.*

Jennifer Brickhouse saw them holding hands, and Stuart DeHann saw them holding hands, and I hold on to that.

3

Jumping the Fence

Marjorie Rose Hakala

Out of the daily feedings and training and classes and animal-visitor encounters of a zoo, there is little that makes it into the news. The stuff that gets the public's attention and brings out the journalists tends to fall into three categories: 1) An animal was born. 2) An animal died. 3) The barriers broke down. Something got out of the zoo, or someone got in.

Births and deaths are reliable; they happen to every creature in the zoo and every person on the planet. Check the obituaries in the same newspapers, or the ambulance runs, or the society pages. But the escape stories are something else. These were never guaranteed to happen. They are disruptions of a sort found in few other places. To stage an escape, you need a cage.

A few years ago, my mother was by herself at the Point Defiance Zoo in Tacoma, Washington. It was an overcast weekday and there was hardly anyone there, so she was on her own when she got to the musk ox enclosure. She must have caught the eye of one of the musk oxen; when he saw her looking at him, he got onto his hind legs, putting his front legs on the railing that ran around the interior of the enclosure, and with one of his front hooves he smashed the glass wall between them.

Mom backed off in a hurry and wasn't hurt, and the break wasn't enough to allow the animals to escape. But she couldn't find anyone to tell about what had happened, so it was up to whatever staff member happened across it to clean up the glass lying on the ground, showing that the pane had been broken from the inside, and to consider whether something ought to be done about the musk oxen.

The same thing must have happened to other people. At the Ranua Wildlife Park in Finland, I saw a sign that said, "Watch out, the musk ox can push the fence. Please, keep your head and hands outside of the enclosure." I wondered how to interpret this information. Can they push the fence *over*? Do they like to push their legs *through* it? Either way, if the musk oxen decide to push on the fence, aren't we at risk even without sticking our heads and hands into their territory?

I told this story at a social gathering and a woman I know volunteered a story of her own. She was in dental school at the University of Minnesota in the late 1970s. She belonged, informally, to the dental fraternity on campus (there was no dental sorority). One night she was out with two of her fraternity brothers, both of whom were a little bit drunk, and they rode their bicycles to Saint Paul's Como Zoo shortly before closing. Inside the zoo, they went up to the ostrich enclosure and saw that there was a nest holding two eggs just inside the fence. The fence was basic, straight-up-and-down, without any inward curve or barbed wire at the top. Hey, said the slightly drunk dental fraternity brothers. We dare you to climb over the fence and steal that egg.

And she did, without stopping to consider. She climbed the fence and dropped down onto the other side, where the eggs, a foot and a half in circumference, were lying out in the open. She picked one of them up and then realized that she had been seen. Not by a person: by the ostrich. Ostriches, it is worth mentioning at this juncture, run faster than any other two-legged animal—over forty miles per hour at a sprint. A nest robbery is probably a good occasion for a sprint. The ostrich took off in the direction of my friend; my friend scrabbled up the fence, dropped the egg to her friends below, and jumped down herself, and all of them took off on their bikes. They weren't pursued, and the egg theft, as far as she or I can tell, was never reported in the news. This is the sort of thing that can happen in a zoo that is truly open to the public, unwalled and unguarded: sometimes members of the public drop in and help themselves.

According to some sources, dead dogs and cats used to be accepted as admission to the Tower of London menagerie, in place of the fee of three halfpence. If visitors brought an animal, it would be fed to the lions while the people watched. It was a treat to see this happen.

When I worked at the International Wolf Center in northern Minnesota, we had a special program every week called "What's for Dinner?" where guests could watch as the wolf pack got fed a roadkill deer. Sometimes there was a fetus in the deer's womb. Sometimes a wolf peed on a portion of food to claim it. Some of our guests found this disgusting. One demanded to know why we didn't put live deer in the enclosure for the wolves to hunt. My coworker told him there would be an ethical problem with doing that. He said, "Sounds more like a pussy problem."

On a visit to the Bronx Zoo in 2012, I was just in time to see the penguins get fed. I got a little lost on the way there, distracted by the old stone buildings and the peacocks wandering the grounds freely with their tails dragging behind them, and when I finally passed through the hanging plastic flaps that curtained off the penguin exhibit, I was startled by the quiet I found there. It was an outdoor area, housing Magellanic penguins from South America, not Antarctic penguins that would have needed ice. Only some low fiberglass walls separate the penguins from the spectators. It's not too hard, I suppose, to pen in a flock of short and flightless birds. A zoo employee was standing on the island among the birds in tall galoshes, carrying a bucket of fish. The skinny and speckled penguins stood around her and craned their necks up toward the fish in her bucket. She distributed the food carefully, fairly. One of the birds got harried away by its fellows, and the keeper went after it, crouched down, and fed it some pieces of fish while keeping the others away. Some of the penguins made a little noise, honking like geese or braying like donkeys, but the keeper ignored them and went about her work, peaceful and long-legged like a heron among the squat penguins. She ignored the people watching her, and we were quiet in return. The whole thing was so simple that I was surprised it had been put on the schedule of programs for the day. It wasn't a showy intrusion. The zookeeper looked like she belonged in there, like she had crossed a barrier that none of us could cross.

The Bronx Zoo did have an escape in recent years. In a story reminiscent of *Harry Potter*, an Egyptian cobra got out of its case and went missing. The story alternately delighted and unsettled the public nationwide. Someone started a "@BronxZoosCobra" Twitter feed detailing the snake's adventures in New York City: attending a Yankees game, ordering bagels, and riding the ferry to Ellis Island. After all the hoopla, it turned out the snake had barely even escaped: it was eventually found in the World of Reptiles building where it had always lived, "coiled in a secluded dark corner" according to the *New York Times*. A peahen escaped the same zoo less than a month later and got off the zoo property entirely. But this was a less remarkable escape: peafowl wander the grounds of the Bronx Zoo freely, usually staying close to where they are fed, and this one chose to leave. She was apprehended inside a garage in the Bronx.

We trust in impermeable boundaries in zoos, but the entire experience depends on permeability. We go to the zoo in the hope that something meaningful is passing through the glass, between the bars, or over the moat. We want to see the animals and for them to see us back. But we don't want them to respond to us the way most animals instinctively would, by running away or (if they're musk oxen who don't like eye contact) by breaking the glass. The International Wolf Center has microphones inside the wolf enclosure connected to speakers in the building, so that visitors can hear the wolves despite the walls and soundproof glass between them. The guests inside the building sometimes howl at the wolves in hope that they'll respond. Usually the wolves can't hear and don't howl back, but they can see the guests and respond to their presence. Toward the end of the tourist season when I worked there, I often saw the wolves come out of hiding two minutes after the last visitors had left the building. The visitors who howled imagined a dialogue with the wolves, but if they could really make themselves heard, the result would be a wolf pack under constant stress, taking out aggression on each other because they couldn't take it out on whoever was making those assertive noises, impinging on their territory.

Harmless animals might escape the most often, but bigger ones can get out too. Casey the gorilla escaped from Como Zoo in May of 1994. He didn't hurt anybody in his brief time outdoors, and he was soon shot with a tranquilizer dart and coaxed back to the gorilla enclosure. A gorilla that escaped from the Dallas Zoo in 2004 injured four people and was shot to death by police officers.

What fascinates me about my mother's musk ox story is that it represents a breakdown in the basic relationship between a spectator and a zoo animal. If the musk ox was angry because my mother was looking at it, well: looking at animals is the entire purpose of a zoo. A zoo animal you can't look at is failing the most basic element of its job. There are other reasons wild animals are kept in captivity: for breeding and species conservation, or for behavioral research. But zoo animals are there to be seen. This is the one deciding characteristic that sets a zoo aside from a wildlife preserve, a research center, or a national park.

I have noticed that thinkers about zoos often bring other senses than sight into their analysis, in an attempt to explain how what happens there is more than what happens when we watch TV. Nature writer Diane Ackerman, in an op-ed contribution to the *New York Times*, suggested that zoos are, among other things, a treasury of smells, "from the sweet drops that male elephants dribble from glands near their eyes in mating season to the scent signposts of lions, hyenas and other animals." Personally, I am skeptical that more than one in a million zoo visitors notices the smell of male elephants' glandular expressions. Humans are not very appreciative of animal smells in general: witness the wrinkling of noses where a male lion has been marking his territory. A connection is being made here, but it is tempered with disgust—a dodgy basis for building bridges between species. Touch is incorporated occasionally, carefully, with domestic species or safe, small animals like chinchillas and non-biting snakes. I don't yet know of any zoo that usefully incorporates the sense of taste into its educational programming. Out of the traditionally defined five senses, sight and hearing are the two we use to experience a zoo, and these are the same senses we can apply to a nature program on TV.

But stories of rupture and escape suggest the application of other senses than the traditional five. Jumping back from a musk ox's foot—or from an animal that looks like it is attacking but can't—we engage our flight reflexes, our sense of our limbs, our haptic sense of the space around us. We enter into a different relationship with the animals from the one we would have if we were more separated from them.

On the night of April 24, 1979, a group of young men broke into Como Zoo and raised some hell, throwing rocks at the polar bears, breaking a goose's neck, and stealing one of the ducks that lived in the bird pond. One of the polar bears, a female named Kuma who had lived at the zoo for twenty-three years, died after being struck in the head by a concrete block.

The public reaction was swift and condemnatory. A $2,600 reward was offered, with money donated by the Como Zoo Society, Humane Society,

City Council, and a local millionaire. A local beer company with a bear mascot offered to pay for a replacement polar bear. About a hundred citizens called the zoo to say how upset they were, some of them breaking down in tears on the phone, and hundreds more called the police with leads. Within twenty-four hours of the break-in, the police followed one of the tips and apprehended seven suspects. One of them was still carrying around a live duck from the zoo in the trunk of his car.

"I'm surprised people are so concerned about an animal," a police captain said to the *Saint Paul Pioneer Press*. "We have an old lady knocked down, her purse snatched and her arm broken, and you don't hear from the public about that. But the people calling today are really incensed about this thing."

After that, letters poured in to the local papers making excuses for the outrage. Everyone was eager to explain why the public was so concerned about the attack. These letters said by turns that humans needed to acquire "a basic and needed awareness for all living things," or that "we should be glad that people can still feel outrage over such a thing." Someone said the public mourning for Kuma offered "a ray of hope for a return to decency."

These comments suggest that animals are a natural locus of moral concern for humans, one of the most basic things we are expected to care about. But this has generally not been the case at all. One letter to the editor claimed, "Everyone knows killing bears is wrong," but this statement posits a version of "everyone" that leaves out the hundreds of hunters to whom the state would issue bear permits that fall. "Other animals don't senselessly murder members of their own species," one letter-writer claimed. This is true mostly because the idea of "murder" is based on the assumption of a human actor. Predators fight over food and territory; rabbits are rather famous for eating their young; nature as a whole produces life upon life upon life, and over and over those lives end in being consumed, or else they escape to die of starvation or disease. But the zoo is supposed to be safe from brutality. People look into the zoo as if they are looking back toward childhood, or toward Eden. "We should be glad that people can still feel outrage over such a thing": *still*, when adulthood has hardened us; *still*, in a fallen, carnivorous world.

Of course predation and death persist in zoos—how could they not? When I was eleven years old and a frequent visitor at the Minnesota Zoo, I learned that a flamingo there had grown back its clipped feathers sooner than expected, escaped from its enclosure, and flew to the cage next door to visit the Komodo dragons. One of the dragons promptly ate it. Zookeepers seemed sanguine about the incident when they spoke to the press. "This was a gourmet meal for her," one spokeswoman said. The dragon, a female named Maureen, had been eating poorly since her arrival at the zoo, so the flamingo was her first good meal in months.

If the flamingo hadn't flown the coop, the dragons would have been fed rats instead. Carnivory is more or less inevitable; it can be schooled but not eliminated. And animals that transgress their own borders are not cause for outrage or even, in many cases, concern. The devoured flamingo did not have a name or any distinguishing personal characteristics. But the stories do make an impression. I still remember that one, twenty years later. It was a startling dose of real violence in a peaceful place.

When the preferred zoo designs involved barred cages and concrete walls, a zoo was a spectacle of mastery. The King of England's lions were not put on display out of interest in natural history; they were a symbol of the king and his kingdom. Their violence was part of the appeal.

In modern zoos, animal violence is minimized where possible; where unavoidable it is explained as part of the food chain; and humans avoid becoming complicit in it. A dragon may eat a flamingo, but it will never be *fed* one. And while humans exert more influence over the natural world than we ever have before, we no longer go to the zoo to witness human mastery. We are in control of so much, now, that taking charge is no longer as interesting as it was. We'd rather pretend we are witnessing a wilderness that has nothing to do with us. Staff aren't bound by the rules, and animals are innocent of them, but dare to harm a zoo animal and you'll learn what kind of crime you have committed: not only a violent act but a violation of a sanctum.

It's possible to create the illusion of a zoo without barriers, using moats and ditches and camouflage fencing to make it look as if all the animals are living in one habitat together, and we're together with them too. The lion lies down with the lamb, or at least, the lion lives near a herd of gnu and doesn't kill them. It's a vision of a world where everyone is free of cages and cells and also completely safe. Building a fence and tearing one down are both acts of violence against the ideal of peaceful freedom, an ideal that could never be realized unless we redesigned the whole menagerie of earth. We build an illusion of that world instead and gaze in, our hands against the glass, hoping the barrier will hold, wondering if today is the day when it will break.

4

To Keep an Ear to the Ground

Barbara Hurd

> Put your ear down close to your soul and listen hard.
> —ANNE SEXTON

In China long ago, people hid drums inside holes they'd dug along ancient roadways. To put an ear to the ground was to bend down, miles, maybe days, later and listen for the deep percussion of the enemy's boots approaching.

In Antarctica, marine biologists, stretched out on their bellies with their heads turned sideways on the ice, heard—down there in the deep, dark cold—the ancient songs of penguins.

Sometimes when I put my ear to the ground, I make my own arbitrary rules: No listening for anything I might expect. No listening for anything that has a plan for me. No listening to anything that knows I'm listening. No pretending to listen to what bores me utterly. One day late last summer, when Samantha and I were walking along the river near Warnick's Point, we lay down in a fern-filled clearing, turned our heads sideways, and pressed our ears to the ground. Above us, the fronds waved like small green flags of allegiance to a country with no congress, to a time when listening to the soul might have meant saving your life.

More rules: No listening to blather. No not listening to her. So when she, ear to the ground, whispered, "Meemi, what are we doing?" I added another rule: No making her listen to what might be my blather. I said nothing about the soul. "Listening to the dirt," I whispered back, and she, happy as any five-year-old for a reason to lie on the ground, stopped wiggling again.

255

If we'd had better ears to the ground that day in the woods, we might have actually heard the unexpected: a rapid series of snaps, a soft popping, a whispered rat-a-tat. Ears cannot widen, but eyes can, and ours might have, as we turned our heads this way and that and tried to find the source of that light smattering sound. Not rain or bird droppings, not cricket wings or leaf fall. No enemy or ancient song, as the scout and the scientist have been trained to hear, though I might argue that poor listening can also, in fact, be both. How often, after all, have our own deaf ears been a cause of hostility and longing?

We lay there for a full three minutes and heard at first just the whish of ferns and, higher up, occasional bird song.

For days, my walks had been full of pinnae and rachis, the difference between lobed and toothed, and the determination to distinguish between evergreen and spinulose wood ferns. And it's not just the language that boggles. The difference between them, for example, is the relative size of the innermost lower pinnule of basal pinnae below the costa. Between the pages of my *Field Guide to Ferns* I'd stuffed fronds, sketches of fronds, and notes about rhizomes and stipes. At night for the last week I'd been lying awake, the windows open, the forest just a few steps away, and reseeing those wide swaths of green out there, which had looked for years like wild swaths of green but which had begun now to split into clumps of emerald and fir and sage gray. To spend time in the woods these past few days was to be on my knees, ticking off the distinctions—color, spore patterns, blade shape—and to know the comforts of taxonomies, of things in their proper place.

"I think this one's a bracken," a friend said, pointing, one day when we were out, calf deep in the undergrowth. To our right, the ridge rose steeply, its flanks a blurry mess of maple and oak. To our left, the trout-laden Savage River gurgled under hemlocks. But in front of us that fern usurped center stage, became the puzzle I wanted to solve. Silently, I ran down the checklist and finally announced, "Nope, brackens have blades in three parts." Sometimes things keep dividing and subdividing, not just the frond and the field guide's method of keying but my smug notions of accomplishment: knowing ferns is a higher skill, I'd decided that week, than knowing wildflowers, which is more complicated than knowing the names of mushrooms: the former, in fact, is better than the latter unless you're lost in the woods and starving. And on it went, until I had, in a few seconds of taxonomic nitpicking, removed myself from that walk, my friend, that lush ferny valley into which I love to disappear. I know, I know: God's in the details. But so's the devil, and that day—maybe increasingly every day—what I want more than heaven or hell is this resounding earth.

*   *   *

Two hours away the Phipps Conservatory in Pittsburgh devotes a whole room to ferns. They spill into the damp walkway, tower overhead, rise in clumps and spread in swaths, some new, some ragged. After the next-door Orchid Room with its splashes of color and audible human gasps of delight, people move through the Fern Room quietly, barely stopping. In the hour I sat and stood and strolled there one day, the only conversation took place between two men obviously waiting for others in their party still lingering among the orchids. "Investment," I overheard. And "digital," "three years," and "fast turnaround." Talk, I assumed, about doing something now which might pay off in the future. Meanwhile nothing in this room would attract birds or bees or butterflies or any other means of reproduction. When it comes to building for the future, ferns are on their own. To scatter their spore, they need only a bit of moisture, the slightest breeze.

To see the largest ferns—Tasmanian Tree Ferns, the label said—I, who'd left my field guide at home this time, had to crane my neck. Its rhizome, instead of lying horizontal on or under the ground, rose from its hairy base straight up almost to the ceiling, where it flared into a canopy of fronds close to fifteen feet across. *This is the forest primeval*, Longfellow intoned. *Bearded with moss, and in garments green, indistinct in the twilight*, but I, standing under the tallest one, thought of a time more primeval then even that of *Evangeline*, a languorous time, 350 million years ago, before birds and blossoms, when nothing strode and overhead was only the swish of fronds the size of small trees and the wing hum of giant dragonflies, a time when hundred-foot-high club mosses creaked in overhead breezes. To keep an ear to the ground in that ancient world would have meant long, slow times of silence, broken only by the occasional slurp of mud under the feet of giant centipedes and, from the earliest ferns, periodic spurts of spores so large their plunk to the ground might have been cause for alarm.

Had we humans, still 349 million years off in the future, been there, we might have noted the quiet intimacy with rain, its invitations to hunker down, the huddles of green, damp feet, and dark corners, the kind of place,

Loren Eiseley says, in which you strain to hear *the undernote of long-dead activity, of something that lingered, that would linger till the last stone had fallen, something that would not go away.*

Isn't this, finally, what the soul—whatever it is—wants: neither the past nor the future (it isn't interested in time) but the attentive ear of the one whose life it makes restless? It doesn't want story; it wants to hear itself.

As I surreptitiously flipped a fern pinnule over to look for spores, a young woman entered the room, sat down quietly on a mossy stone bench, unbuttoned her blouse, and lifted her baby to bared breast. A giant frond arched over and in front of them so that from where I stood, the baby's head, bald, and the breast, pale, almost shone from behind a feathery veil, both of them half-hidden by the drooping, dripping, green mantle of too much musing. The blouse draped open, the baby's mouth widened, and as the woman leaned her head back against the bench, her face went slack. Memorize this, I told myself, this palimpsest, this momentary juxtaposing of tattered and fresh, this adjacency of images that might mean the kind of resonance I long for is occasionally possible.

5

Of Smells

Michel de Montaigne

It has been reported of some, as of Alexander the Great, that their sweat exhaled an odoriferous smell, occasioned by some rare and extraordinary constitution, of which Plutarch and others have been inquisitive into the cause. But the ordinary constitution of human bodies is quite otherwise, and their best and chiefest excellency is to be exempt from smell. Nay, the sweetness even of the purest breath has nothing in it of greater perfection than to be without any offensive smell, like those of healthful children, which made Plautus say of a woman:

> *Mulier tum bene olet, ubi nihil olet.*
> ["She smells sweetest, who smells not at all."
> —PLAUTUS, *MOSTEL*, I. 3, 116.]

And such as make use of fine exotic perfumes are with good reason to be suspected of some natural imperfection which they endeavor by these odors to conceal. To smell, though well, is to stink:

> *Rides nos, Coracine, nil olentes*
> *Malo, quam bene olere, nil olere.*
> ["You laugh at us, Coracinus, because we are not scented;
> I would, rather than smell well, not smell at all."
> —MARTIAL, VI. 55, 4.]

And elsewhere:

> *Posthume, non bene olet, qui bene semper olet.*
> ["Posthumus, he who ever smells well does not smell well."
> —Idem, ii. 12, 14.]

I am nevertheless a great lover of good smells, and as much abominate the ill ones, which also I scent at a greater distance, I think, than other men:

> *Namque sagacius unus odoror,*
> *Polypus, an gravis hirsutis cubet hircus in aliis*
> *Quam canis acer, ubi latest sus.*
> ["My nose is quicker to scent a fetid sore or a rank armpit,
> than a dog to smell out the hidden sow."
> —Horace, *Epod.*, xii. 4.]

Of smells, the simple and natural seem to me the most pleasing. Let the ladies look to that, for 'tis chiefly their concern: amid the most profound barbarism, the Scythian women, after bathing, were wont to powder and crust their faces and all their bodies with a certain odoriferous drug growing in their country, which being cleansed off, when they came to have familiarity with men they were found perfumed and sleek.

'Tis not to be believed how strangely all sorts of odors cleave to me, and how apt my skin is to imbibe them. He that complains of nature that she has not furnished mankind with a vehicle to convey smells to the nose had no reason; for they will do it themselves, especially to me; my very mustachios, which are full, perform that office; for if I stroke them but with my gloves or handkerchief, the smell will not out a whole day; they manifest where I have been, and the close, luscious, devouring, viscid melting kisses of youthful ardor in my wanton age left a sweetness upon my lips for several hours after. And yet I have ever found myself little subject to epidemic diseases, that are caught, either by conversing with the sick or bred by the contagion of the air, and have escaped from those of my time, of which there have been several sorts in our cities and armies. We read of Socrates, that though he never departed from Athens during the frequent plagues that infested the city, he only was never infected.

Physicians might, I believe, extract greater utility from odors than they do, for I have often observed that they cause an alteration in me and work upon my spirits according to their several virtues; which makes me approve of what is said, that the use of incense and perfumes in churches, so ancient and so universally received in all nations and religions, was intended to cheer us, and to rouse and purify the senses, the better to fit us for contemplation.

I could have been glad, the better to judge of it, to have tasted the culinary art of those cooks who had so rare a way of seasoning exotic odors with the relish of meats; as it was particularly observed in the service of the king of Tunis, who in our days—[Muley-Hassam, in 1543.] —landed at Naples to have an interview with Charles the Emperor. His dishes were larded with odoriferous drugs, to that degree of expense that the cookery of one peacock and two pheasants amounted to a hundred ducats to dress them after their fashion; and when the carver came to cut them up, not only the dining-room, but all the apartments of his palace and the adjoining streets were filled with an aromatic vapor which did not presently vanish.

My chiefest care in choosing my lodgings is always to avoid a thick and stinking air; and those beautiful cities, Venice and Paris, very much lessen the kindness I have for them, the one by the offensive smell of her marshes, and the other of her dirt.

6

On Touching Ground

Jericho Parms

Deep within the galleries of the Metropolitan, a glass wall case barely contains the wild form of a racehorse. Veiny grooves mark the horse's flank and haunches, its powerful shoulders, crest, the forelock of its mane. The tail extends like a petticoat train in its cantering wake. Head high, the horse is poised, proud.

Perhaps even more than his dancers, more than his nude women bathing, horses captured the heart of Edgar Degas. Yet they all shared similar traits—in their ephemeral postures, in their show jumps and pliés, in the strength and energy of their legs cast in bronze. I peer in close. All four of the horse's hooves are suspended in midair.

Degas's bronze is polished, near black. The light catches the horse's muscular limbs, like white wax on obsidian, the patent leather shoes I wore as a girl in the city, or the riding boots I packed when we traveled west to Grandfather's ranch. Christmas in Arizona rarely brought snow. The desert floor left a coat of dust on my rubber soles.

In the mornings I helped Grandfather in the tack shed. The straw-scented air from the paddock mingled with the damp, industrial interior that sheltered old oil drums, mud-caked basins, ropes, harnesses, thrush ointments, and salve. I followed as he worked, measuring feed buckets, dragging water to the trough, grooming the remaining mares as their black marble eyes and mahogany bay coats shimmered in the sun.

* * *

I read in the newspapers that the wild mustangs are on the run again. Nearly thirty thousand horses still roam the open range. Each fall the papers grapple to tell the story of the annual rundown and removal of horses from public grazing lands. Decades since Congress passed the Wild Horse and Burro Act in 1971, prohibiting the capture of wild horses by machine for commercial sale, the *New York Times* described the latest roundup as "horse versus helicopter here in the high desert." Each year the occasion stirs controversy and I find myself, a world away, awaiting the whinny and squeal of the Manhattan-bound #1 train on my way to work at the museum, enmeshed in following the debate. For every advocate that warns of the damage—foals separated from their mothers, yearlings caught in the stampede—a straight-talking rancher heralds the old days of feral pursuit, when "a cowboy really wasn't a cowboy if you didn't rope a wild horse." The horses no longer vie against lasso-wielding cowboys and Indians; the Bureau of Land Management and its band of modern ranchers run down the horses with low-flying helicopters into makeshift corrals. Degas may have captured his racehorse in trot, but what of a wild-blooded mustang on the run?

Bronze bears no witness to a horse's speed. Whether by breeding or birthright, a horse is a runner, surrendering only to the curl and surge of its legs, to its hooves drumming the ground like thunder, to its mane fanning as it leans into each turn. I imagine the uneven terrain as a mere notion beneath their hooves, the same way the cracks in the concrete had no impact on me as I skipped down city streets; of no consequence were the tar pebbles and schist that got caught in my worn tennis shoes when I ran.

*   *   *

Out west, we sprinted like thoroughbreds. *Equus caballus.* Born of the same pedigree, my older brother and I were three years apart and an uneven match as we raced the dirt roads of my grandfather's Tucson ranch. I trailed, breathless. The warmth rose in my legs; my pulse quickened. My feet propelled me down the straight towards Grandfather's angled figure, his blue jeans pale with the dust of my brother's victory. But there he was, still palming his Stetson, its buckle gleaming as he swept his arm, waving me to the finish, A deep "whoa, whoa" sounded from his chest as I came to a stop in his arms. Leaning against his hip, my legs tingled—a slow sequence toward stillness—with each recaptured breath.

* * *

In 1878, Eadweard Muybridge—pioneer of the moving image—shot a series of photographs at the racetracks in Palo Alto, California. The images, *Horse in Motion*, revealed for the first time that there is a moment during a horse's trot when all four hooves simultaneously leave the ground. The previously unobserved phenomenon caused a sensation. Muybridge toured Europe with his signature biunial lantern slides to present his sequence, which proved that artists, by depicting at least one hoof on the ground, had been misrepresenting the true movement of horses for ages.

Degas's horse is true to life. The artist frequented the Longchamp Racecourse in Paris to observe the racing breeds. He studied Muybridge's photographs and, by placing a supporting post beneath the horse's abdomen, molded each leg faithfully aloft. *Horse Trotting, Feet Not Touching Ground* is sleek, agile. But it is not on the run. Notice the upright neck and slightly gapped muzzle. Notice the stately curve from the crest to the loins and hindquarters, between the shoulders and breast—ribs open, posture squared, well trained, *rehearse*d. Degas has mastered a refined, elegant trot.

* * *

In the museum, a girl enters the gallery where I linger after a lunch break. She scans the collection in a nearby wall case—*Horse Balking, Horse Rearing, Horse at Trough*—and then turns suddenly and increases her clip toward the adjacent gallery where a bronze dancer stands poised. Tiptoeing around the base, the girl peers up at the statuette fashioned with a corset and crinoline skirt. The statue's braided hair, cast in wax from a horsehair wig, is held by a bow of white satin. The dancer's legs support the upright carriage of her stance—fourth position, is it?—her right leg extending forward to present the inner line of her slippered foot while her left remains grounded. From behind, one can see her arms are locked close along the curve of her torso; her hands are cupped *a derrière*.

The Little Fourteen-Year-Old Dancer is modeled after the young ballerina Marie van Goethem, who became Degas's signature model and muse for his scrutiny of the female form in motion. Her figure, and those of several smaller dancers exhibited nearby, reveals the nuances of youth with subtle majesty—the soft tension between a prepubescent slouch and a choreographed style. Notice the *Dancer Putting On Her Stocking*, or another, *Looking at the Sole of*

Her Right Foot, their nascent curiosity and preoccupation, the truth of their form—over their loveliness—revealing grace. From a distance, I can see that the bronze of the dancer's skin is tinted lighter than the trotting horse before me, more brown than black, like an equine coat of chestnut or roan, like the Sonoran sands after a heavy rain.

*   *   *

At dusk, my grandfather and I walked away from the white adobe ranch house, along the back acres of his land. I skipped alongside him, keeping pace in the lines of his Bill Hickok shadow, which lay like a paper doll against the ground. And I, his devoted Calamity Jane. After a while, he stopped to square his legs and shoulders, as I grabbed his arms and stepped onto his boot tops. There, we waltzed. His white hair feathered around his head; his Buddy Holly glasses slid down his nose as he laughed. He smelled of pipe tobacco, hay bales, leather, and liniment—far from the cufflinks and fresh-laundered lapels he might have worn to white-tie affairs after he married my grandmother and settled back east. We danced until dark, his spurs scrawling arabesques in the dust, my feet safely elevated atop his. I could have been Marie van Goethem herself. The young dancer's head tilts upward. In the museum, as I stand before her, my own neck cranes. The statuette's eyes appear half-closed, as if wishing, or remembering, or searching to find her pose—like a rider feeling for balance on a saddle or a child seeking treasures of the past.

*   *   *

It's funny really, all this talk of horses. I was hardly the vision of a girl one might imagine on a horse: blue eyes and tight ponytail, beige riders and good posture. Nor was I the plaid-shirted cowgirl type with authentic chaps and true-buckle riding boots. With my blond nappy curls and hand-me-downs, I may have been more akin to a horse than a rider. Born of a black father and white mother whose marriage in 1976 (nearly a decade after *Loving v. Virginia* struck down laws opposing interracial marriage) never really garnered approval from the *familie*s, each camp fearing how hard it might be for *the children*.

*   *   *

Before dark, my brother and I marked "X" in the grainy desert soils. Kneeling in the rocky arroyo, we staked our claim in the prospect of fool's gold and muscovite to add to the growing museum of specimens we brought back to the city: flint arrowheads and fossil shells, horseshoes and snake skins, a handful of sharks' teeth buffed and blackened from the Gulf Coast of Mexico. We collected what we could. Back home, we became the curators, turning the windowsills of our bedroom into showcases, testimonies of a land otherwise odd and foreign to us "city kids." And what we couldn't bring back I recorded in the archives of memory: Grandfather's dalmatian prancing among the horses; a gestating mare bedding down in straw; the first steps of a newborn foal, gray-moistened with life, eager to unfold its legs, to stand, wobble, run. This became our gallery, evidence of the expanse of life and what it meant to dream.

*   *   *

Degas had his evidence. He learned about movement from the sequential photographs of Muybridge, the world-class racing breeds at Longchamp, and van Goethem and her classmates at L'École de Danse of the Paris Opera. Degas molded his horses with the same painstaking observation as he did his female figures: a galloping stride captured with equal scrutiny as a woman's step from a bath or a ballerina's pointe work. In the same way Muybridge revealed the nature of human and animal locomotion—a *Horse and Rider Galloping*, a *Woman Opening a Parasol, Man and Woman Dancing a Waltz*— Degas revealed the common repertoire of movement, of finesse.

Perhaps that is why children seem to appreciate the Degas galleries. They filter in and out with wide eyes, parents somewhere in tow, or enter with the brisk run-walk of field trip excitement. They peer at the pastel canvases of dancers stretching at the barre, or the bronze statuettes midpirouette. The girls finger-brush their hair and retie their ponytails, mimicking the footwork. One girl demonstrates a *pas-de-bourèe* shift to *demi-plié*. The museum's wood floor creaks beneath her. Another presses close against the wall case to better see the horses. She shimmies her shoulders, and I hear a faint "neigh" escape her pouty lips. I wonder what she sees, what world inhabits Degas's racehorse, what fate awaits her memories. Her fingers and nose leave breathy smudges that slowly vanish from the glass.

Much of what we know is emblematic: the glory of the West, the icon of a wild horse. Most of what we see is representation: the aesthetic of a captured pose, the inner compositions of how and why we remember. But some things we know because they are part of us: the long limbs and piano fingers I inherited from my grandfather, his high-arched feet and his curiosity, too. And some things we only know by observing: sequential images, dominant traits, language used to classify, shape, and mold.

For my grandfather's part, it was a simple choice to live in the Sonora—to "go west" as he did—from the valleys of Pennsylvania to the Arizona plains where, in the late 1930s, he worked his way through college. And there, by chance, he met my grandmother, the fair-skinned, blonde-bobbed young woman on an English saddle, who was traveling on a sorority vacation. Grandfather rescued her from a runaway horse. I've imagined the story more than once: a harem of Bettys and Dorothys touring the desert on horseback, when one takes off from the caravan. Did my grandmother will her horse to gallop, or did it take off beneath her? Did Grandfather feel his horse's hooves aloft as he followed in pursuit? The two of them later settled back east, but they always plotted to retire, as they did in the mid-1970s, on the same land where they first surveyed their courtship.

I, too, moved west for college, and then for a while I just kept going: West to Southwest, Central America, and eventually Europe, moving between the backcountry and the boroughs, and always returning to New York. I sometimes wonder to what extent I was still running in search of the thrill I felt twirling atop my grandfather's boots or racing toward a mirage.

We never know how much we inherit from the past. How far did the early stagecoaches travel to stake claims on new land? How far did Degas voyage through the Parisian racetracks and ballet theaters to capture his forms? How far ahead did my grandfather plan to escape the domestic landscape of the suburbs and cities, to return to his unfettered freedom?

*　*　*

Few sights compare to that of a wild mustang, *Equus ferus*. First introduced to the Americas by Spanish conquistadors, many of the feral horse breeds left free on the range descended from cavalry horses once bred for their size and strength. Grandfather, docent of my curiosity, taught me of the wild horses—*los mesteños*, the stray, the "ownerless"—of what they teach us about resilience and grace. For those he owned on the ranch—retired quarter horses and show breeds—we rehearsed every act of their care: testing the water temperature, tasting the feed. We sampled the liniment, too, used to cool the horses in the Tucson heat. I watched him as he rubbed it into his own skin. "Whatever is good enough for the horses" was good enough for him. So I tried it too, massaging a dab on my knees and ankles, kneading the thin muscles along my shins. The balm tingled and burned. My skin felt like ice (not just cold, but colorless), polished, sleek. I almost believed that we could feel what the horses felt, that our legs could know what their legs knew: about the difference between a trot and a run, between mere movement and dancing—that freedom is different from flight.

And maybe we are among those untamed and unclassified, neither domestic nor wild—half-breeds given just enough training in the world to watch our backs in the city before we are let free to live and graze with abandon, forming our own names for things that exist between extremes (neither the saddle nor the shoe, wax nor the obsidian).

Sometimes I think that as long as the horses are left free to roam, memory, too, may exist unbound. Yet each fall bands of mustangs are corralled into holding pens. Of those that survive the stampedes, some will be trapped and tamed, preserved as keepsakes or insignia, like the cast of an infant's shoe enclosed in a museum vitrine. Some will be broken and trained like the ballerina forced to shed her youth. But some will run like the racehorses of Longchamp, like a runaway stallion courting romance, and escape to another year, trotting, until the day their feet touch ground.

7

Perdition

Kristen Radtke

8

The Night My Mother
Met Bruce Lee

Paisley Rekdal

Age sixteen, my mother loads up red tubs of noodles, teacups chipped and white-gray as teeth, rice clumps that glue themselves to the plastic tub sides or dissolve and turn papery in the weak tea sloshing around the bottom. She's at Diamond Chan's restaurant, where most of her cousins work after school and during summer vacations, some of her friends, too. There's Suzy at the cash register, totaling up bills and giving back change, a little dish of toothpicks beside her and a basket of mints that taste like powdered cream. A couple of my mother's cousins are washing dishes behind the swinging kitchen door, and some woman called Auntie #2 (at her age, everyone is Auntie and each must take a number) takes orders at a table of women that look like Po Po's mah-jongg club. They don't play anymore. They go to the racetrack.

The interior of Diamond Chan's restaurant is red: red napkins, red walls, red carp in the tank and in signature seals on the cheap wall hangings. Luck or no luck, it's like the inside of an esophagus. My mother's nails are cracked, kept short by clipping or gnawing, glisten only when varnished with the grease of someone else's leftovers. Still, she enjoys working here, its repetitive actions, the chores that keep her from thinking. The money my mother earns will soon get sucked into the price of a pink cashmere sweater for Po Po's birthday, along with a graduation photo of herself, also in a pink sweater, pearls, her face airbrushed fog-rose at the cheeks and mouth.

Graduation? Unlike her brothers, she knows she's going to college. Smith, to be exact, though without the approval of the school counselor. "Smith is . . . expensive," the school counselor told my mother only yesterday, which is why my mother is slightly irritated now, clomping around under the weight of full tubs of used dishes. "Smith is not for girls like you." What does she plan to be when she grows up? "A doctor?" my mother suggests. Um, no. "Nursing. Or teaching, perhaps, which is even more practical. Don't you think?"

My mother, who is practical above all things, agreed.

So it's the University of Washington in two years with a degree in education. Fine. She slams down full vials of soy sauce onto each table, makes sure the nozzle heads are screwed on exactly. Someone the other week stuck chewing gum up under the lid of one, and my mother had to dig it out with an old chopstick and then forgot to fully tighten the lid. Black, sweet-smelling pool on the white tablecloth. Seeing it, she could feel the back of her throat fill up with salt. Smith is not for girls like her.

"Cindy!" someone shouts. The kitchen door swings open. A momentary view: white chef shirts stained with red and brown grease. A woman wiping her brow with the back of her hand.

It is not, my mother would argue, the fact she could be denied the dream of Smith so much that someone should *tell* her she could be denied it. My mother knows the counselor was hinting at some limitation my mother would prefer to ignore. Still, she is whiter than white, should intelligence be considered a pale attribute. Deep down she understands she has a special capacity for work; she likes it, she's good at it, she excels at school and its predictable problems. Hers is a discipline entirely lacking in the spirits of whatever *loh fan* may sneer or wonder at her in study hall; to be told by a fat, dyed-blond guidance counselor she may be inferior? The monkey calling the man animal.

Now out of the kitchen erupts the newcomer, a smatter of duck fat and ash. Like everyone here, he's someone's cousin's cousin, though he talks like he's got marbles piled in his mouth.

"I come from Hong Kong," he told my mother on break in the alley. "From *real* Chinese." Is there a substitute? He leers at Suzy, waves his hand dismissively over the carved dragon beams, the waitresses gossiping in English. He's two years older than my mother, lean, high-cheekboned, shaggy-headed. He has big plans for himself. He likes to whip his arms and legs around in the kitchen, threaten the other busboy. Already he's dropped a dish, insulted the cook, cut his thumb on a knife blade. He smells funny.

"Mr. B.O. Jangles," Suzy calls him. "Kung Fooey."

"What the hell the matter with him?" growls Auntie #2. "I never seen nobody act like that before."

"It's all the rage in China," my mother says. She is repeating what he told her in a tone of voice that is meant to seem sarcastic but comes out another way. All the rage. In China.

She stacks more dishes in her tub. From the kitchen comes a high-pitched human squawk and the sound of something clattering to the floor. He's going to get fired soon and my mother is never going to Smith. A waitress scurries out of the kitchen, bearing more food, a panicked look on her face. My mother stands and watches the kitchen door swing in place behind her back. Back and forth, back and forth, back and forth.

Around age thirteen, for summer vacation I come down with laziness heretofore unheard of in a child. I doze in bed till noon at least, stay up every night watching bad movies or reading. Sometimes, if it's a bad enough movie and she is not teaching the next morning, my mother wakes and joins me.

Tonight is *Enter the Dragon*. I remember it because a year or two ago when it came out, all the boys on the block bought numchucks. We smacked our backs with the sticks on chains, left thumb-thick bruise prints on our rib cages. Jeff down the street still has the movie poster, still tells people he has a black belt in karate.

My mother and I watch Bruce Lee set foot on the island, followed closely by the playboy and the black man who will die after the banquet and all his women. Bruce Lee narrows his eyes, ripples his chest muscles underneath his white turtleneck.

"I knew him," my mother tells me. "I worked with him in a restaurant when I was in high school."

"Really?" This is now officially the only cool thing about her. "What was he like?"

"I don't remember. No one liked him, though. All that kung fu stuff; it looked ridiculous. Like a parody."

We watch in the dark as Bruce Lee confronts himself, over and over. In the hall of mirrors, his bloody chest and face seem outlined in silver. He is handsome and wiry; he caws at his opponents like an ethereal avenger. I peek at my mother beside me on the sofa. In the television light, her broad face twists into an expression I do not recognize. Then the light flickers, changes, makes her ordinary again.

9

The Coroner's Photographs

Brent Staples

My brother's body lies dead and naked on a stainless steel slab. At his head stands a tall arched spigot that, with tap handles mimicking wings, easily suggests a swan in mourning. His head is squarish and overlarge. (This, when he was a toddler, made him seem top-heavy and unsteady on his feet.) His widow's peak is common among the men in my family, though this one is more dramatic than most. An inverted pyramid, it begins high above the temples and falls steeply to an apex in the boxy forehead, over the heart-shaped face. A triangle into a box over a heart. His eyes (closed here) were big and dark and glittery; they drew you into his sadness when he cried. The lips are ajar as always, but the picture is taken from such an angle that it misses a crucial detail: the left front tooth tucked partly beyond the right one. I need this detail to see my brother full. I paint it in from memory.

A horrendous wound runs the length of the abdomen, from the sternum all the way to the pubic mound. The wound resembles a mouth whose lips are pouting and bloody. Massive staplelike clamps are gouged into these lips at regular intervals along the abdomen. This is a surgeon's incision. The surgeon was presented with a patient shot six times with a large-caliber handgun. Sensing the carnage that lay within, he achieved the largest possible opening and worked frantically trying to save my brother's life. He tied off shattered vessels, resectioned the small intestine, repaired a bullet track on the liver, then backed out. The closing would have required two pairs of hands. An assistant would have gripped the two sides of the wound and drawn them together while a second person cut in the clamps. The pulling together has made my brother's skin into a corset that crushes in on the abdomen from all sides. The pelvic bones jut up through the skin. The back is abnormally arched from the tension. The wound strains at the clamps, threatening to rip itself open. The surgeon worked all night and emerged from surgery gaunt, his greens darkened with sweat. "I tied off everything I could," he said, and then he wept at the savagery and the waste.

This is the body of Blake Melvin Staples, the seventh of my family's nine children, the third of my four brothers, born ten years after me. I know his contours well. I bathed and diapered him when he was a baby and studied his features as he grew. He is the smallest of the brothers, but is built in the same manner: short torso but long arms and legs; a more than ample behind set high on the back; knocking knees; big feet that tend to flat. The second toe is also a signature. It curls softly in an extended arc and rises above the others in a way that's unique to us. His feelings are mine as well. Cold: The sensation moves from my eyes to my shoulder blades to my bare ass as I feel him naked on the steel. I envision the reflex that would run through his body, hear the sharp breath he would draw when steel met his skin. Below the familiar feet a drain awaits the blood that will flow from this autopsy.

The medical examiner took this picture and several on February 13, 1984, at 9:45 A.M. The camera's flash is visible everywhere: on the pale-green tiles of the surrounding walls, on the gleaming neck of the spigot, on the stainless steel of the slab, on the bloody lips of the wound.

The coroner's report begins with a terse narrative summary: "The deceased, twenty-two-year-old Negro male, was allegedly shot by another person on the premises of a night club as a result of a 'long standing quarrel.' He sustained multiple gunshot wounds of the abdomen and legs and expired during surgery."

Blake was a drug dealer; he was known for carrying guns and for using them. His killer, Mark McGeorge, was a former customer and cocaine addict. At the trial Mark's lawyer described the shooting as a gunfight in which Blake was beaten to the draw. This was doubtful. Blake was shot six times: three times in the back. No weapon was found on or near his body. Blake's gunbearer testified that my brother was unarmed when Mark ambushed and gunned him down. But a gunbearer is not a plausible witness. A drug dealer known for shooting a rival in plain public view gets no sympathy from a jury.

The jury turned back the prosecution's request for a conviction of murder in the first degree. Mark was found guilty of second-degree murder and sentenced to seven years in jail. Five years for the murder. Two years for using the gun.

Blake is said to have cried out for his life as he lay on the ground. "Please don't shoot me no more. I don't want to die." "*Please don't shoot me no more. I don't want to die.*" His voice had a touch of that dullness one hears from the deaf, a result of ear infections he suffered as a child. The ear openings had narrowed to the size of pinholes. He tilted his head woefully from side to side trying to pour out the pain. His vowels were locked high in his throat, behind his nose. This voice kept him a baby to me. This is the voice in which he would have pleaded for his life.

The coroner dissects the body, organ by organ:

HEART:	300 grams. No valve or chamber lesions. Coronary arteries show no pathologic changes.
LUNGS:	900 grams combined. Moderate congestion. Tracheobronchial and arterial systems are not remarkable.
LIVER:	1950 grams. There is a sutured bullet track at the interlobar sulcus and anterior portion of the right hepatic lobe. There has been moderate subcapsular and intraparenchymal hemorrhage.
SPLEEN:	150 grams. No pathologic changes.
KIDNEYS:	300 grams combined. No pathologic changes.
ADRENALS:	No pathologic changes.
PANCREAS:	No pathologic changes.
GI TRACT:	The stomach is empty. Portions of the small bowel have been resected, along with portions of the omentum. The bowel surface is dusky reddish-brown, but does not appear gangrenous.
URINARY BLADDER:	Empty.
NECK ORGANS:	Intact. No airway obstructions.
BRAIN:	1490 grams. Sagittal and serial coronal sections show no discrete lesions or evidence of injury.

SKULL: Intact.

VERTEBRAE: Intact.

RIBS: Intact.

PELVIS: There is a chip fracture of the left pubic ramus, and there is
            also fracturing of the right pubic ramus. There is extensive
            fracturing of the left femur, and there is a through-and-
            through bullet wound of the right femur just below the
            hip joint.

The coroner describes the wounds in detail. The surgical incision and its grisly clamps are dismissed in a single sentence. The six bullet holes receive one full paragraph each. The coroner records the angle that each bullet traveled through the body, the organs it passed through along the way, and where it finally came to rest. With all this to occupy him, the coroner fails to note the scar on Blake's left hand. The scar lies in the webbing between the thumb and index finger and is the result of a gun accident. A shotgun recoiled when Blake fired it and drove the hammer deep into the web, opening a wound that took several stitches to close.

I saw the wound when it was fresh, six weeks before Blake was murdered. I was visiting Roanoke from Chicago, where I then lived. I sought Blake out to tell him that it was time to get out of the business and leave Roanoke. The signs of death were everywhere; his name was hot in the street. Blake and I were making small talk when we slapped each other five. Blake clutched his hand at the wrist and cried out in pain. Then he showed me the stitches. This ended the small talk. I told him that he was in danger of being killed if he didn't leave town.

Staples men have been monolinguists for generations. We love our own voices too much. Blake responded to my alarm by telling me stories. He told me about the awesome power of the shotgun that had injured him. He told me about making asses of the police when they raided his apartment looking for drugs. The door of his apartment was steel, he said; they'd sent for a tow truck to pull it from its frame. Inside they found him twiddling his thumbs in the bathroom. He'd flushed the cocaine down the toilet. The night he told me these stories was the last time I saw him alive.

Six weeks later my brother Bruce called me with the news. "Brent, Blake is dead," he said. "Some guy pulled up in a car and emptied out on him with a magnum. Blake is dead." I told myself to feel nothing. I had already mourned Blake and buried him and was determined not to suffer his death a second time. I skipped the funeral and avoided Roanoke for the next three years. The next time I visited my family I went to see the Roanoke Commonwealth Attorney and questioned him about the case. He was polite and impatient. For him, everything about the killing had been said. This, after all, had been an ordinary death.

I asked to see the files. A secretary brought a manila pouch and handed it to the Commonwealth Attorney, who handed it to me and excused himself from the room. The pouch contained a summary of the trial, the medical examiner's report, and a separate inner pouch wrapped in twine and shaped like photographs. I opened the pouch; there was Blake dead and on the slab, photographed from several angles. The floor gave way, and I fell down and down for miles.

10

Because, the Ferguson Verdict

Ira Sukrungruang

Because, in 1978, we were the first Thai family in a working class neighborhood of Chicago, predominantly inhabited by Polish and Irish. Because we found our mailbox off its post every weekend, the aluminum dented in the shape of a baseball bat. Because rotten eggs splattered the white siding of our bi-level, which my mother scrubbed until she could see the pale of her face. Because someone scrawled on our driveway, *Chinks Go Home*, in shaving cream that stained and stayed on the concrete for weeks. Because at the tile factory off Archer Avenue my father got into a fight. Because a co-worker said he talked funny, and he was tired of everyone telling him he talked funny, and so he punched the offender in the face, who was as white as some of the floor tiles the factory churned out. Because we owned a gun, a heavy silver one with a leather handle, a safeguard against anyone out to do us harm. Because we believed everyone was out to do us harm. Because my father chased two boys away with the gun one night, his splayed feet slapping the concrete, his voice screaming obscenities until he was hoarse. Because those boys kept ding-dong-ditching our home till past midnight. Because we called the police and they never showed. Because I was four and endlessly crying, and my mother couldn't shush me, so she pressed me hard to her chest, so hard my nose bled. Because a year later I found the gun in my father's briefcase of important things, and I picked it up and pulled the trigger and nothing happened, but in my brain there was a bang that silenced robins. Because my mother's first true purchase in the country, a '74 Thunderbird, was stolen, and the police did nothing except laugh at her accent. Because they told her if she learned to speak better they'd take her more seriously, that if she wanted to live in America, she should speak like an American. Because my mother felt a smidgen of glee when she saw a police officer wheeled into the emergency room where she worked as an RN, but she did her job anyway. Because she knew a nurse's job was right and thankless. Because her brother in Thailand was a police officer and his job was right and thankless. Because, despite herself, all police officers were not those police officers and those police officers were far and few between; we just managed to always find them. Because a year later, the Thunderbird was found in pieces in the parking lot of an abandoned steel factory. Because my family was referred to as chink, gook, jap, words that in no way referenced us but we carried the wounds they carved anyway, like etchings in the pale bark of a cypress. Because words had the ability to crumble us. Because the word "bitch" uttered by the white three-year-old boy behind our house forced my mother to enroll me in Tae Kwon Do, so I could defend her honor. Because honor was what we had left. Because we clung to our honor like a safety blanket. Because honor sometimes made me do stupid things like breaking windows and blowing up mailboxes, like punching a little boy in the nose for calling my mother a bitch. Because honor is linked to pride, which is linked to stupidity. Because sometimes we were stupid. Because once on a spring day I was surrounded by white boys who beat me down and someone stole the Buddha hanging around my neck. Because I was eight. Because I was not white. Because I spoke with an accent. Because a white man with receding hair stood in his driveway and watched the beating before complaining that I tore up his grass in my attempt to kick free. Because no matter how hard I was taught to kick and punch at the dojo, it never seemed hard enough, bloody enough. Because it never managed to restore anything, but instead let guilt settle in the stomach, heavy and laden, like the brick I launched at the house across the street from the Chicago Thai Buddhist temple, after news that a monk was hit with a rock and had to get ten stitches on his brow. Because police officers did not come then either. Because I was angry. Because I was scared. Because it seemed I loved hiding in the shadows more than standing in the light. Because the light exposed my fear of the world. Because my fear of the world started with my mother's familiar line, heard over and over throughout my life: "You are not like them. Always remember that." Because I learned they are not like them either. Because we are always looking for an answer, a reason why things happen, why there is so much hate in the world, in a country, in a city, in a home. Because the word "because" demands cause and effect, demands sequential understanding, though in the face of hate there is only cause, cause, cause. Because the effect is this country on the brink of chaos. Because we are looking for some sense in senselessness. Because we need to be saved. Because, despite our anger bubbling over, I cling to the belief that we are able to love. Because of Buddha. Because of God. Because of Allah. Because we are human, blood and biology, and able to show empathy and forgiveness and understanding, the flowers of humanity about to burst under great duress. Because of Emmett Till or Rodney King or Vincent Chin or Kuanchung Kao, who police officers shot because they feared his martial arts moves. Because of the history we carry within us, a history that, no matter how much we want to deny it, is part of the genetic make-up of our being. Because we carry all these histories, heavy and burdened. Because we share this body of history, which joins—never separates—us. Because here, in my palms, are all of the social and political injustices enacted on our planet. Because here, under my fingernail, is the debris from centuries of war. Because here, on the tip of each hair follicle, are the names of the deceased, slain because of race or gender or sexual orientation. Because here, inside the cavity of my ear, are tears shed. Because here, in my heart, is our heart, beating, beating, beating.

Because. Because. Because.

11

First

Ryan Van Meter

Ben and I are sitting side by side in the very back of his mother's station wagon. We face glowing white headlights of cars following us, our sneakers pressed against the back hatch door. This is our joy—his and mine—to sit turned away from our moms and dads in this place that feels like a secret, as though they are not even in the car with us. They have just taken us out to dinner, and now we are driving home. Years from this evening, I won't actually be sure that this boy sitting beside me is named Ben. But that doesn't matter tonight. What I know for certain right now is that I love him, and I need to tell him this fact before we return to our separate houses, next door to each other. We are both five.

Ben is the first brown-eyed boy I will fall for but will not be the last. His hair is also brown and always needs scraping off his forehead, which he does about every five minutes. All his jeans have dark squares stuck over the knees where he has worn through the denim. His shoelaces are perpetually undone, and he has a magic way of tying them with a quick, weird loop that I study and try myself, but can never match. His fingernails are ragged because he rips them off with his teeth and spits out the pieces when our moms aren't watching. Somebody always has to fix his shirt collars.

Our parents face the other direction, talking about something, and it is raining. My eyes trace the lines of water as they draw down the glass. Coiled beside my legs are the thick black and red cords of a pair of jumper cables. Ben's T-ball bat is also back here, rolling around and clunking as the long car wends its way through town. Ben's dad is driving, and my dad sits next to him, with our mothers in the back seat; I have recently observed that when mothers and fathers are in the car together, the dad always drives. My dad has also insisted on checking the score of the Cardinals game, so the radio is tuned to a staticky AM station, and the announcer's rich voice buzzes out of the speakers up front.

The week before this particular night, I asked my mother, "Why do people get married?" I don't recall the impulse behind my curiosity, but I will forever remember every word of her answer—she stated it simply after only a moment or two of thinking—because it seemed that important: "Two people get married when they love each other."

I had that hunch. I am a kindergartener, but the summer just before this rainy night, I learned most of what I know about love from watching soap operas with my mother. She is a gym teacher, and during her months off she catches up on the shows she has watched since college. Every summer weekday, I couldn't wait until they came on at two o'clock. My father didn't think I should be watching them—boys should be outside, playing—but he was rarely home early enough to know the difference, and according to my mother, I was too young to really understand what was going on anyway.

What I enjoyed most about soap operas was how exciting and beautiful life was. Every lady was pretty and had wonderful hair, and all the men had dark eyes and big teeth and faces as strong as bricks, and every week there was a wedding or a manhunt or a birth. The people had grand fights where they threw vases at walls and slammed doors and chased each other in cars. There were villains locking up the wonderfully haired heroines and suspending them in gold cages above enormous acid vats. And, of course, it was love that inspired every one of these stories and made life on the screen as thrilling as it was. That was what my mother would say from the sofa when I turned from my spot on the carpet in front of her and faced her, asking, "Why is he spying on that lady?"

"Because he loves her."

In the car, Ben and I hold hands. There is something sticky on his fingers, probably the strawberry syrup from the ice cream sundaes we ate for dessert. We have never held hands before; I have simply reached for his in the dark and held him while he holds me. I want to see our hands on the rough floor, but they are visible only every block or so when the car passes beneath a streetlight, and then for only a flash. Ben is my closest friend because he lives next door, we are the same age, and we both have little brothers who are babies. I wish he were in the same kindergarten class as me, but he goes to a different school—one where he has to wear a uniform all day and for which there is no school bus.

"I love you," I say. We are idling, waiting for a red light to be green, a shining car has stopped right behind us, so Ben's face is pale and brilliant.

"I love you too," he says.

The car becomes quiet as the voice of the baseball game shrinks smaller and smaller.

"Will you marry me?" I ask him. His hand is still in mine; on the soap opera, you are supposed to have a ring, but I don't have one.

He begins to nod, and suddenly my mother feels very close. I look over my shoulder, my eyes peeking over the back of the last row of seats that we are leaning against. She has turned around, facing me. Permed hair, laugh lines not laughing.

"What did you just say?" she asks.

"I asked Ben to marry me."

The car starts moving forward again, and none of the parents are talking loudly enough for us to hear them back here. I brace myself against the raised carpeted bump on the wheel well as Ben's father turns left onto the street before the turn onto our street. Sitting beside my mom is Ben's mother, who keeps staring forward, but I notice that one of her ears keeps swiveling back here, a little more each time. I am still facing my mother, who is still facing me, and for one last second, we look at each other without anything wrong between us.

"You shouldn't have said that," she says. "Boys don't marry other boys. Only boys and girls get married to each other."

She can't see our hands, but Ben pulls his away. I close my fingers into a loose fist and rub my palm to feel, and keep feeling, how strange his skin has made mine.

"Okay?" she asks.

"Yes," I say, but by accident my throat whispers the words.

She asks again. "Okay? Did you hear me?"

"Yes!" This time nearly shouting, and I wish we were already home so I could jump out and run to my bedroom. To be back here in the dark, private tail of the car suddenly feels wrong, so Ben and I each scoot off to our separate sides. "Yes," I say again, almost normally, turning away to face the rainy window. I feel her turn too as the radio baseball voice comes back up out of the quiet. The car starts to dip as we head down the hill of our street; our house is at the bottom. No one speaks for the rest of the ride. We all just sit and wait and watch our own views of the road—the parents see what is ahead of us, while the only thing I can look at is what we have just left behind.

12

Math 1619

Gwendolyn Wallace

Show all of your work clearly and thoroughly. You may use an approved calculator, but the use of a tablet is not permitted. Once you have completed the problems, hand your test to the white man seated at the front of the classroom.

1. When a black girl has a question in physics class about double slits, does she not ask her question (and instead writes "HELP" on her paper next to the problem) because:

   a. everyone else seems to understand the new concept.
   b. she believes the students in her class will think that she is bad at physics *because* she is black and female.
   c. when she was ten years old, she told her parents that she was trying her best in school. They told her that her best wasn't good enough because people would always think poorly of her because she is black and female. They said that she had to do twice as well in order to get half of the credit. She isn't doing twice as well in physics, but pretending she doesn't have any questions may have the same effect.
   d. with so few black girls at her boarding school she represents her whole race and can't let the white and Asian students in her class leave Physics 230 with the idea that all black girls are inherently bad at physics.
   e. All of the above.

2. A black girl is born light-skinned, but grows 0.8 shades darker each summer when she goes to Chattanooga, Tennessee. There, she plays all day under the beating sun in the waterpark, as water squirts from the mouths

of giant rock animals. If her hairdresser believes she is too dark when she is 4 shades darker than she is currently, and her aunt's standard for too dark is 1.2 times that, and her mother's standard is when her daughter is only 1 shade lighter than herself, how old will the girl be when all three people tell her to stop playing out in the sun? When will the black girl start carrying an umbrella with her when the sun is out?

3. Below is a graph of the black girl's pulse when she sees the blonde-haired woman slowly approach her from behind as she's buying a Mother's Day card. This is her first time getting followed in a store. The black girl is in a J.Crew sweater and jeans. The girl remembers to take her hands out of her pockets and slow her breathing. She softens any hardness in her eyes anyone could claim to see. The black girl smiles. The adjacent graph shows how close the saleswoman is getting to her over time. Find the speed of the girl's pulse when the saleswoman is ten feet away from her.

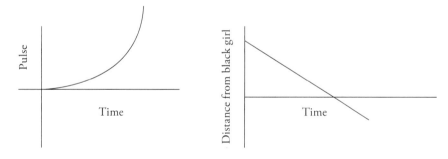

4. By the eighth grade, the black girl knows to sit at the front of the classroom once history class approaches the year 1619. That way she can't see everyone staring at her when their conversation about the start of slavery in America begins. She makes a promise to herself never to be associated with the slaves in her history textbook. Because the black girl can't subtract her skin, create a function that will let the black girl subtract everything else she thought was "too black" about herself within three years. She could start by subtracting her black friends, subtracting rap music from her phone, or subtracting any sort of confidence she has. She could even start by adding a whole new group of white friends or perfect manners or fancy sweaters. Get creative! There are many different correct approaches and answers.

5. *Credit will be assessed on the use of a fully algebraic approach to solve this problem.* The first time the black girl tells her mother she wants to be white, it is in the car. The girl's hair is thinning from the seven years of relaxer, and she tries to push one of the limp strands behind her ear. Her mother yells at her, saying, "You can't do that, you know! You're not white!" The black girl whispers, "I wish I was," from the back seat. Her mother cries when she hears her. The second time she tells her mother she wants to be white is while attending a gymnastics camp where she becomes, for the first time, acutely aware of how black she is in the room of white faces. She calls her mother crying on the phone the very first night, says it would be easier if she looked like everyone else at camp. Her mother cries that time too. In seventh grade at summer camp, a white girl tells the black girl that she is the "whitest black girl (she has) ever met." The black girl takes it as a compliment. In eighth grade, she thinks that if she avoids all black people, she won't be associated with them. If she acts white enough, maybe she won't get followed, won't be thought of as ugly, won't be thought of as angry. In ninth grade when she comes to her fancy boarding school, she promises herself she'll have no black friends. In tenth grade, when a stranger insists the girl is in a "black prep posse," she runs sobbing to the health center to the small, cozy room of a very nice white female counselor. She tries her best to explain how she doesn't feel black enough. The counselor recommends she talk to a black teacher. She never does. In eleventh grade her friend tells her that the guy she likes "doesn't date black girls." If she is seventeen now, how long will it take her to think she is beautiful? (Hint: All of your answers must be doubled because she is black *and* female.)

   How does your answer change if:

   a. she is not a light-skinned black girl, but a dark-skinned black girl?
   b. her parents never talked to her about how race would impact her life?
   c. her hair is nappy?

Extra Credit: The black girl and her mother are traveling from their home (Point X) to a wedding (Point Y), winding down the back roads of Connecticut. The mother asks the daughter how she and her husband could do a better job of raising the girl's brother as a black boy (note that the presence of male privilege in this equation may change your problem-solving strategies). The mother apologizes for not giving her daughter any culture, any roots to hang on to, and no concept of how to embrace her blackness. She says she is scared for her children. "What can we do differently for your brother?" she asks the girl, pleading. If the car can go 55 mph on the highway but only 25 mph on the dirt roads, how long does the black girl have to explain to her mother that she doesn't think there's anything her parents can do to make growing up black less painful?

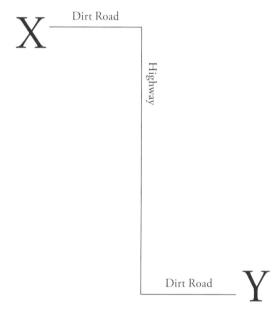

Appendix I

Good Habits for Healthy Writers

Writing is a practice of attention.

—JANE HIRSHFIELD

These days, whenever I ask a colleague or a friend the simple question, "How are you?" the answer inevitably arrives as one terse word: *busy*. And they *are* busy: with work, with deadlines, with family, and with errands that seem to multiply rather than abate. As I let them go on their busy ways, I can feel my own busyness fluttering up in response; I rush to type in one more thing on my smartphone app's to-do list. As I do so, I'm barely aware that my breathing has become more shallow and rapid, and my shoulders have begun to creep up to my ears.

And throughout all this, the news keeps jutting into my line of sight. My neck begins to tense, my head starts to ache, and a vast weariness overtakes my body. By the time I get home, I barely have enough energy to make dinner, much less even think about writing. And worse: I've barely noticed the world around me, hardly taken in the details of life that could provide the impetus for writing in the first place. I've been walking in a fog of stress and amorphous anxiety.

So today, I take a breath. I sit up straight, roll my shoulders back, and look out the window. My copper beech tree is shedding its brilliant leaves. A small breeze jitters the branches, and they wave in a pattern that looks almost choreographed. As I glance at the base of the tree, my busy mind wants to note that I need to rake all the spent leaves—and that I've already missed the opportunity to do so before the rains come—but I allow that thought to drift by, for now. For now, I just want to look, take in this temporary beauty before it's gone.

—BRENDA

In an instructional book such as this one, we aim to provide lots of good, practical information that can help you generate and revise your writing. But often such instruction can neglect or gloss over a fundamental skill we all need to cultivate: the ability to create the space in our lives—and our minds—for writing in the first place. All the instruction on the use of sensory detail or ways to research won't matter unless we're able to actually create the structures we need to slow down, focus, make space for writing, and pay attention.

Such a skill has become even more imperative, and more difficult, in a world that has become increasingly cluttered. We're available for interruption seemingly 24/7, and our gaze can become shortsighted: limited to the distance between us and our screens. Finances can become strained if we choose writing over other work, or when we can't find good-paying work in the first place. We have families and other obligations, all calling to us at the same volume. As Felicia Rose Chavez writes in her article, "The Mental Load: Honoring Your Story Over Your To-Do List":

> I'm always choosing. Which mental load is it today? Man the kitchen table and forgo the rest, knowing that if I choose writing over housework, I'll suffer the physical manifestation of my to-do list, evidence that I'm a bad wife, a bad mother, a bad Chicana? Or else forgo the writing and suffer the heat-hot psychological cargo of golden stories burning bright?

There are so many obstacles to writing, and we're not necessarily taught how to take care of ourselves or how to foster an observant frame of mind. When and if we do so, we prioritize not only the products of writing, but also the practices that help reduce stress and enhance our ability to be patient observers and patient writers.

Practice, Practice, Practice

If we think about writing as a practice, we can liken it to the ways artists, musicians, and athletes incorporate practice as an essential aspect of their work. They make practice part of their routines—sketching, playing scales, running drills. What are the ways we can form practices to increase our stamina and skills in writing?

Practices of Mind and Body

The first order of business? *Breathe.* It seems almost too simple: we breathe all the time, right? But becoming aware of our breathing—this literal lifeline between inner and outer worlds—can be the key to settling down and settling in to your writing.

Breathing is one of the few functions of the body that is both conscious and unconscious. The body will happily keep on breathing, whether you're aware of it or not, but you can also bring your attention to the breath and direct it in powerful ways. Jon Kabat-Zinn, founder of the secular Mindfulness-Based Stress Reduction (MBSR) program, draws on the basic teachings of many spiritual leaders to show how simple mindfulness practices can benefit both body and mind. He writes of the breath as the foundation of these practices in his book *Mindfulness for Beginners:*

> Take the breath, for instance. We take it so much for granted. . . . Suzuki Roshi referred to its coming in and going out over and over again as a "swinging door." And since we can't leave home without this vital and mysterious "swinging door," our breathing can serve as a convenient first object of attention to bring us back into the present moment. . . . It is an ideal anchor for our wayward attention.

There are dozens of breathing awareness exercises available, and a quick search on the internet will lead you to some helpful resources (see also the list of resources at the end of this chapter). They take just a few minutes, and the more you practice, the more you will find yourself automatically turning to the breath as a way to "reset" yourself and your day. By coming back to the self, you also create the space to be more observant: both of the world around you and of the associations your mind makes. This is the fodder for writing.

Moments of Transition

We often feel as though we are moving nonstop through our days, barely remembering how we got from one place to the next. But in reality dozens of moments give us opportunities to stop and take a breath.

1. Become aware of the moments of transition that occur in your day. These can be as simple as moving from one room to another, from one classroom to another, leaving the house, entering the house, getting in your car, leaving your car, waiting in line at a store, and so on.
2. The next time you're aware that you are in a moment of transition, slow down and pause for a few seconds.
3. Take a deep breath. Reset yourself.
4. Notice something in your environment, just observing life around you for a moment.
5. Continue on with what you are doing.

One easy way to begin this practice, if you drive, is to use the unbuckling of your seatbelt as a reminder. Park your car, and before you automatically unbuckle the seatbelt, breathe three times. You'll be surprised at how effective this practice can be, and it takes less than a minute. And you can use any opportunity—an elevator ride, a stoplight, waiting for your coffee order—as a moment of intentional transition, breath, and observation.

Desk Yoga
Writers spend *a lot* of time at their desks. And perhaps you also spend time sitting at a desk in your job or your studies. Our bodies can suffer from sitting too much, and an unhappy body can often lead to an unhappy mind.

1. Take notice of your posture when you are working at a desk. Are you sitting up straight or are you hunched over? How are you holding your neck? Where are your shoulders?
2. Set a timer. Every twenty minutes or so, take a moment to sit up, roll your shoulders back, adjust the position of your neck. Take an intentional breath.
3. There are many online programs and books available that can offer you simple stretches that take just a few minutes and that you can do at your desk. One of our favorites is "Desk Yoga" by yoga teacher Rodney Yee. You'll want stretches that counteract the unhealthy postures: chest openers, side stretches, etc. (Of course, don't do anything that feels uncomfortable or causes pain.)

Dealing with Technology

For many of us, digital technologies are intricately woven in with our daily lives. We're writing at our computers, which are linked to the internet, and we have our cell phones that keep us in constant connection with both our local and global communities. Technology isn't a negative thing, per se, but the omnipresence of technology makes it easy for our devices to take over and become distractions. They can also become an underlying source of stress and anxiety.

The answer is not necessarily to abandon use of technology; such a thing just isn't possible anymore. But we can, perhaps, become a bit more aware of how and when we're using technology intentionally (helpful) and not-so-intentionally (unhelpful).

A good resource for dealing with technology is the book *Mindful Tech: How to Bring Balance to Our Digital Lives* by David Levy. Much of the material came out of his work with the Association for Contemplative Mind in Higher Education (another great resource), and his observations on how digital technologies were affecting his students. He supplies many possible avenues for becoming aware of ourselves in relationship to our everyday online habits and using that awareness to shift their power over us.

By doing these kinds of observations, you might find yourself making some simple changes. For example, maybe you allow yourself a half-hour in the morning without any input from the online world. Try it for a week, observe how you feel. Or you set a timer while you're working—twenty-five minutes, say—and can only go online when the time is up. Or perhaps you go a little further, instituting an "Internet Sabbath" where you don't go online for one day each week. Or a weekend "offline retreat." The important thing is to experiment and find whatever works for you.

Practices of Reading

Many of us became writers because we loved to read. As children, we often might have been found tucked away in a favorite hiding place, reading for hours on end. Reading itself can be a profound way to find moments of still-ness and absorption in the midst of busyness.

Unfortunately, for some of us, the time and space to read deeply can feel in short supply and reading online can foster the habit of skimming.

Reading as Preparation for Writing

One way to prioritize reading is to see it as an essential preparation to the act of writing. Such a perspective may enable you to set aside the time necessary to read in a focused way. And as with the breathing practices offered previously, you don't have to set aside wide swaths of time for this; just a half hour, or even fifteen minutes, would do nicely.

Most important is the *way* you will read. You can certainly read for pleasure, but as writers-in-training you'll also be reading to learn how the authors you love do what they do. Following is a practice adapted from the ancient ritual of *Lectio Divina*.

1. While reading, make note of a passage that feels especially strong (vibrant, alive).
2. Reread the passage aloud, slowly.
3. Take note of what you hear when you read it aloud (rhythms, images, sounds, etc.)
4. What "speaks" to you in this passage? Why did it stand out to you?
5. If you're so inclined, you can keep what is sometimes referred to as a "commonplace book": a journal to write down these passages and your responses to them.

Reading as a Writer

As avid readers, we often read for content first, taking in the story and the images for pleasure. As writers striving to learn from our reading, we need to do a second read that analyzes *how* the writer achieved his or her effects (and think about how we can "steal" some of those techniques).

Preceding the Anthology, we provided you a handy list called "Reading as a Writer." You can use these questions just for yourself, as part of your reading practice, but you can also use these ideas as part of a group or class. They will focus your reading on techniques and skills you might practice for your own purposes. A good way to learn from other writers is to emulate their craft, much the way an athlete will study game tapes, or artists might make copies of the masters as preparation for their own work.

Practices of Writing

All writers have their own tried-and-true writing routines, and what works for one person may not work at all for another. So the only way to find the writing practices that work for you is to experiment and be open to changing things up. Try writing every day at a particular time and place to make it part of your daily routine (this can be for fifteen minutes or several hours). Or set aside two hours once a week, on the weekend. Or carry a notebook wherever you go, jotting down ideas and observations as they come to you.

The poet and essayist Lia Purpura has said to her students: "Touch your work every day." This touch—staying in contact, even if for only a brief hello—helps create momentum, keeping your writing mind engaged. Kim Stafford, in his essay "Writing Daily, Writing in Tune," likens daily writing practice to the way a musical instrument holds the vibration of song long after the music has stopped:

> An instrument dies if not played daily. A guitar, a violin, a lute chills the air for the first fifteen minutes of fresh play. It will need to be quickened from scratch. But the fiddle played every day hangs resonant on the wall, quietly boisterous when first it is lifted down, already trembling, anxious to speak, to cry out, to sing at the bow's first stroke. . . . The instrument is in tune before the strings are tuned.

The key word for any routine, though, is *practice.* Not all writing sessions will produce viable work, and production might not be the point. The practice of writing aims to be just that: a training that makes you stronger. And as with any practice, you need to do it regularly to see results. As Bonnie Friedman writes in her book *Writing Past Dark: Envy, Fear, Distraction, and Other Dilemmas in the Writer's Life:* "Talent is not rare. What's rare is the devotion and stamina to keep writing, and the ability to build on the successes that your work already displays. Caring for the writerly self is a decisive component in being able to keep writing, and writing better."

Many writers feel they need solitude to write. They can write only in isolation, with no noise or interruption. Others enjoy writing by themselves, but in the midst of daily life (notice all the laptops and solo writers you see in your local coffee shop!). And still others have found that it helps to write with other writers who give both support and accountability to the writing routine. And you may find that what worked for you in the past no longer works so well; you can keep evolving your practice as your writing self evolves.

In Chapter 14, "The Power of Writing Communities," we give you some ideas on how to develop and use writing groups, writing contracts, and writing challenges to help you generate new work. Look back to that chapter and see what small steps you can take now to find the support you need.

FOR FURTHER READING

Resources Available Online

- You can search "apps for stress reduction" and find several different kinds of apps to use on your phone or computer.
- *The Center for Contemplative Mind in Higher Education* offers several different articles, guided meditations, and practices.
- "Desk Yoga" by Rodney Yee. Short four-minute stretches you can do at your desk.

Print Resources

- *The Writing Life* by Annie Dillard
- *Writing Past Dark: Envy, Fear, Distraction, and Other Dilemmas in the Writer's Life* by Bonnie Friedman
- *Writing Down the Bones: Freeing the Writer Within* by Natalie Goldberg
- *Writing Begins with the Breath: Embodying Your Authentic Voice* by Larraine Herring
- *Bird by Bird: Some Instructions on Writing and* Life by Anne Lamott
- *Mindful Tech: How to Bring Balance to Our Digital Lives* by David Levy
- *The Mindful Writer: Noble Truths of the Writing Life* by Dinty Moore
- *The Pen and the Bell: Mindful Writing in a Busy World* by Brenda Miller and Holly J. Hughes
- *The Muses Among Us: Eloquent Listening and Other Pleasures of the Writer's Craft* by Kim Stafford
- *The Creative Habit: Learn It and Use It for Life* by Twyla Tharpe
- *Full Catastrophe Living: Using the Wisdom of Your Body and Mind to Face Stress, Pain, and Illness* by Jon Kabat-Zinn

Appendix II

Resources for Writers

Time and Money

Time and money: two essential things that can be in short supply for sustaining a productive writing life.

Time

For focused, intensive writing time, consider applying for a residency at a writers' or artists' colony. Most of these provide time and space for writing at no or nominal charge (including meals). Besides the benefit of sustained writing time, you also will meet other writers and artists who will inspire and support your work. Lists of retreat centers can be found online, at websites such as Association of Writers and Writing Programs (AWP) and *Poets & Writers* magazine. (Both organizations also have wonderful print journals, as well.) Be on the lookout for retreats that cater to your demographic: some offer special residencies for working mothers, for example, or for writers who live in a particular state or region.

You can also create your own retreat for a day, a weekend, a week, or longer by renting a place by yourself or, ideally, with others. Many writers also create "virtual retreats": a group agrees to spend anywhere from a day to a weekend with a predetermined writing schedule and goals; each member checks in regularly via email or on a blog with what has been accomplished. Some even write together, virtually, by using a video conference-calling app, so that they can feel more connected as they work in their own spaces. If you are in a writing class, arrange to meet a small group of peers outside of class time for generative writing; not only will you gain more focus and inspiration, you might also forge lasting writerly friendships.

Money

Grants and fellowships exist to help support your writing. Both AWP and *Poets & Writers* list grants, prizes, and fellowships; you can also search online with the phrase "grants for writers" and come up with many good sources. Often there are fairly large grants available for specific types of writers (younger writers, certain ethnic groups, religion, geographic region, etc.). Large grants—such as the National Endowment for the Arts (NEA), the Guggenheim, the Whiting Foundation, the Lannan Foundation, and the Rona Jaffe Award—exist, but they require you to establish your work in literary journals first. Some grants you can't even apply for, but anonymous panelists nominate your work. So you need to have your writing out there in the public eye. (See Chapter 15, "Publishing Your Creative Nonfiction.")

Credits

Index

Abbey, Edward, 104
abstract language, 174
Ackerman, Diane, 40
adjective/adverb "purge," 198
"Adorable Things" (Shōnagon), 130–131
The Adventures of Huckleberry Finn (Twain), 35, 38
"After Yitzl" (Goldbarth), 175
"Afternoon of an American Boy" (White), 10–11
"Against Technique" (Lott), 159
The Age of Missing Information (McKibben), 72–73
agenting approach, in workshop, 206–207
agents, literary, 222
Als, Hilton, 74
Andrew, Elizabeth Jarrett, 195–196
Angela's Ashes (McCourt), 29
animals, 40–41
Another Bullshit Night in Suck City (Flynn), 142–143
Arsdale, Sarah Van, 35
The Art of the Personal Essay (Lopate), 103, 104, 153
arts, 69–77
  moving image, 71–73
  music as, 73–74

and "reading narratives," 74–75
  visual, 70–71
Association of Writers and Writing Programs (AWP), 220, 299, 300
attention to details, 81
audience, 197, 226
Aurelius, Marcus, 103
author bios, 226
autobiographical comics, 131–132

"Backtalk" (Hoffman), 108
Baldwin, James, 56, 112
Ballering, Zoe, 92–93
Barnes, Kim, 23
Beard, Jo Ann:
  and attention to detail, 6, 172–174
  and braided form, 127
  and dialogue, 176–178
  and memory, 8
Beavis, Catherine, 142
"Because, the Ferguson Verdict" (Sukrungruang), 52, 125, 279–281
Bechdel, Alison, 132
Beckett, Samuel, 142
beginnings, 130
"Behind the Screen" (Beard), 6

Bellingham Review, 139, 143, 233

Berry, Wendell, 38–40, 42

The Best American Essays 2008, 108

Between the World and Me (Coates), 60–61

biographer, stance of a, 25–26

bios, author, 226

Bird, Isabella, 104

Biss, Eula, 129, 154–156

Blake, William, 142

blanket-statement dodge, 161–162

blogs, 144–145

"Blood; Quantum" (Geller), 61–62

Bluets (Nelson), 125–126

Bly, Nellie, 104

bodies, 59–67

differences between, 64–65

and gender/sexual identity, 62–64

and race, 60–62

body image, 15–16

The Body of the Dead Christ in the Tomb (painting), 115

book proposals for publication, 224–227

Book View Café, 228

Borich, Barrie Jean, 63

Botany of Desire: A Plant's-Eye View of the World (Pollan), 80

Bouldrey, Brian, 115

Boully, Jenny, 55, 154–156

"A Boundary Zone" (Hesse), 105

braided essays, 126–127

Braiding Sweetgrass: Indigenous Wisdom, Scientific Knowledge, and the Teachings of Plants (Kimmerer), 39–40

breadcrumbing, 220–221

breathing, for stress reduction, 293–295

Bresland, John, 115

Brevity (online journal), 61, 122

Brown, Michael, 52

Bucak, A. Papatya, 122

"Buckeye" (Sanders), 12–13

"Burl's" (Cooper), 184–185

Burroway, Janet, 179

Bush, Vannevar, 144

Byron, George Gordon, 214

Canterbury Tales (Chaucer), 142

Capote, Truman, 141

Cappello, Mary, 80–81, 84

Castro, Joy, 61

Center for Pacific Northwest Studies (Western Washington University), 90

challenges of creative nonfiction, 151–168

fact vs fiction as, 156–161

pact with reader as, 152–156

protecting oneself as, 161–162

solutions to, 162–164

writing from life as, 152

"A Chapter on Ears" (Lamb), 104

chapter-by-chapter outlines, 225

character development, 175–176

Chaucer, Geoffrey, 142

Chavez, Felicia Rose, 292

The Checklist Manifesto: How to Get Things Right (Gawande), 80

"Choom" (Boully), 154–156

Christman, Jill, 40

cinematic scenes, 13–14
Citizen Potawatomi Nation, 39
"The Clan of One-Breasted
    Women" (Williams), 82–83, 165
cliché, 174, 180
Coates, Ta-Nehisi, 60–61
Colbert, Stanley, 212
collage structure, 124–126
collections of essays, 222–223
command voice, 181
competition, 226
complexity, 83–85
consciousness, human, 39
"Consider the Lobster" (Wallace),
    109–110
containers, 184–187
Cooper, Bernard:
    omission of characters by,
        160–161
    and point of view, 154–155
    and profluence, 184–185
    and sound, 11, 28
    "The Fine Art of Sighing,"
        243–244
    on writing process, 199
cooperative presses, 228
"The Coroner's Photographs"
    (Staples), 25, 185–186, 274–278
cover letters, 221, 233
Cowley, Abraham, 110
Crazy Brave (Harjo), 141–142
Creative Nonfiction (journal), 86
cross-genre writing, 141–142
"Cubist Mother" (Ross), 123–124
cueing the reader, 162–163
cultural identity, 26–27

D'Agata, John, x, 153
Davenport, Guy, 69
de Gutes, Kate Carroll, 64
"Dead Christ" (video essay), 115
Deadpool (film), 163
decentering, 144
Deleuze, Gilles, 144
desk yoga, 294
detail(s):
    attention to, 81
    specificity and, 173–174
    storytelling with, 5–8
dialogue, 176–177
Dickens, Charles, 113
Dickinson, Emily:
    on flood subjects, 84
    and humor, 187
    "Tell all the truth but tell it
        slant," v
    and truth, ix, 102
Didion, Joan:
    and collage structure, 125
    in essay tradition, 104
    on framing, 106
    on immersion, 86
    and looping essays, 186
    and New Journalism, 108–109
    and point of view, 154–155
    and sensory detail, 9–10
digital literature, 143–144
Dillard, Annie:
    and animals, 40–41
    on poetry vs. prose, 169, 178
    and scientific research, 85
disability, as identity, 64–65
discussion, 204–207

dodging, 161–162
Doty, Mark, 62
"A 'Downwinder' in Hiroshima"
    (Williams), 30
Doyle, Brian, 53, 183–184,
    245–246
drafting, 194–195
"The Drama Bug" (Sedaris), 187
Duncan, David James, 4–5

earliest memory, 4–5
eBay, 131
Edgeworth, Maria, 104
editing, 231–235
Ehrlich, Gretel, 33
Einstein, Albert, 85
The Electric Kool-Aid Acid Test
    (Wolfe), 108–109
The Elements of Style (Strunk), 174
Elkin, Stanley, 149
Emerson, Ralph Waldo, 38
emotional truth, 158–160
The Empathy Exams (Jamison),
    112
Encyclopedia of an Ordinary Life
    (Rosenthal), 129–130
endings, 130
Enter the Dragon (film), 72
"An Entrance to the Woods"
    (Berry), 42
epistrophe, 183
essays:
    braided, 126–127
    collage, 124–126
    collections of, 222–223
    flash, 121–123

"hermit crab," 127–130
of ideas, 111–112
looping, 185–186
lyric, x, 120–131, 181
meditative, 110
micro, 123–124
nonce, 130–131
object, 111
personal (*see* personal essays)
radio, 114
video, 115
Essays (de Montaigne), 103
"essays in disguise" (Plutarch and
    Seneca), 103
Essays in Idleness (Kenkō), 103
essays of ideas, 111–112
exposition, 170–173

factual truth, 158–160
Faery, Rebecca, 121
Fallaci, Oriana, 88–89
family, 23–32
    biographer, stance of a, 25–26
    and cultural identity via food,
        26–27
    issues with writing about, 28
    motives for writing about, 30
    permission to write about,
        28–30
    situating yourself in relation to,
        24
*Family Resemblance: An Anthology
    and Exploration of Eight Hybrid
    Literary Genres* (eds. Sulak and
    Kolosov), 142
Faulkner, William, 237

feedback, 204
"Fifty Ways to Be a Brilliant Mom
    Without Having a Baby" (blog),
    145
"The Fine Art of Sighing"
    (Cooper), 11, 27, 154–155,
    243–244
Firebird (Doty), 62
"First" (Van Meter), 62, 179–180,
    282–285
first-person narrator, 107
Fisher, M. F. K., 10
flash nonfiction, 121–123
flood subjects, 84
Flynn, Nick, 142–143
food, 26–27
"Forest in the Trees: The
    Challenges of Shaping a Book
    (Not a Collection) of Essays"
    (McClanahan), 223
form, 102, 107–114
"A Four-Hundred-Year-Old
    Woman" (Mukherjee), 36–37
"The Fourth State of Matter"
    (Beard), 127, 172–173,
    177–178
fourth wall, breaking of, 163–164
Fowler, Gene, 194
*Fragments: Memories of a Wartime
    Childhood* (Wilkomirski), 159
framing, 106–107
Frankenstein (Shelley), 214
Franzen, Jonathan, 113
Frey, James, 159–160
Friedman, Bonnie, 297
Fries, Kenny, 64, 65

"From Soup to Nuts" (Tandoh), 27
Fun Home: A Family Tragicomic
    (Bechdel), 132
Fussell, Paul, 43, 44

Gawande, Atul, 80
Gay, Roxane, 15
Geller, Danielle, 61–62
gender identity, 62–64
Gerard, Philip, 79, 224
Glass, Ira, 114
global revision, 195
"Go Ahead: Write About Your
    Parents, Again" (Wilson), 25
Goldbarth, Albert, 175
Goldberg, Natalie, 196
"Goodbye to All That" (Didion),
    9–10, 154–155
"Good-Bye to Forty-Eighth Street"
    (White), 35–36
Gopnik, Adam, 108
Gornick, Vivian, 107, 153
Granta (journal), 41
grants, for writers, 300
graphic memoirs, 131–132
*The Graywolf Annual 3: Essays,
    Memoirs and Reflections* (ed.
    Walker), 103
Guattari, Félix, 144
Guggenheim fellowships, 300
Gutkind, Lee, 86, 151

Hakala, Marjorie Rose, 41, 88,
    247–254
Hamlet, 114
Hampl, Patricia, 157–158

Harjo, Joy, 141–142

Harry Potter series, 212

"Hateful Things" (Shōnagon), 130–131

Hazlitt, William, 104

hearing, sense of, 11

Hemingway, Ernest, 123

Hemley, Robin, 24, 29, 153

"Hereafter in Fields" (Vivian), 110

"hermit crab" essays, 127–130

Hesse, Douglas, 105

Hirshfield, Jane, 291

history, 51–58
    as frame for nonfiction, 52–53
    and perception, 56
    protagonists in, 54–55

Hoffman, Richard, 108

Holbein, Hans, 115

Holocaust, 131–132, 159

home, writing about, 36–37

House Built on Ashes (Rodríguez), 7

"How to Become a Writer" (Moore), 128

Huber, Sonya, 16

Hughes, Ted, 214

Hugo, Richard, 200

human consciousness, 39

humor, 187

Hunger: A Memoir of (My) Body (Gay), 15

Hurd, Barbara:
    and meditative essays, 110
    and research essays, 83–84
    and setting, 87–88
    "To Keep an Ear to the Ground," 255–258

hybrid forms, 142–143

hybrid presses, 228

I Am, I Am, I Am: Seventeen Brushes with Death (O'Farrell), 13–14

"I Cannot Explain My Fear" (Bucak), 122

identity:
    cultural, 26–27
    disability and, 64–65
    and early memories, 4
    gender/sexual, 62–64
    racial, 60–62

illness memoirs, 16–17

image, 179–180

imagination, 157–158

"imagistic endurance," 5–8

immersion research, 86–87

In Cold Blood (Capote), 141

inadvertent revelations, 129

independent publishers, 227

Indra's net, 81

Internet, for research, 90–91

"Internet Sabbath," 295

interrogative voice, 181

interviews, for research, 88–89

intuition, 14–15

"Inventing Peace" (Weschler), 70

Inventing the Truth: The Art and Craft of Memoir (ed. Zinsser), 107–108

The Iowa Review, 164

Istanbul: Memories and the City (Pamuk), 87

"It Wasn't Enough" (Strong), 114

Iyer, Pico, 43

Jamison, Leslie, 112
Jane Eyre (Brontë), 35
Johnson, Jenny, 5
JSTOR, 90–91
"Jumping the Fence" (Hakala), 41, 88, 247–254
Just Breathe Normally (Shumaker), 224
"Just This Once" (Shumaker), 224
juxtaposition, 124, 139

Kabat-Zinn, Jon, 293
Karr, Mary, 163–164
Keller, Helen, 9
Kenkō, 103
Kennedy, John, 123
Kesey, Ken, 109
Khan Academy, 91
Khomeini, Ayatollah, 89
Kimmerer, Robin Wall, 39–40, 42
King, Susan, 140
King Lear (Shakespeare), 142
Kingston, Maxine Hong, 113–114
Kitchen, Judith:
  and character development, 175
  on hybrid form, 142
  and point of view, 178
  on publishing, 231
Klaus, Carl, 126
"The Knife" (Selzer), 171–172
Knopp, Lisa, 162
Kotre, John, 4
Koul, Scaachi, 26–27
Kundera, Milan, 51, 52
Kushner, Tony, 203, 204
Kuusisto, Stephen, 59

Lamb, Charles, 104
Lamott, Anne, 187
Lannan Foundation, 300
Le Guin, Ursula K., 228
"Leap" (Doyle), 53, 183–184, 245–246
"Leaves from the Mental Portfolio of a Eurasian," 54–55
Lectio Divina, 296
Lejeune, Philippe, 153
LeMay, Eric, 143
Lenney, Dinah, 111
Letters Like the Day: On Reading Georgia O'Keeffe (Sinor), 75
Levy, David, 295
The Liar's Club (Karr), 163–164
libraries, 89–90
The Lifespan of a Fact (D'Agata), 153
Listening to the Savage: River Notes and Half-Heard Melodies (Hurd), 83–84
literary agents, 222
literary journalism, 108–110
literary journals, 218–219
LitLine (website), 220
"Living Like Weasels" (Dillard), 40–41
Living Revision: A Writer's Craft as Spiritual Practice (Andrew), 195–196
looping essays, 185–186
Lopate, Phillip, 103, 104, 153
Lott, Bret, 159
Lying: A Metaphorical Memoir (Slater), 163
lyric essays, x, 120–131, 181

Madden, Patrick, 131
The Made-Up Self: Impersonation in the Personal Essay (Klaus), 126
Mailer, Norman, 108–109
main clause, 176
Mairs, Nancy, 64–65
"Man and Boy" (Sutin), 139, 175
Maps to Anywhere (Cooper), 160
Margolick, David, 74
marketing, 226–227
"Marketing Memory" (Cooper), 160–161
Martone, Michael, 131
"Math 1619" (Wallace), 62, 128–129, 286–289
Maus I (Spiegelman), 131–132
Maus II (Spiegelman), 131–132
McClanahan, Rebecca, 223
McCourt, Frank, 29
McKibben, Bill, 72–73
mechanics of personal essays, 105
Meditations (Aurelius), 103
meditative essays, 110
"Memoir? Fiction? Where's the Line?" (Schwartz), 158–159
memoirs, 107–108
memory, 3–22
   and body image, 15–16
   earliest, 4–5
   and illness memoirs, 16–17
   and imagination, 157–158
   and "imagistic endurance," 5–8
   metaphorical, 8
   muscle, 8–9
   senses of, 9–15
   "shocks" of, 5, 108, 173

"Memory and Imagination" (Hampl), 157–158
"The Mental Load: Honoring Your Story Over Your To-Do List" (Chavez), 292
metaphor, 82, 161, 179–180
metaphorical memory, 8
"Michael Martone's Leftover Water" (Madden), 131
micro essays, 123–124
A Million Little Pieces (Frey), 159–160
Mindful Tech: How to Bring Balance to Our Digital Lives (Levy), 295
Mindfulness for Beginners (Kabat-Zinn), 293
Mindfulness-Based Stress Reduction (MBSR), 293
mixed media, 137–147
   blogs/social media as, 144–145
   cross-genre writing as, 141–142
   digital literature as, 143–144
   hybrid form as, 142–143
   scope of, 137–140
Momaday, N. Scott, 3
"moments of being," 5, 83
moments of transition, 293–294
money, as resource, 300
Montaigne, Michel de:
   in essay tradition, 103–104
   on his process, 110, 119
   "Of Smells," 259–261
Moore, Lorrie, 128
Morábito, Fabio, 111
The Moth: True Stories Told Live (radio show), 114

Mount Baker, 34

moving image arts, 71–73

Mrs. Dalloway (Woolf), 181–182

Mukherjee, Bharati, 36–37

muscle memory, 8–9

music, 73–74

My Lesbian Husband: Landscapes of a Marriage (Borich), 63

Nabokov, Vladimir, 193

NaMeWriMo (National Memoir Writing Month), 215

Nan A. Talese, 159

NaNoWriMo (National Novel Writing Month), 215

NaPoWriMo (National Poetry Writing Month), 215

National Endowment for the Arts (NEA), 300

nature writing, 37–42

Nelson, Maggie, 125–126

New Journalism, 108–110

New Pages (website), 220

Nguyen, Beth, 205

"The Night My Mother Met Bruce Lee" (Rekdal), 26, 62, 72, 270–273

"No Name Woman" (Kingston), 113–114

Nola: A Memoir of Faith, Art, and Madness (Hemley), 153

nonce forms, 130–131

The Noonday Demon (Solomon), 109

The Normal School (magazine), 71

"Notes of a Native Son" (Baldwin), 56, 112

"Nuns Fret Not at Their Convent's Narrow Room" (Wordsworth), 121

object essays, 111

"Object Lessons" (Bloomsbury Books), 111

The Object Parade (Lenney), 111

"Of Greatness" (Cowley), 110

"Of Smells" (Montaigne), 10, 259–261

O'Farrell, Maggie, 13–14

On Autobiography (Lejeune), 153

"On Being a Cripple" (Mairs), 65

"On the Pleasure of Hating" (Hazlitt), 104

"On Touching Ground" (Parms), 71, 126–127, 262–268

online journals, 219

Oprah's Book Club, 159

Orwell, George, 104, 126

outlines, chapter-by-chapter, 225

Packing for Mars: The Curious Science of Life in the Void (Roach), 86

"The Pain Scale" (Biss), 129

Pain Woman Takes Your Keys, and Other Essays from a Nervous System (Huber), 16

Pamuk, Orhan, 87

Paper Lion (Plimpton), 86

Paris Review, 86

Parker, Dorothy, 182

Parms, Jericho, 71, 126–127, 262–268

participatory research, 86–89
"The Pat Boone Fan Club"
    (Silverman), 74
"People Are Starving" (Rivecca),
    15, 178–179
"Perdition" (Radtke), 14, 131, 269
"perhapsing," 162
"Perhapsing: The Use of
    Speculation in Creative
    Nonfiction" (Knopp), 162
personal essay(s):
    essays of ideas as, 111–112
    meditative essays as, 110
    memoirs as, 107–108
    New Journalism as, 108–110
    object essays as, 111
    radio essays as, 114
    sketches/portraits as, 113–114
    video essays as, 115
personal essays, 101–117
    forms of, 102
    framing in, 106–107
    mechanics of, 105
    tradition of, 103–104, 107–114
personality, 106
perspective, 165
Petrie, Lindsay, 180
photography, 106
pitfalls of creative nonfiction,
    164–166
place-based research, 87–88
Plath, Sylvia, 214
Plimpton, George, 86
Plutarch, 103
poetry, 181–184
Poets & Writers magazine, 299, 300

point of view, 177–179
Polidori, John William, 214
Pollan, Michael, 80
pop-culture references, 72
porosity, 81
portraits, 113–114
A Postcard Memoir (Sutin), 71,
    139–140
practices, 292–298
    of mind and body, 293-295
    of reading, 295-296
    of writing, 297-298
A Prairie Home Companion (radio
    show), 114
present tense, 5–6
primary sources, 91–92
privileged observers, 54
profluence, 184
pronouns, 177–179
proofreading, 234
prose, 197–200
protagonists, 54–55
Proust, Marcel, 9, 75
publication, 217–230
    book proposals for, 224–227
    of books, 222–227
    breadcrumbing, 220
    literary agents in, 222
    researching, 220–221
    self-directed, 227–228
    in small presses, 227
    submission for, 221–222
    targeting work toward, 220
    venues for, 218–219
PubMed, 90
Pulitzer Prize, 131–132

the "punch" (end words), 198–199
Purpura, Lia, 297

racial identity, 60–62
radio essays, 114
Radtke, Kristen, 14, 131, 269
Rambo (film), 43
reading as a writer, 239-241, 296
reading, practices of, 295–296
"Reading History to My Mother"
    (Hemley), 24, 29
"reading narratives," 74–75
*Refuge: An Unnatural History of
    Family and Place* (Williams),
    82–83
Rekdal, Paisley:
    and family, 28
    and imagination, 25–26
    "The Night My Mother Met
        Bruce Lee," 270–273
    and pop-culture references, 72
    and race, 62
Remembrance of Things Past
    (Proust), 9, 75
representative scenes, 172–173
research, 79–97
    attention to detail in, 81
    developing skills for, 89–92
    escalating complexity in, 83–85
    immersion, 86–87
    interviews as, 88–89
    of key events, 82–83
    metaphors in, 82
    participatory, 86–89
    place-based, 87–88
    research maps, 92–94

scientific/technical, 85
    in topical nonfiction, 80–81
retreats, for writers, 299
"revenge prose," 164–166
revision, 195–200
rhythm, 181–184
Rivecca, Suzanne, 15, 178–179
Roach, Mary, 85, 86
Rodríguez, José Antonio, 7, 8, 12
Rona Jaffe Award, 300
Roosevelt, Franklin, 123
Rose, Phyllis, 74–75
Rose Metal Press, 142
Rosenthal, Amy Krouse, 129–130
Ross, Michelle, 123–124
Rowling, J. K., 212

*Safekeeping: Some True Stories from
    a Life* (Thomas), 164
Salon magazine, 132
Sand, George, 54
Sanders, Scott Russell, ix, 12–13
SASE (self-addressed stamped
    envelope), 221–222
Savarese, Ralph James, 59
"search and destroy" (*to be* verbs),
    197-198
scene, 130, 170–173
Schwartz, Mimi, 29, 158–159
scientific research, 85
Sedaris, David, 187
self-directed publication, 227–228
Self-Publishing Review, 228
Selzer, Richard, 171–173, 176, 177
Seneca Review, x, 121
Seneca the Younger, 103

senses, 9–15
September 11 terrorist attacks, 113, 183
setting(s):
  as characters, 35–36
  home as, 36–37
  nature as, 37–42
settings, 33–49
  and travel writing, 42–44
  witnesses of, 44–45
sexual identity, 62–64
Shakespeare, William, 114, 142, 187
Shapes of Native Nonfiction (eds. Warburton and Washuta), 102
Shelley, Mary, 214
Shelley, Percy, 214
"shocks of memory," 5, 108, 173
Shōnagon, Sei, 103, 130–131
"A Short Essay on Being" (Boully), 55
Shumaker, Peggy, 224
sight, sense of, 13–14
Silverman, Sue William, 74
Sin Far, Sui, 54–55
Sinor, Jennifer, 75
"Sir, Ma'am, Sir: Gender Fragments" (de Gutes), 64
The Situation and the Story (Gornick), 107
"sixth" sense, 14–15
Six-Word Memoirs (journal), 123
sketches, 113–114
Slater, Lauren, 163
"The Sloth" (Christman), 40

"Slouching Towards Bethlehem" (Didion), 125
small presses, 227
smell, sense of, 9–10
The Smoking Gun (website), 159
social media, 144–145
Solomon, Andrew, 109
Sontag, Susan, 194, 217
specific scenes, 172–173
specificity, 173–174
Spiegelman, Art, 131–132
Stafford, Kim, 297
Stallone, Sylvester, 43
Staples, Blake, 186
Staples, Brent, 25, 185–186, 274–278
Staring Back: The Disability Experience from Inside Out (Fries), 64
Stegner, Wallace, 106
Stieglitz, Alfred, 75
The Story of World War II's Heroic Army of Deception (Gerard), 224
Strange Fruit: The Biography of a Song (Margolick and Als), 74
"Street Haunting" (Woolf), 186
Strong, Charlene, 114
structures, 184–187
Strunk, William Jr., 174
subjectivity, 207
submissions, 221–222, 234–235
Submittable (online submission manager), 220
Sukrungruang, Ira:
  "Because, the Ferguson Verdict," 279–281

and collage structure, 62, 125
and formative moments, 52
on race, 61
Sutin, Lawrence, 71, 137, 139–140, 175
Swallow: Foreign Bodies, Their Ingestion, Inspiration, and the Curious Doctor Who Extracted Them (Cappello), 80–81
"Swimming Pool Hedonist," 82
syntactic symbolism, 182

taglines, 162
Talese, Gay, 108–109
Tandoh, Ruby, 27
targeting your work, 220, 226
taste, sense of, 10–11
technical research, 85
technology, dealing with, 295
TED talks, 91
Textbook (Rosenthal), 129–130
Thelma and Louise (film), 73
themes, 130
"therapist's couch prose," 164–166
"There's No Recipe for Growing Up" (Koul), 26–27
"A Thing Shared" (Fisher), 10
"Things of This Life" (Kitchen), 175, 178
This American Life (radio show), 114
Thomas, Abigail, 164
Thoreau, Henry David, 37–40, 104
time, as resource, 299
"Time and Distance Overcome" (Biss), 154–156
titles, 123

"To Keep an Ear to the Ground" (Hurd), 40, 83–84, 87–88, 110, 255–258
Toolbox (Morábito), 111
topical nonfiction, 80–81
touch, sense of, 12–13
tradition of personal essays, 103–104, 107–114
transcendentalists, 38
transition, moments of, 293–294
travel writing, 42–44
Treading the Maze: An Artist's Book of Daze (King), 140
Triquarterly (journal), 115
Trueblood, Kate, 213
truth, 155–161
Truth Serum (Cooper), 160

The Vampyre (Polidori), 214
Van Meter, Ryan, 5, 62, 179–180, 282–285
venues for publication, 218–219
Vermeer, Johannes, 70
video essays, 115
Video Night in Kathmandu (Iyer), 43
virtual retreats, 299
visual arts, 70–71
Vivian, Robert, 110

Walden; or, Life in the Woods (Thoreau), 38, 104
Walker, Scott, 101, 103
Wallace, David Foster, 109–110
Wallace, Gwendolyn, 62, 128–129, 286–289
Warburton, Theresa, 102

Washuta, Elissa, 102
Weschler, Lawrence, 70–71
Western Washington University, xi, 233
Where the Bluebird Sings to the Lemonade Springs (Stegner), 106
Whetham, Jen, 82
White, E. B., 10–11, 35–36, 126
White Gloves: How We Create Ourselves Through Memory (Kotre), 4
Whiting Foundation, 300
whole truth, 160–161
Wilkomirski, Binjamin, 159
Williams, Terry Tempest, 30, 82–83, 165
Wilson, Tarn, 25
Winfrey, Oprah, 159–160
Winterson, Jeanette, 99
witness, stance of, 30, 44–45, 53–54, 183, 253
Wolfe, Tom, 80, 108–109
Woolf, Virginia, 5, 181–182, 186
Wordsworth, William, 121
"The World as I See It" (Einstein), 85
"Writing About Family: Is It Worth It?" (Schwartz), 29
writing communities, 203–216
    checklist for, 210–212
    creating, 212–213
    discussion in, 204–207

feedback in, 204
    guidelines for, 208–209
    small vs. large, 209
    as writing practice, 214–215
"Writing Daily, Writing in Tune" (Stafford), 297
Writing Fiction (Burroway), 179
writing from life, 152
Writing Past Dark (Friedman), 297
writing practice, 214–215
writing process, 193–201
    drafting in, 194–195
    revision in, 195–200
writing skills, 169–191
    in character development, 175–176
    in dialogue, 176–177
    in humor, 187
    in image/metaphor, 179–180
    and point of view, 177–179
    in rhythm, 181–184
    in scene/exposition, 170–173
    in specificity/detail, 173–174
    in structures/containers, 184–187

The Year of Reading Proust: A Memoir in Real Time (Rose), 75
Yee, Rodney, 294
yoga, desk, 294
YouTube, 71

Zinsser, William, 107–108

About the Authors

BRENDA MILLER is the author of five essay collections including *Season of the Body, Listening Against the Stone* and *An Earlier Life*, which received the Washington State Book Award for Memoir. Her creative nonfiction appears in leading literary journals and has received six Pushcart Prizes. She also coauthored *The Pen and the Bell: Mindful Writing in a Busy World* with Holly J. Hughes. Brenda is a professor of English at Western Washington University, and associate faculty at the Rainier Writing Workshop. In her spare time, she fosters dogs with Happy Tails Happy Homes, volunteers with Whatcom Hospice, and eats fabulous meals with her colleague Suzanne Paola.

SUZANNE PAOLA is the author of, most recently, *Make Me a Mother* (W. W. Norton) and the digital chapbook *Curious Atoms: A History with Physics*. She is also the author of *Body Toxic: An Environmental Memoir, A Mind Apart: Travels in a Neurodiverse World*, the novella *Stolen Moments*, and four books of poetry. Awards for her poetry and prose include a *New York Times* Notable Book, an American Book Award, a *Library Journal* Best Science Book of the Year, a Lenore Marshall Award finalist, an Oprah Bookshelf pick, and a Pushcart Prize. She lives in Bellingham, Washington, and is the editor-in-chief of the *Bellingham Review*. She teaches in jails and juvenile facilities with the group Underground Writing, and loves spending time, especially if it's eating or petting dogs, with her colleague Brenda Miller.